W9-CDY-549

Instantly DELICIOUS

250+ ESSENTIAL INSTANT POT® RECIPES

Instantly DELICIOUS

250+ ESSENTIAL INSTANT POT® RECIPES

Oxmoor House®

Published by Oxmoor House, an imprint of Time Inc. Books
225 Liberty Street, New York, NY 10281

Editorial Assistant: Lauren Moriarty
Project Editor: Lacie Pinyan
Design Director: Melissa Clark
Photo Director: Paden Reich
Senior Designer: Alana Hogg
Photographers: Erin Adams, Johnny Autry, Iain Bagwell, Robbie Caponetto, Jennifer Davick, Stephen DeVries, Alison Miksch, Victor Protasio, Becky Luigart-Stayner, Hector Manuel Sanchez
Prop Stylists: Cindy Barr, Kay E. Clarke, Elizabeth Demos, Lindsey Lower, Claire Spollen
Food Stylists: Marian Cooper Cairns, Margaret Monroe Dickey, Erin Merhar
Recipe Developers and Testers: Julie Christopher, Cooking Light Test Kitchen, Oxmoor House Test Kitchen, Southern Living Test Kitchen
Senior Production Manager: Greg A. Amason
Assistant Production and Project Manager: Kelsey Smith
Copy Editor: Adrienne Davis
Proofreader: Julie Gillis
Indexer: Mary Ann Laurens
Fellow: Holly Ravazzolo

ISBN-13: 978-0-8487-5941-4
Library of Congress Control Number: 2018941159
First Edition 2018
Printed in the United States of America
10 9 8 7 6 5 4 3 2 1

We welcome your comments and suggestions about Time Inc. Books.
Please write to us at:
Time Inc. Books
Attention: Book Editors
P.O. Box 62310
Tampa, Florida 33662-2310

Time Inc. Books products may be purchased for business or promotional use. For information on bulk purchases, please contact Christi Crowley in the Special Sales Department at (845) 895-9858.

CONTENTS

WELCOME

Who doesn't want to save time in the kitchen? Thanks to the Instant Pot®'s pressure cook setting, you can quickly cook dried beans, "bake" a cake, or have a pot roast on the table in less than an hour. And on the days when slow cooking sounds more appealing, simply set a stew to cook. The Instant Pot® is popular for a reason—it's a multitasking guru that's worth carving out a spot for on the counter.

This book starts at the beginning with a hardworking Basics chapter (page 12) that includes some of the Instant Pot® community's most frequently requested recipes for everything from "Roast" Turkey Breast (page 27) to Poached Eggs (page 17). We show you how meal-prep staples, such as Pressure Cooker Rotisserie-Style Chicken (page 26), transform into easy weeknight meals like Greek Pizza with Chicken and Artichokes (page 97).

When it comes to a grab-and-go breakfast, simple and satisfying recipes for Plain Yogurt (page 14) and Greek Yogurt (page 15) set you up for a successful morning. Perhaps you've wondered what to do with the leftover whey. In response to this common conundrum, we created recipes such as Wheat 'n' Honey Dinner Rolls (page 49) and Pumpkin Bread (page 53) that give you delicious solutions to use up your whey.

The Instant Pot®'s versatility saves you time during dinner without sacrificing flavor. Flip to Meatless Mains (page 162) to find family-friendly favorites like Southern-Style "Baked" Macaroni and Cheese (page 168). Browse easy side options, including Lemony Steamed Kale (page 181) and Hot Texas Caviar (page 202), or whip up a one-pot weeknight meal such as Easy Chicken and Dumplings (page 110). We recommend ending on a sweet note with a wedge of Bourbon-Pecan Cake (page 244).

Our best Instant Pot® advice: Use it to make your life easier. Throw dinner together in between soccer practice and ballet. Save money on everyday staples like yogurt and broth. Serve a crowd-pleasing appetizer, or quickly satisfy your chocolate cravings with a decadent dessert. Whether you are new to the Instant Pot® community or looking for recipes to add to your repertoire, you'll find plenty of inspiration in these pages.

WHAT IS THE INSTANT POT®?

The Instant Pot® is a programmed multipurpose appliance that is a pressure cooker, slow cooker, rice cooker, yogurt maker, steamer, sauté pan, and more. It cooks meals faster and remembers your most recent settings for a personalized cooking experience. And it saves time cooking foods such as dried beans, stews, and meats.

PRESSURE COOKING IN THE INSTANT POT®

1. Connect power cord. The LED display shows "OFF" indicating that it's in standby state. Follow the cooking preparations on page 11.
2. Select a cooking function, e.g. [Rice], [Soup], [Meat/Stew], etc. (Steam release handle should be in "Sealing" position.) Once a function key is pressed, its indicator lights up. (Within 10 seconds after pressing a function key, you can still select other function keys or adjust cooking time.)
3. Select cooking pressure. All functions except [Rice] default to "High Pressure." For [Rice] function, the default is "Low Pressure."
4. Select cooking time. You may use the [+] or [-] key to fine-tune cooking time to the minutes specified in your recipe. Any previously used cooking settings, including fine-tuned times, pressure, and temperature, are stored once you change the default settings, even after the Instant Pot® is unplugged. To reset to factory default settings, see Instruction Manual.
5. Cooking starts automatically 10 seconds after the last key press. Three audible beeps will sound to indicate the cooking process has begun. The LED display shows "On" indicating that the preheating state is in progress. Once the cooker reaches working pressure, the LED display changes from "On" to the programmed cooking time. The cooking time counts down to indicate the remaining time in minutes.
6. When the pressure cooking cycle finishes, the cooker beeps and automatically goes into the "Keep Warm" cycle, called Auto "Keep Warm" Cycle.

SLOW COOKING IN THE INSTANT POT®

1. Connect the cooker to the power outlet. The LED display shows "OFF" indicating that it's in standby state. Follow the cooking preparations on page 11.
2. Press the [Slow Cook] function key. (Steam Release Handle should be in "Venting" position.)
3. Change cooking time between 0.5 and 20 hours by pressing the [+] or [-] key.
4. Select the desired cooking mode by repeatedly pressing the [Slow Cook] key to select temperature ("Less" for LOW; "Normal" for MEDIUM; "More" for HIGH).
5. Cooking starts automatically 10 seconds after the last key is pressed.
6. When the cooking finishes, the cooker beeps and goes into the Auto "Keep Warm" Cycle for 24 hours.

SAUTÉING

The lid must be off when using the "Sauté " function. Press the [Sauté] key. For safety reasons, the maximum operation time of one "Sauté" cycle is 30 minutes. Select the cooking temperature among "Normal", "More," and "Less" modes with the [Sauté] key. The "Normal" mode is suited for regular sautéing or pan-searing. The "More" mode is for stir-frying, blackening meat at a higher temperature, or reducing liquids. The "Less" mode is suitable for simmering liquids or thickening delicate sauces.

HOW TO RELEASE PRESSURE

Quick Pressure Release:

Turn the steam release handle to the "Venting" position to let out steam until the float valve drops down. Please be aware that Quick Pressure Release is not suitable for food with large liquid volume or high starch content (e.g. oatmeal, porridge, sticky liquids, starchy soups, etc.). Food content may splatter out from the steam release. Use Natural Pressure Release instead.

Natural Pressure Release:

Allow the cooker to cool down naturally until the float valve drops down. This may take 10 to 15 minutes or even longer, depending on the amount of food inside. The cooker will not go into Auto "KEEP WARM" Cycle until the pressure has been released. Some recipes call for a specifically timed Natural Pressure Release.

See page 10 for more pressure release method details.

INSTANT POT® FEATURES

PROGRAMS	DUO	DUO +	NOTES
Manual (on older models)	✓		Use the [Manual] key for pressure cooking when custom time and/or pressure level is desired.
Pressure Cook	✓		Replaces the [Manual] custom pressure cooking program key on newer models.
Slow Cook		✓	This is a non-pressure cooking program. You may also use the Instant Pot® glass lid in this setting. Slow Cook using a choice of 3 heat levels (Less=WARM), (Normal=LOW); (More=HIGH).
Sauté	✓	✓	Use "Less"mode for simmering, thickening, and reducing liquids; "Normal" mode for pan-searing, and "More" mode for stir-frying or browning meat. Never have the lid on when sautéing. Maximum time is 30 minutes as a safety precaution.
Pressure Level	✓	✓	Use repeated presses of this key to toggle selection to Low or High Pressure. Do not fill the inner pot more than ⅔ full. For food that expands during cooking, such as rice or dried vegetables, do not fill the inner pot more than ½ full.
Adjust (on older models)	✓		Use [Adjust] to change heat level modes ("Less", "Normal", "More") for [Sauté], [Slow Cook], and [Yogurt] programs and to extend or shorten preprogrammed cook-time duration.
Time Control Keys [+/-]	✓	✓	Use [+/-] to fine tune changes in pressure cooking times in 1 minute increments. Press and hold to add or subtract rapidly, or press once for each minute of desired change. Also use [+/-] to change slow cook time, yogurt incubation time, or bread proofing time in 30-minute increments.
Rice	✓	✓	On the DUO, [Rice] is pre-programmed at Low Pressure for cooking regular and parboiled rice. Cooking duration is automatic depending on volume in cooker and cannot be changed. [Rice] on the DUO PLUS is an automated program, but pressure level can be changed. On both models, turn [Keep Warm] off to prevent overcooking.
Porridge	✓	✓	Use for rice porridge and hot cereal grains. Do not use Quick Pressure Release for these foods as thick liquid may spatter out and block the pressure release valve.
Yogurt	✓	✓	Use "More" mode to scald milk to 180°F for yogurt; use "Normal" mode to incubate yogurt; use "Less" mode to proof yeast doughs.
Cake (on some models)		✓	Adjust cooking time for different recipes. "Less" mode for lighter moist cakes; "Normal" mode for denser moist cakes; "More" mode for New York-style cheesecakes.
Egg (on some models)		✓	Preset times are intended for extra large eggs. Adjust cooking time with multiple presses of the [Egg] key to account for different egg sizes, quantity, and desired degree of doneness.
Multigrain	✓	✓	Choose different time modes based on type of grain and desired texture.
Steam	✓	✓	Use the trivet provided to elevate food above the water, and use the Quick Pressure Release method to prevent food from overcooking. Use for vegetables, fish, and seafood and to reheat leftovers in heat-proof containers.
Soup ("Soup/Broth" on some models)	✓	✓	Using this key keeps soups and broths clear due to lack of boiling motion while pressure cooking.
Sterilize		✓	Use to sterilize utensils and to pasteurize dairy products.
Poultry (on older models)	✓		On newer models, cook poultry with the Meat/Stew program key using "Less" mode. Change time as desired using the [+/-] key. Poultry can also be cooked at High Pressure using either [Manual] or [Pressure Cook] depending on model.
Meat/Stew	✓	✓	Choose different time modes based on the meat texture desired. "More" mode is programmed for longer cook time and is for fall-off-the-bone meat texture.
Beans/Chili	✓	✓	Choose different time modes based on the bean texture desired. Soaked, dried beans will take shorter cook time than unsoaked beans.
Keep Warm/ Cancel	✓	✓	On older models, automatic [Keep Warm] can be turned off by a second press of desired program key before program starts. Press [Keep Warm/Cancel] to turn cooker off. On some newer models, [Keep Warm] and [Cancel] are two separate keys. Repeated presses of the [Keep Warm] key toggles among low, medium, and high heat modes. [Cancel] turns the cooker off.
Timer/Delay Start	✓	✓	The [Timer] key on older models functions the same as [Delay Start] on newer models. See product manual for instructions.

EQUIPMENT LIST

The popularity of the Instant Pot® means there are many accessories now available but don't let the options overwhelm you. Take stock of what you have (you may already own an 8-inch cake pan and silicone cupcake liners) before you start shopping. The most commonly used equipment in this book is listed below.

COLLAPSIBLE STEAMER BASKET

This type of steamer basket has legs, so a trivet is not necessary to elevate food above the water. It's ideal for steaming vegetables and making hard-cooked eggs. Look for one with an extendable handle so you can easily remove it from the Instant Pot®.

TEMPERED GLASS LID

Pop the glass lid on the Instant Pot® to keep your food warm after it finishes cooking, or use it to monitor your meal while it slow cooks. A glass lid is also helpful when making yogurt or heating water.

TALL AND SHORT TRIVETS

Trivets elevate your food so that you can hard-boil eggs or cook Pot in Pot (PIP). (For more on Pot in Pot cooking, see page 11.) The tall trivets create a second layer, which is helpful for cooking food like potatoes underneath.

EXTRA SEALING RINGS

The silicone rings are sometimes smelly after cooking intense-flavored foods, so keep extra rings on hand to separate desserts from savory dishes.

CORNING CASSEROLES

This versatile dish is used to cook Southern-Style "Baked" Macaroni and Cheese (page 168).

ROUND CASSEROLE DISH WITH LID

Used with the Pot in Pot technique, the material of this dish should be heat-proof or ovenproof, such as high-temperature silicone, heat-proof glass, or ceramic.

EXTRA INNER POT

Having an extra inner pot around is handy when you have yogurt chilling in the fridge and want to cook dinner.

7-INCH SPRINGFORM PANS

This pan ensures the sides of cheesecakes, such as Triple-Chocolate Cheesecake (page 239), stay intact. You'll also use the pans to make Tofu Lasagna (page 172).

8-INCH CAKE PAN

You'll use this common kitchen staple to cook Spiced Carrot Cake (page 251).

8-INCH PUSH PAN

This serves as an alternative to a 7-inch springform pan when cooking cheesecakes.

6-CUP BUNDT PAN

A half-sized Bundt pan is a perfect fit for the 6-quart Instant Pot®. Use it to "bake" cakes and quick breads. It can be used for many recipes calling for an 8- x 4-inch loafpan.

6-OUNCE CUSTARD CUPS

Tempered glass custard cups are an excellent choice to cook eggs or individual servings in the Instant Pot®. Glass conducts heat evenly, and the rounded bottoms make perfectly-shaped poached eggs.

6-OUNCE RAMEKINS

Pumpkin Pie Custards with Gingersnap Topping (page 242) cook in these handy ramekins.

SILICONE CUPCAKE LINERS

These colorful molds, possibly already in your pantry, are used to make German Chocolate Mini Cheesecakes (page 234).

OVEN GLOVES OR LINED RUBBER GLOVES

Using lined rubber gloves (such as Spontex Bluettes) instead of oven mitts allows you greater dexterity when removing items from inside of a hot Instant Pot®.

QUICK SOLUTIONS FOR YOUR INSTANT POT® PROBLEMS

PROBLEM:

You poured your White Chicken Chili ingredients into the Instant Pot® without adding the inner pot.

SOLUTION:

Add your food to the inner pot before placing it in the Instant Pot®. Except when sautéing, it is often easier to put ingredients in the inner pot first, wipe the outside of the inner pot clean, and then place it back in the cooker. You'll be slurping soup in no time.

PROBLEM:

Your Quick Pressure Release knob has a tendency to splatter.

SOLUTION:

Foamy foods, such as grains or beans, are prone to splattering when Quick Pressure Release is used. Try using Natural Pressure Release instead. Or, release pressure gradually. With your fingers held to the side, or with a wooden spoon, carefully turn the Pressure Valve handle to "Venting." Steam will begin escaping from the top of the valve. See chart below for more information on pressure release methods.

NATURAL PRESSURE RELEASE
Natural Pressure Release, also known as NR, occurs when cooking time is over and pressure is allowed to decrease on its own. Because the pressure is gradually released, there is less chance of splattering. This method is usually used for starchy foods, large liquid volumes, and meat.

TIMED PRESSURE RELEASE
Certain recipes call for a specifically timed Natural Pressure Release, which asks that you let the pot sit for an allotted time before turning the valve to release the remaining pressure.

QUICK PRESSURE RELEASE
This method quickly stops the cooking process to prevent overcooking. Quick Pressure Release, also known as QR, is best for food that needs to finish fast, such as quick-cooking vegetables and delicate seafood.

SLOW PRESSURE RELEASE
Pressure is manually released in short bursts, making Slow Pressure Release ideal for foamy food or when your pot is full.

PROBLEM:

You used hot water and your food ended up undercooked.

SOLUTION:

Using hot liquid in a recipe that calls for cold liquid shortens the overall cooking time because pressure begins to build as the liquid heats and cook time starts when pressure is reached. To avoid gooey grains and raw meat, stick to cold liquid when called for, or adjust the cooking time accordingly.

PROBLEM:

You filled the pot with macaroni and cheese goodness—all the way up to the Max Line.

SOLUTION:

Overfilled pots can clog the Venting Knob. A good rule of thumb when pressure cooking in the Instant Pot®: keep the inner pot less than ⅔ full. For foods that expand during pressure cooking (such as beans), ½ full is a good guideline. If you accidentally overfill the pot, use Natural Pressure Release to avoid a sticky situation.

PROBLEM:

You want to start developing your own Instant Pot® recipes but don't know how much liquid to use.

SOLUTION:

If there's not enough liquid, the Instant Pot® will not be able to generate enough steam to pressurize the pot. If there's too much liquid, the overall cooking time will increase and result in overcooked food. There must be a minimum of 1 to 1½ cups liquid in the pot for it to pressurize properly.

FOLLOW THESE STEPS WHEN PRESSURE COOKING IN THE INSTANT POT® FOR GREAT RESULTS EACH TIME.

1 Open the lid: Grasp the lid handle, and rotate approximately 30 degrees counterclockwise in the direction of "Open" until the ▼ mark on the lid is aligned with the ▲ mark on the cooker base.

2 Remove the inner pot from the cooker: Except when sautéing, it is easier to add food and liquid to the inner pot while it is out of the cooker. Clean and wipe the outside of the inner pot, and remove objects from inside the cooker before returning the inner pot to the cooker.

3 Add food and liquid to the inner pot: For all pressure cooking programs, the total amount of precooked food and liquid should NEVER exceed ⅔ of the inner pot capacity. For non-pressure cooking programs, do not fill past the MAX line. For foods with high starch content, such as oatmeal, porridge and sticky liquids, do not fill the inner pot past the ½ mark.

4 Close the lid and position the "Pressure Valve" properly: When running any of the programs except "KEEP WARM," "SAUTÉ," "SLOW COOK," or "YOGURT," align the pointed end of the steam release handle to "Sealing" position. The "SAUTÉ" function must be used without the lid.

5 Select cooking function, and program the cooker: Press the desired function key. Adjust pressure, temperature, and cook times according to the directions in your recipe.

WHAT IS PIP?

Pot in Pot (PIP) cooking allows you to pressure cook traditionally oven-only recipes that don't contain liquid, such as Southern-Style "Baked" Macaroni and Cheese (page 168) or Bourbon-Pecan Cake (page 244). You can also use the PIP method to reheat leftovers or cook several dishes at the same time. Just remember that the recipes you cook together must have the same pressure cook time.

BASICS

6-QUART

PLAIN YOGURT

MAKES: 2 QUARTS | HANDS-ON: 10 MINUTES | INCUBATE: 8 HOURS | CHILL: 12 HOURS

You can easily make your own yogurt in the Instant Pot® using milk of any fat percentage (fat-free, 1% low-fat, 2% reduced-fat, or whole) or even reconstituted nonfat dry milk. For a starter, choose a plain, unsweetened yogurt of which you like the taste. You can continue to use a reserved portion of each batch as the starter for the next.

2 tablespoons plain yogurt with active live cultures, room temperature (see Tips)

2 quarts milk

1. Place the yogurt in a 1-cup glass measuring cup; stir well. Cover and let stand while preparing the milk.

2. Pour the milk into the inner pot of a 6-quart Instant Pot®. Lock the lid; turn Pressure Valve to "Venting." Press YOGURT [More]. (You should see the word "boil" on the display.) Stirring the milk occasionally will help prevent hot spots on the bottom of the pot. When the milk reaches 180°F, the word "yogt" will appear, and the Instant Pot® will beep. Stir well, and check that the milk registers at least 180°F but not more than 185°F on a thermometer. If temperature is less than 180°F, press YOGURT [More], and repeat the cycle.

3. Open the lid. Remove the inner pot from the cooker, and place on a wire rack to cool to 110° to 115°F, stirring occasionally.

4. Stir the yogurt, and gradually stir in ½ cup of the warm milk, about ¼ cup at a time, stirring until smooth after each addition. Pour into the remaining milk in the pot, and stir well. Place the pot in the cooker. Lock the lid.; turn Pressure valve to "Sealing" or "Venting." Press YOGURT [Normal]. Set the timer for 8 hours.

5. When time is up, the Instant Pot® will beep, "yogt" will appear on the display, and the cooker will go into standby mode.

6. Test to see if the yogurt is set: Insert a clean spoon into the center of the mixture, and, without stirring or otherwise disturbing the rest of the mixture, remove a spoonful to taste. Yogurt should be the texture of custard and taste mildly tart. (Yogurt will continue to thicken and become slightly more tart as it chills.) If the yogurt is not set, or you desire a more tart product, press YOGURT [Normal]; set time for an additional 1 to 2 hours, and test again.

7. When the yogurt is ready, remove the pot from the cooker, being careful not to disturb the set. Cover and chill 12 hours or overnight.

8. Transfer the yogurt to smaller containers if desired, or strain to make Greek Yogurt (page 15), and store in the refrigerator up to 1 month.

TIPS:

You may set the inner pot in a large bowl of cold, not ice, water to hasten cooling to 110° to 115°F. Stir often, and check the temperature after stirring.

...

It's best to start with commercial plain yogurt the first time. Make sure it contains active live cultures and does not contain gelatin, sugar, or thickeners. Save some yogurt from each batch to culture the next. You can freeze it in 2-tablespoon portions in airtight containers. Thaw in the refrigerator and bring to room temperature before use.

GREEK YOGURT

MAKES: ABOUT 1 QUART | HANDS-ON: 10 MINUTES | CHILL: 2 HOURS

Greek yogurt is thick and creamy as a result of straining plain yogurt. Try it instead of sour cream on top of baked potatoes or chili. It's also delicious layered in parfaits. Choose your favorite stir-in, such as berries, coconut, or peanut butter, to sweeten, flavor, or add texture.

Plain Yogurt (page 14)
Cheesecloth, muslin, or coffee filters

1. Set a fine-mesh sieve over a 2-quart glass measure or large glass bowl. Line the sieve with several layers of cheesecloth or muslin, or overlap several coffee filters to fit the sieve. Spoon the yogurt into the prepared sieve; cover and chill 2 hours or until yogurt is desired thickness. Reserve the whey (the clear liquid in the bowl) for another use.

2. Transfer the yogurt and whey to separate clean containers; cover and store in the refrigerator up to 1 month.

NOTE: Straining will lessen the volume of yogurt by about half, depending on how thick you like it.

TIP:

Use your leftover whey in these sweet treats:

Bran-Oat Muffins with Apricots and Pecans (page 54)
Farm House Yogurt Bread (page 51)
Pumpkin Bread (page 53)
Wheat 'n' Honey Dinner Rolls (page 49)
Prune Snack Cake (page 250)
Chocolate Almond Cake (page 243)
Bourbon-Pecan Cake (page 244)
Butter Cake (page 246)

6-QUART

HARD-COOKED EGGS

SERVES: 12 | HANDS-ON: 4 MINUTES | UNDER PRESSURE: 8 MINUTES | QUICK PRESSURE RELEASE

The Instant Pot® "boils" eggs beautifully, and they are so easy to peel! It can take some experimentation to find the sweet spot for your altitude and the size and number of eggs you like to cook, but this method works for 12 cold Grade A Large eggs at an altitude of less than 1,000 feet.

1 cup cold tap water
12 refrigerator-cold large eggs
Ice

1. Pour the 1 cup cold tap water into the inner pot of a 6-quart Instant Pot®. Insert tiered or stackable trivets, or a steamer basket on top of the included Steam Rack with the handles in the "up" position, into the pot. Carefully place the eggs in the steamer basket or on the trivets.
2. Lock the lid; turn Pressure Valve to "Sealing." Turn off KEEP WARM. Press STEAM [High Pressure]; cook for 8 minutes. Open the cooker using Quick Pressure Release (page 7).
3. While the eggs cook, fill a large bowl with ice and water. When the cook time is up, transfer the eggs to the ice water to stop the cooking process. Peel and serve hot, or cool completely and store, unpeeled, in the refrigerator up to 2 weeks.

TIP:

The STEAM [High Pressure] setting is best for temperature-sensitive eggs or veggies. These foods will begin cooking even before the full pressure level is reached, so it's important that pressure is reached quickly. The STEAM setting more quickly comes to pressure by heating continuously, whereas the PRESSURE COOK setting pressurizes by heating intermittently and takes longer.

6-QUART

POACHED EGGS

SERVES: 4 | HANDS-ON: 2 MINUTES | UNDER PRESSURE: 2 MINUTES | QUICK PRESSURE RELEASE

Many variables can affect the results when poaching eggs in the Instant Pot®, including the number and size of the eggs, the thickness and type of material of your egg cups (whether glass or silicone), the starting temperature of the water, and even the size of the Instant Pot® being used. The following method works for four Grade A Large eggs in ovenproof glass custard cups at an altitude of less than 1,000 feet.

Cooking spray
1¼ cups cold tap water
4 refrigerator-cold large eggs

1. Coat 4 (6-ounce) custard cups with cooking spray. Place 1 tablespoon of the cold water in each cup. Crack 1 egg into the water in each cup.

2. Pour the remaining 1 cup cold water into the inner pot of a 6-quart Instant Pot®. Set the Steam Rack in cooker with the handles folded under the rack. Place 3 custard cups on top of the rack. Set the remaining custard cup in the center on top of the first 3 cups.

3. Lock the lid; turn the Pressure Valve to "Sealing." Turn off KEEP WARM. Press STEAM [High Pressure]; cook for 2 minutes or until desired degree of doneness. Immediately open the cooker using Quick Pressure Release (page 7). Carefully lift egg cups from the cooker, and remove the eggs from the cups using a slotted spoon.

TIP:

Because water on top of poached eggs can make the eggs appear underdone, it's best to test doneness by pressing the yolks lightly with the back of a coffee spoon. If more doneness is desired, lock the lid, press KEEP WARM, and let stand for an additional minute or so; then, test again. (Do not return to pressure and add time because by the time pressure is regained, the eggs will be overcooked.)

◂ CLASSIC DEVILED EGGS

SERVES: 24 | HANDS-ON: 15 MINUTES | CHILL: 1 HOUR

If you want to up your deviled eggs game, try one of the four variations.

12 Hard-Cooked Eggs (page 16), peeled
½ cup mayonnaise
1½ teaspoons white wine vinegar
1½ teaspoons Dijon mustard
⅛ teaspoon kosher salt
Dash of hot sauce (optional)
Garnishes: Paprika, fresh chopped chives (optional)

1. Cut eggs in half lengthwise, and carefully remove yolks, keeping egg whites intact.

2. Grate egg yolks using the small holes of a box grater. Mash together yolks, mayonnaise, and next 3 ingredients. Add more salt or hot sauce, if desired.

3. Spoon or pipe yolk mixture into egg whites. Cover and chill at least 1 hour or until ready to serve. Garnish with paprika and chives, if desired.

AVOCADO-TARRAGON

Prepare recipe as directed in Steps 1 and 2. Mash together 1½ ripe avocados and 3¾ teaspoons fresh lime juice. Stir avocado mixture and 1 teaspoon dried tarragon into yolk mixture. Add salt and pepper to taste. Spoon or pipe yolk mixture into egg white halves. Top with desired amount of fresh flat-leaf parsley leaves.

SMOKED SALMON, LEMON, AND CAPERS

Prepare recipe as directed in Steps 1 and 2; stir 1½ tablespoons finely chopped drained capers, ¾ teaspoon loosely packed grated lemon rind, 1 tablespoon lemon juice, ¼ teaspoon black pepper, and ⅛ teaspoon kosher salt into yolk mixture. Spoon or pipe yolk mixture into egg white halves. Top with desired amount of smoked salmon.

SPINACH, POPPY SEED, AND BACON

Prepare recipe as directed in Steps 1 and 2; stir ¾ cup frozen chopped spinach, thawed; 4½ teaspoons grated red onion; and 4½ teaspoons poppyseed dressing into yolk mixture. Spoon or pipe yolk mixture into egg white halves. Top with chopped cooked bacon.

TROUT CAVIAR-HORSERADISH

Prepare recipe as directed in Steps 1 and 2; stir 3¾ teaspoons prepared horseradish into yolk mixture. Spoon or pipe yolk mixture into egg white halves. Top each egg half with ¾ teaspoon trout caviar.

SPICY SOUTHWESTERN DEVILED EGGS

SERVES: 24 | HANDS-ON: 15 MINUTES | CHILL: 1 HOUR

Choose your favorite mustard to adjust the flavor to your liking.

12 Hard-Cooked Eggs (page 16), peeled
6 tablespoons mayonnaise
2 to 4 tablespoons pickled sliced jalapeño chiles, minced
1 tablespoon mustard
½ teaspoon ground cumin
⅛ teaspoon table salt
Garnish: Chopped fresh cilantro (optional)

Cut the eggs in half lengthwise, and carefully remove the yolks. Mash the yolks; stir in the mayonnaise, jalapeño chiles, mustard, cumin, and salt. Spoon or pipe the egg yolk mixture into the egg halves. Cover and chill at least 1 hour or until ready to serve. Garnish with the cilantro, if desired.

3- OR 6-QUART

HOW TO COOK RICE

The Instant Pot® takes away many a rice-cooking woe: no more boil-overs, no more gummy or crunchy grains, no more pot watching. Make a large batch so you have extra rice on hand for a quick weeknight meal. Just be sure to keep the ratio of rice to water 1:1.

BROWN BASMATI RICE OR LONG-GRAIN BROWN RICE

MAKES: 4 CUPS | HANDS-ON: 1 MINUTE
UNDER PRESSURE: 15 MINUTES
5-MINUTE NATURAL PRESSURE RELEASE

1½ cups brown basmati rice or long-grain brown rice
1½ cups water

Stir together the rice and water in a 3- or 6-quart Instant Pot®. Lock the lid; turn Pressure Valve to "Sealing." PRESSURE COOK [High Pressure] for 15 minutes. Allow a 5-Minute Natural Pressure Release (page 10). Turn Pressure Valve to "Venting" to release remaining pressure. Fluff rice with a fork.

WHITE BASMATI RICE

MAKES: ABOUT 2½ CUPS | HANDS-ON: 1 MINUTE | UNDER PRESSURE: 6 MINUTES
10-MINUTE NATURAL PRESSURE RELEASE

1 cup white basmati rice
1 cup water

Stir together the rice and water in a 3- or 6-quart Instant Pot®. Lock the lid; turn Pressure Valve to "Sealing." PRESSURE COOK [High Pressure] for 6 minutes. Allow a 10-Minute Natural Pressure Release (page 10). Turn Pressure Valve to "Venting" to release remaining pressure. Fluff rice with a fork.

JASMINE RICE

MAKES: 2½ CUPS | HANDS-ON: 1 MINUTE
UNDER PRESSURE: 3 MINUTES
10-MINUTE NATURAL PRESSURE RELEASE

1 cup jasmine rice
1 cup water

Rinse the rice until the water runs clear; drain well. Combine the drained rice and 1 cup water in the inner pot of a 3- or 6-quart Instant Pot®. Lock the lid; turn Pressure Valve to "Sealing." PRESSURE COOK [High Pressure] for 3 minutes. Allow a 10-Minute Natural Pressure Release (page 10). Turn Pressure Valve to "Venting" to release any remaining pressure. Fluff rice with a fork.

Risotto with
Tomato Topping,
page 219

6-QUART

COOKED QUINOA

MAKES: ABOUT 5 CUPS | HANDS-ON: 7 MINUTES | UNDER PRESSURE: 1 MINUTE
10-MINUTE NATURAL PRESSURE RELEASE

Quinoa is an amazingly versatile and nutritious protein-packed grain that works well for breakfast, lunch, and dinner. It looks similar to couscous and is an easy substitute for rice, but it has a distinct, nutty flavor of its own. The natural coating on quinoa, called saponin, can taste bitter, so it's important to purchase pre-washed quinoa or rinse it yourself.

2 cups pre-washed quinoa
2 cups water

1. Remove the lid from a 6-quart Instant Pot®. Press SAUTÉ [Normal]. Add the quinoa, and cook, stirring constantly, until toasted and fragrant, about 5 minutes. Stir in the 2 cups water.
2. Lock the lid; turn the Pressure Valve to "Sealing." PRESSURE COOK [High Pressure] for 1 minute. Allow a 10-minute Natural Pressure Release (page 10). Turn the valve to "Venting" to release the remaining pressure.
3. Fluff the quinoa with a fork. Use immediately, or cool completely, divide into 1- to 2-cup freezer containers, and freeze up to 3 months.

TIP:

Toasting is not absolutely necessary, but it makes for a fluffier texture when using quinoa for salads or as a pilaf side dish.

6-QUART

VEGETABLE STOCK

MAKES: ABOUT 2½ QUARTS | HANDS-ON: 15 MINUTES | UNDER PRESSURE: 60 MINUTES
60-MINUTE NATURAL PRESSURE RELEASE

Homemade vegetable stock is much more flavorful than store-bought options, and the Instant Pot® makes it easy. Collect and freeze veggie trimmings to use in this simple stock. If you have leftover mushroom stems and trimmings, add them to the pot as well. To control the sodium level, skip the salt, and instead season to taste when using the stock in a recipe.

- 2 large onions, coarsely chopped (about 4 cups)
- 7 large celery stalks, coarsely chopped (leaves included)
- 6 large parsley sprigs, stems cut into large pieces
- 6 whole cloves
- 6 whole peppercorns
- 5 large carrots, peeled and coarsely chopped
- 3 large scallions, root ends removed and cut into 1-inch pieces
- 2 large garlic cloves, smashed
- 1 large bay leaf
- ¾ teaspoon dried Italian seasoning, crushed
- 10 cups water
- Table salt (optional)

1. Combine all ingredients, except salt, in the inner pot of a 6-quart Instant Pot®.

2. Lock the lid; turn Pressure Valve to "Sealing." PRESSURE COOK [High Pressure] for 60 minutes. Let cooker stand without opening until the pressure drops completely, or at least 1 hour. Open the cooker, and transfer the inner pot to a wire rack. Turn off the cooker. Cover the stock, and let cool just until warm. Strain the stock, discarding solids; stir in salt to taste, if desired. Transfer to rigid plastic freezer containers, allowing a 1-inch headspace. Cover and cool completely. Store in the refrigerator up to 1 week, or freeze up to 1 year.

6-QUART

CHICKEN BONE BROTH

MAKES: ABOUT 3 QUARTS | HANDS-ON: 35 MINUTES | UNDER PRESSURE: 120 MINUTES
CHILL: 24 HOURS | 60-MINUTE NATURAL PRESSURE RELEASE

While meat stocks are clear, bone broth is somewhat cloudy because it's richer in flavor and nutrients. You can collect cooked bones over time and store them in the freezer to use in this broth. You can also add raw boney parts leftover from cutting up whole chickens. For consistency in flavor, you may choose to omit salt in this recipe and add salt to the recipes in which the broth is used.

2 (2½ to 3-pound) rotisserie chickens
2 large celery stalks, sliced
2 cups coarsely chopped onion
½ teaspoon dried Italian seasoning, crushed
6 whole black peppercorns
3 quarts water
Table salt (optional)

1. Bone the chickens, placing the skin and bones in the inner pot of a 6-quart Instant Pot®. Reserve the meat for another use. Add the celery, onion, Italian seasoning, and peppercorns. Pour in the 3 quarts water.

2. Lock the lid; turn Pressure Valve to "Sealing." PRESSURE COOK [High Pressure] for 120 minutes. Let the cooker stand in "Keep Warm" mode for 60 minutes before opening the cooker. (The pressure may have completely dropped before that time, but do not open the cooker for a full 60 minutes.)

3. Open the cooker, and transfer the inner pot to a wire rack to cool just until warm. Strain the broth, discarding solids; stir in salt to taste, if desired. Transfer the stock to rigid plastic freezer containers, allowing a 1-inch headspace, or into a large bowl. Cover and let cool completely. Chill overnight.

4. Skim the solidified fat from the top of the broth. Use immediately, or cover freezer containers with lids, and freeze up to 1 year.

3- OR 6-QUART

COOKED BONELESS CHICKEN BREASTS OR THIGHS

MAKES: ABOUT 5 CUPS COOKED CHICKEN AND 2½ CUPS BROTH | HANDS-ON: 10 MINUTES
UNDER PRESSURE: 12 MINUTES | 5-MINUTE NATURAL PRESSURE RELEASE

Cooked chicken is a convenient ingredient to have on hand to easily make last-minute meals. Pressure cooking ensures tender, juicy meat that is easily chopped or shredded for soups, sandwiches, or casseroles. This recipe freezes well, up to 1 year, so you can make extra and store for a later date.

- **1 (14.5-ounce) fat-free, lower sodium chicken broth**
- **2 pounds skinless, boneless chicken breast halves or thighs**
- **½ medium onion, coarsely chopped**
- **2 celery stalks, coarsely chopped**
- **¼ teaspoon Italian seasoning**
- **¼ teaspoon black pepper**

1. Place all ingredients in the inner pot of a 3- or 6-quart Instant Pot®. Lock the lid; turn Pressure Valve to "Sealing." PRESSURE COOK [High Pressure] for 12 minutes. Allow a 5-Minute Natural Pressure Release (page 10). Turn Pressure Valve to "Venting" to release remaining pressure.

2. Remove the chicken from the pot, reserving the broth. Let cool slightly. Chop or shred the chicken with 2 forks; divide into freezer containers. Add a small amount of the reserved broth to each container. Use immediately, or freeze up to 3 months. Pour the remaining broth into containers, allowing a 1-inch headspace. Use immediately, store in the refrigerator up to 10 days, or freeze for up to 1 year.

TIP:

While the chicken is warm, use an electric mixer to quickly shred it for sandwiches or soups. Stir in your favorite bottled barbecue sauce for a quick sandwich filling.

6-QUART

PRESSURE COOKER ROTISSERIE-STYLE CHICKEN

SERVES: 4 | HANDS-ON: 15 MINUTES | UNDER PRESSURE: 25 MINUTES
NATURAL PRESSURE RELEASE

Thanks to the Instant Pot®, it doesn't take much longer than a run to the supermarket to cook your own rotisserie-style chicken. This tender, juicy bird yields about 3 cups skinned and boned chicken and 3 cups rich, tasty broth. Chill the broth to make removing the fat easier. Save and freeze the carcass to have on hand for a batch of Chicken Bone Broth (page 24).

1 (3½- to 3¾-pound) whole frying chicken
1 tablespoon Greek seasoning
¾ teaspoon garlic powder
¾ teaspoon paprika
½ teaspoon dried Italian seasoning
1 tablespoon olive oil
1 (14.5-ounce) can reduced-sodium chicken broth

1. Pat the chicken dry with paper towels. Combine the Greek seasoning, garlic powder, paprika, and Italian seasoning in a small bowl. Rub the seasoning mixture over the entire chicken and inside the body cavity.

2. Remove the lid of a 6-quart Instant Pot®. Add the oil. Press SAUTÉ [Normal].

3. When the oil is shimmering, place the chicken, breast side down, in the pot. Cook 5 minutes to brown. Turn the chicken over, and cook 2 minutes. Pour chicken broth around the chicken to avoid washing off the herb mixture.

4. Lock the lid; turn Pressure Valve to "Sealing." PRESSURE COOK [High Pressure] for 25 minutes. Turn off the cooker.

5. Allow a complete Natural Pressure Release (page 7). Remove the chicken from the pot. Let stand 10 minutes before carving. If desired, you may remove the skin and bones and chop the chicken for another use.

TIP:

If desired, you can broil the chicken on a rack in a shallow pan after cooking to crisp and brown the skin. Watch closely to prevent burning.

6-QUART

"ROAST" TURKEY BREAST

SERVES: 6 TO 8 | HANDS-ON: 20 MINUTES | UNDER PRESSURE: 30 MINUTES
NATURAL PRESSURE RELEASE

Add this easy "roast" turkey to your meal prep repertoire. You can thinly slice the tender turkey for quick sandwiches, or chop for filling soups or hearty casseroles. The broth turns into a gravy that tastes delicious with the turkey breast or poured over mashed potatoes.

1 (4½-pound) frozen whole bone-in turkey breast, thawed
1 tablespoon olive oil
1½ teaspoons garlic powder
1 teaspoon table salt
¼ teaspoon paprika
¼ teaspoon black pepper
1 (14.5-ounce) can reduced-sodium chicken broth
½ teaspoon dried Italian seasoning
1 large celery stalk
½ medium onion, coarsely chopped into ½-inch pieces
Cooking spray
⅓ cup all-purpose flour (optional)
Freshly ground black pepper

1. Remove and discard the gravy pouch from the turkey breast, if present. Pat the turkey dry with paper towels. Rub the olive oil over the entire surface of the turkey. Combine the garlic powder, salt, paprika, and ¼ teaspoon pepper; rub onto all surfaces of the turkey.

2. Stir together the chicken broth and Italian seasoning in the inner pot of a 6-quart Instant Pot®. Place the prepared turkey breast on the Steam Rack, skin side up; lower into the pot using the rack handles. Add the celery and onion to the pot around the turkey. Lock the lid; turn Pressure Valve to "Sealing." PRESSURE COOK [High Pressure] for 30 minutes. Allow a complete Natural Pressure Release (page 7).

3. While the turkey cooks, place a rack in a foil-lined sheet pan. Coat the rack and foil with cooking spray.

4. Preheat the broiler.

5. Transfer the cooked turkey to the prepared pan; broil about 5 minutes or until brown. Let stand 10 minutes before carving.

6. If desired, strain the broth into a large saucepan, discarding solids; let cool slightly. Combine about ½ cup of the cooled broth with the ⅓ cup flour, if desired. whisking until smooth. Stir flour mixture into the broth. Bring to a boil; boil, whisking often, until thickened. Stir in freshly ground black pepper to taste.

6-QUART

COOKED DRIED BEANS (UNSOAKED METHOD)

MAKES: ABOUT 5 CUPS BEANS | NATURAL PRESSURE RELEASE

Soaking dried beans shortens cook time and produces a better texture, but you can also cook beans without soaking. Factors such as altitude, liquid volume, and age affect cook times for dried beans, so keep a record of your preferred cook times for future reference.

1 pound (2½ cups) dried beans (see varieties below)
8 cups water
1 tablespoon canola oil
2 teaspoons table salt (optional)

Wash and sort the chosen variety of beans; drain. Combine the drained beans, 8 cups water, oil, and, if desired, salt in the inner pot of a 6-quart Instant Pot®. Lock the lid: turn Pressure Valve to "Sealing." PRESSURE COOK [High Pressure] for the times below. Allow a complete Natural Pressure Release (page 7).

BEAN COOKING TIMES

BEAN TYPE	TIME
Black Beans	20 to 25 minutes
Black-eyed Peas	20 to 25 minutes
Chickpeas (Garbanzo Beans)	35 to 40 minutes
Great Northern Beans	25 to 30 minutes
Kidney Beans, Red	25 to 30 minutes
Kidney Beans, White (Cannellini Beans)	35 to 40 minutes
Lentils (Brown)	15 to 20 minutes
Navy Beans	25 to 30 minutes
Pinto Beans	25 to 30 minutes

6-QUART

COOKED DRIED BEANS (SOAKED METHOD)

MAKES: ABOUT 5 CUPS DRAINED BEANS AND 4 CUPS BEAN LIQUID | HANDS-ON: 8 MINUTES
UNDER PRESSURE: 15 MINUTES | SOAK: AT LEAST 8 HOURS | 10-MINUTE NATURAL PRESSURE RELEASE

Keeping a variety of cooked dried beans in the freezer makes it easy to jump-start recipes, especially soups and stews. Although adding salt while cooking does not significantly affect the cook time or tenderness of dried beans, it does result in much better-tasting beans.

1 pound (2½ cups) dried beans (see bottom right for varieties)
Water for soaking
6 cups water
1 tablespoon canola oil
2 teaspoons table salt (optional)

1. Sort and wash the beans; drain. Place the beans in the inner pot of a 6-quart Instant Pot®. Cover with water to a depth of 2 inches above beans. Lock the lid, and let soak 8 hours or overnight. Drain the beans, discarding the soaking water.
2. Return the beans to the pot. Add the 6 cups water, oil, and, if desired, salt.
3. Lock the lid of the Instant Pot®. Turn Pressure Valve to "Sealing." PRESSURE COOK [High Pressure] for 14 to 16 minutes. Allow a 10-minute Natural Pressure Release (page 10). Turn Pressure Valve to "Venting" to release remaining pressure.
4. Use immediately, or divide cooked beans into 1- or 2-cup rigid freezer containers, and add cooking liquid just to the fill line to allow for expansion. Freeze up to 6 months.

CHOOSE FROM THE FOLLOWING VARIETIES:

Black Beans

Black-eyed Peas

Chickpeas

Great Northern Beans

Red Kidney Beans

White Kidney Beans (Cannellini Beans)

Navy Beans

Pinto Beans

1 tablespoon

2

BREAKFAST, BREADS & BEVERAGES

◂ YOGURT PARFAIT

SERVES: 8 | HANDS-ON: 10 MINUTES | BROIL: 5 MINUTES

Cooking your own granola is much cheaper than purchasing the prepared version. To make your morning a little easier, prepare the granola in advance and store in an airtight container. When it's time for breakfast, all you'll have to do is assemble the parfait.

1 cup old-fashioned rolled oats
¼ cup raw sunflower seeds
¼ cup sweetened flaked coconut
¼ cup chopped walnuts
¼ cup flaxseed meal
½ teaspoon ground cinnamon
¼ teaspoon table salt
2 tablespoons butter, melted
2 tablespoons honey
½ teaspoon vanilla extract
4 cups Greek Yogurt (page 15)
2 cups raspberries or other fresh berries of your choice

1. Place an oven rack on the middle shelf of the oven, about 10 inches below the broiler. Preheat the broiler to high heat.

2. Combine the oats, sunflower seeds, coconut, walnuts, flaxseed meal, cinnamon, and salt on a baking sheet; toss well. Broil 3 minutes or until lightly toasted, stirring every 1 minute. Combine the butter, honey, and vanilla in a small bowl. Drizzle the butter mixture over the oat mixture; toss to coat. Broil the granola an additional 2 minutes or until well toasted, stirring after 1 minute. Remove the granola from the oven; cool on the pan 8 minutes, stirring occasionally.

3. Spoon ½ cup of the yogurt into each of 8 bowls. Top with about ⅓ cup granola and about ¼ cup berries.

MAPLE-PECAN GRANOLA

SERVES: 12 | HANDS-ON: 10 MINUTES | BAKE: 1 HOUR

Try sprinkling this easy granola over Greek Yogurt (page 15) for a light breakfast or late afternoon snack. You can change the flavor by substituting your favorite nut for the pecan pieces.

2 cups rolled oats
½ cup pecan pieces
½ cup maple syrup
¼ cup packed brown sugar
2 tablespoons canola oil
⅛ teaspoon table salt
Cooking spray

Preheat the oven to 300°F. Combine all ingredients, except the cooking spray; spread on a large jelly-roll pan coated with cooking spray. Bake at 300°F for 1 hour, stirring every 15 minutes. Cool completely. Store in an airtight container up to 1 week, or freeze up to 3 months.

FOUR EASY BREAKFAST BOWLS

A few pantry staples elevate the ho-hum flavor of everyday oatmeal, taking it from dull to delicious. These simple but satisfying breakfast options will keep you full for hours.

6-QUART

HEARTY OATS AND GRAINS

SERVES: 8 | HANDS-ON: 4 MINUTES
UNDER PRESSURE: 10 MINUTES
10-MINUTE NATURAL PRESSURE RELEASE

3 cups water
2 cups unfiltered apple cider
1 cup steel-cut oats
1 cup 10-grain "hot cereal" (such as Bob's Red Mill)
½ teaspoon table salt
1½ teaspoons ground cinnamon
1 cup 2% reduced-fat milk, warmed
½ cup maple syrup
1½ cups sliced or cubed apple
½ cup chopped walnuts, toasted (optional)

1. Stir together the 3 cups water, apple cider, oats, grain blend, salt, and cinnamon in the inner pot of a 6-quart Instant Pot®.

2. Lock the lid; turn Pressure Valve to "Sealing." PRESSURE COOK [High Pressure] for 10 minutes. Allow a 10-minute Natural Pressure Release (page 10). Turn Pressure Valve to "Venting" to release remaining pressure.

3. Open the cooker; stir well. Spoon about ⅔ cup oat mixture into each of 8 bowls; top evenly with milk, syrup, apple, and nuts, if desired.

6-QUART

CHERRY-HAZELNUT OATMEAL

SERVES: 6 | HANDS-ON: 7 MINUTES
UNDER PRESSURE: 10 MINUTES
10-MINUTE NATURAL PRESSURE RELEASE

5 cups water
2 cups steel-cut oats
⅔ cup dried Bing or other sweet cherries, coarsely chopped
½ teaspoon table salt
½ teaspoon ground cinnamon
5 tablespoons brown sugar
¼ cup chopped hazelnuts, toasted
2 tablespoons toasted hazelnut oil

1. Combine the water, oats, cherries, salt, and cinnamon in the inner pot of a 6-quart Instant Pot®.

2. Lock the lid; turn Pressure Valve to "Sealing." PRESSURE COOK [High Pressure] for 10 minutes. Allow a 10-minute Natural Pressure Release (page 10). Turn Pressure Valve to "Venting" to release remaining pressure.

3. Stir in 3 tablespoons of the brown sugar and 1 tablespoon of the nuts. Divide the oatmeal among 6 bowls; sprinkle each serving with 1 teaspoon of brown sugar. Top each serving with 1½ teaspoons nuts; drizzle with 1 teaspoon hazelnut oil.

6-QUART

STEEL-CUT OATMEAL WITH APPLES

SERVES: 10 | HANDS-ON: 3 MINUTES
SLOW COOK: 6 HOURS

1 teaspoon coconut oil
4 cups diced Granny Smith apple (about 1 pound)
2 cups gluten-free steel-cut oats (such as Bob's Red Mill)
7 cups water
½ cup honey
½ teaspoon table salt
½ teaspoon ground allspice
1 (13.66-ounce) can light coconut milk
Garnishes: toasted cashews, additional diced Granny Smith apple (optional)

Coat the inner pot of a 6-quart Instant Pot® with the coconut oil. Stir together the apple, oats, water, honey, salt, allspice, and coconut milk in the inner pot. Lock the lid; turn Pressure Valve to "Venting." SLOW COOK [Normal] for 6 hours. Stir well before serving. Garnish with toasted cashews and additional diced apple, if desired.

6-QUART

PEANUTTY MAPLE OATS

SERVES: 6 | HANDS-ON: 10 MINUTES
UNDER PRESSURE: 3 MINUTES
NATURAL PRESSURE RELEASE

1 cup steel-cut oats
3 cups water
1 tablespoon canola oil
⅛ teaspoon table salt
½ cup plus 1 tablespoon reduced-fat peanut butter
1½ cups diced banana
¼ cup pure maple syrup
⅛ teaspoon ground nutmeg

1. Combine the oats, water, oil, and salt in a 6-quart Instant Pot®. Lock the lid; turn Pressure Valve to "Sealing." PRESSURE COOK [High Pressure] for 3 minutes. Open the cooker using Natural Pressure Release (page 7).

2. Stir in peanut butter.

3. Divide the oat mixture among 6 bowls. Top with the diced banana, and drizzle with the syrup. Sprinkle with the nutmeg, and serve immediately.

6-QUART

BROWN RICE CEREAL WITH VANILLA CREAM AND BERRIES

SERVES: 4 | HANDS-ON: 10 MINUTES | UNDER PRESSURE: 23 MINUTES
QUICK PRESSURE RELEASE

The chewy texture of brown rice makes it an ideal grain for warm breakfast cereals. Prepare this on Sunday to simplify your Monday morning routine; it keeps in the refrigerator for up to 3 days.

1 cup uncooked long-grain brown rice
1½ cups water
1 tablespoon canola oil
1 cup fat-free milk
¼ cup heavy cream
3 tablespoons sugar
⅛ teaspoon table salt
1 teaspoon vanilla extract
½ cup fresh blueberries
½ cup fresh raspberries
2 teaspoons grated lemon rind

1. Remove the lid from a 6-quart Instant Pot®. Press SAUTÉ [Normal]. When the inner pot is hot, add the rice. Cook, stirring constantly, 3 minutes or until lightly toasted. Add the 1½ cups water and the oil. Lock the lid; turn Pressure Valve to "Sealing." PRESSURE COOK [High Pressure] for 23 minutes. Turn off the cooker. Open the cooker using Quick Pressure Release (page 7).

2. Divide the rice among 4 bowls.

3. Add the milk, cream, sugar, and salt to the pot. Press SAUTÉ [Normal]; cook, stirring constantly, 2 minutes or until thoroughly heated. Turn off the cooker; stir in the vanilla.

4. Top the rice evenly with the milk mixture. Sprinkle with the berries and lemon rind.

TIP:

For creamier rice, stir the milk, cream, sugar, and salt into the cooked rice in the pot. Lock the lid; turn Pressure Valve to "Venting." Press SLOW COOK [Less]. Cook for 30 minutes; turn off cooker. Remove the inner pot from the cooker, and cool slightly. Stir in the vanilla. Spoon into bowls, and top with the berries and lemon rind.

6-QUART

TOASTED ALMOND AND APPLE QUINOA

SERVES: 4 | HANDS-ON: 5 MINUTES | UNDER PRESSURE: 6 MINUTES
NATURAL PRESSURE RELEASE

Spiked with cherries and loaded with protein and fiber, this easy breakfast will keep you satisfied throughout the morning. You can substitute any apple variety you have on hand for the Braeburn.

⅔ cup slivered almonds
1 cup uncooked quinoa
2 cups water
⅓ cup dried tart cherries
1 tablespoon canola oil
¼ teaspoon table salt
1 teaspoon vanilla extract
1 cup sliced Braeburn apple
1 tablespoon sugar
¼ teaspoon ground cinnamon

1. Remove the lid from a 6-quart Instant Pot®. Press SAUTÉ [Normal]. Add the almonds to the pot; cook, stirring constantly, 2 to 3 minutes or until lightly browned. Remove the almonds from the pot, and set aside.

2. Add the quinoa to the pot; cook 1 minute or until lightly browned, stirring frequently. Stir in the 2 cups water, cherries, oil, and salt. Turn off the cooker.

3. Lock the lid; turn Pressure Valve to "Sealing". PRESSURE COOK [High Pressure] for 6 minutes. Open the cooker using Natural Pressure Release (page 7). Stir in the vanilla.

4. While the cooker stands, combine almonds, apple, sugar, and cinnamon, tossing to coat. Divide quinoa mixture among 4 bowls; top with the apple mixture.

OATMEAL WAFFLES WITH SAUTÉED APPLES

SERVES: 6 | HANDS-ON: 21 MINUTES | BAKE: 6 MINUTES

Sweet cinnamon-apples dress up these sturdy, stick-to-your-ribs waffles. Leftover whey from Greek Yogurt (page 15) makes the waffles extra moist.

1 cup uncooked quick-cooking oats

1 cup apple juice

2 cups just-add-water pancake mix

1 cup Greek Yogurt whey (page 15)

⅓ cup canola oil

½ teaspoon ground cinnamon

2 ounces (¼ cup) butter

2 Gala apples, peeled and sliced

½ cup firmly packed light brown sugar

1. Preheat the oven to 350°F.

2. Place the oats on a jelly-roll pan. Bake at 350°F for 6 to 7 minutes or until toasted, stirring halfway through. Cool for 5 minutes.

3. Microwave the apple juice in a 1-cup glass measuring cup at HIGH 1 minute or just until warm.

4. Combine the pancake mix, whey, oil, cinnamon, toasted oats, and warm apple juice. Cook the batter in a preheated, oiled Belgian-style waffle iron until golden (about ⅓ cup batter per waffle).

5. Melt the butter in a medium nonstick skillet over medium. Add the apple slices and brown sugar to the skillet. Cook, stirring occasionally, 5 to 6 minutes or until the apple is tender and beginning to brown. Serve sautéed apples over waffles.

6-QUART

GROUND CORN BREAKFAST BOWLS

SERVES: 4 | HANDS-ON: 10 MINUTES | UNDER PRESSURE: 25 MINUTES
NATURAL PRESSURE RELEASE

If you prefer thinner grits, stir in 2 to 3 tablespoons of additional milk at the end.

1 cup stone-ground cornmeal

3¾ cups water

1 cup 2% reduced-fat milk

1 tablespoon canola oil

1 garlic clove, chopped

½ teaspoon table salt

½ teaspoon Worcestershire sauce

⅛ teaspoon ground red pepper

4 ounces reduced-fat sharp Cheddar cheese, shredded (about 1 cup)

Garnish: ¼ cup chopped scallions

1. Combine the cornmeal, 2 cups of the water, milk, oil, and garlic in a 4-cup glass measure. Pour the remaining water into the inner pot of a 6-quart Instant Pot®. Place the Steam Rack in cooker. Place the 4-cup glass measure on top of the rack.

2. Lock the lid; turn Pressure Valve to "Sealing." PRESSURE COOK [High Pressure] for 25 minutes. Open the cooker using Natural Pressure Release (page 7). Turn Pressure Valve to "Venting" to release remaining pressure.

3. Stir in the salt, Worcestershire sauce, and pepper. Gradually add ¾ cup of the cheese, stirring until cheese melts. Spoon grits into 4 bowls. Garnish with chopped scallions and remaining shredded cheese.

6-QUART

SOUTHERN GRITS

SERVES: 4 | HANDS-ON: 3 MINUTES | UNDER PRESSURE: 18 MINUTES | QUICK PRESSURE RELEASE

A Southern staple, grits are a delicious departure from oatmeal or cereal in the morning.

4 cups water

1 cup white, yellow, or speckled stone-ground grits

½ teaspoon table salt

¼ teaspoon freshly ground black pepper

Butter

1. Pour the 4 cups water into the inner pot of a 6-quart Instant Pot®. Add the grits and salt, stirring well. Lock the lid; turn Pressure Valve to "Sealing." Press PORRIDGE [High Pressure]. Cook for 18 minutes.

2. Open cooker using Quick Pressure Release (page 7). Add the pepper, stirring well. Top each serving with a pat of butter.

6- OR 8-QUART

HUEVOS RANCHEROS

SERVES: 4 | HANDS-ON: 15 MINUTES | UNDER PRESSURE: 0 MINUTES
QUICK PRESSURE RELEASE

Make-Ahead Poached Eggs (recipe below) are a tremendous time-saver in this savory breakfast. Store the cooked eggs in the refrigerator for up to 5 days until you are ready to serve the Huevos Rancheros. A garnish of cilantro adds fresh flavor, but you can omit it if you'd like.

1 (14½-ounce) can seasoned fire-roasted salsa-style diced tomatoes, undrained
1 (15-ounce) can black beans, undrained
1 Cubanelle pepper, seeded and chopped
½ cup frozen whole kernel corn
¼ teaspoon ground cumin
8 commercial tostada shells
4 Make-Ahead Poached Eggs (see recipe at right)
¼ cup thinly sliced scallions
¾ cup (3 ounces) shredded Mexican Style Four-Cheese Blend
¼ cup chopped fresh cilantro

1. Stir together the tomatoes, black beans, Cubanelle pepper, corn, and cumin in the inner pot of a 6- or 8-quart Instant Pot®.

2. Lock the lid; turn Pressure Valve to "Sealing." Press STEAM [High Pressure]; set time for 0 minutes. Immediately open the cooker using Quick Pressure Release (page 7).

3. While the bean mixture cooks, heat the tostada shells in the oven according to package directions; keep warm.

4. After opening the lid of the Instant Pot®, carefully nestle drained Make-Ahead Poached Eggs into the hot bean mixture. Cover the pot, and let stand 1 to 2 minutes or until eggs are just warm. (Do not overheat.)

5. Place 2 tostada shells, overlapping slightly, on each of 4 plates. Spoon ¾ cup bean mixture down the center of the shells on each plate. Sprinkle each serving with 1 tablespoon scallions. Top each serving with 1 poached egg, and sprinkle with 3 tablespoons cheese and 1 tablespoon cilantro. Serve immediately.

NOTE: You may substitute 2 cups cooked dried black beans (page 28) with about ¼ cup of the cooking liquid for the canned beans, and 1 large Anaheim chile, seeded and chopped, for the Cubanelle pepper, but the heat level can vary from mild to spicy.

MAKE-AHEAD POACHED EGGS

SERVES: 4 | HANDS ON: 10 MINUTES

If you have perfected preparing poached eggs in your Instant Pot® (page 17), you can chill them according to this method, too. Just be sure to cook the eggs by either method so that the yolks remain tender.

1 teaspoon table salt
4 very fresh large eggs

1. Place a collapsible vegetable steamer with a center handle into a 3-quart saucepan, and fill the pan with water to 1½ to 2 inches above the bottom of the steamer. Stir in the salt. Place the pan over medium-low heat until the water is barely simmering.

2. Fill a 3-quart bowl with very cold water, adding a few ice cubes, if necessary; set aside.

3. Break the eggs, 1 at a time, into a custard cup. Transfer each egg to a fine wire-mesh sieve; drain off the watery portion of the egg, and place in a bowl. Placing the rim of the bowl close to the surface of the simmering water, carefully slip the eggs, 1 at a time, into the simmering water. After the eggs have stood in the water for about 15 seconds, carefully turn them over with a rubber spatula or slotted spoon. Cook 3 to 4 minutes, turning the eggs several times, until the whites are firm and the yolks are still tender.

4. Lift the steamer with the eggs from the pan using the center handle of the steamer, and set the steamer along with the eggs into prepared cold water. If using right away, just leave the eggs in the cold water bath. If making ahead, gently transfer the chilled eggs to a storage container partially filled with cold water. Finish filling the container with cold water. Cover and store in the refrigerator up to 5 days.

JOSIE'S SPECIAL SCRAMBLE

SERVES: 1 | HANDS-ON: 12 MINUTES

Transform your leftover Polynesian Turkey Loaf (page 114) into a quick supper or filling breakfast for one. To make additional servings, simply multiply the recipe up to 4 times. For a heartier meal, serve with a toasted slice of buttered Farm House Yogurt Bread (page 51).

FOR 1 SERVING

2 large eggs

2 dashes of garlic powder

2 dashes of ground nutmeg

2 dashes of table salt

2 teaspoons butter

1 (⅓-inch-thick) slice chilled Polynesian Turkey Loaf (page 114), cut into ⅓-inch pieces

1½ cups loosely packed baby spinach, coarsely chopped

Freshly ground black pepper

Grated fresh Parmesan cheese

1. Whisk together the eggs, garlic powder, nutmeg, and salt in a medium bowl until no egg white is visible.

2. Melt the butter in a medium-size, well-seasoned cast-iron skillet, or nonstick skillet, over medium-high. Add the turkey loaf cubes, and cook, stirring often with a spatula, just until beginning to brown, about 2 minutes. Reduce heat to medium. Stir in the spinach; cook, stirring constantly, until spinach wilts, about 1 minute.

3. Reduce heat to medium-low. Add the egg mixture; cook, without stirring, until the mixture begins to set on the bottom. Draw the spatula across the bottom of the skillet to form curds. Continue until the egg mixture is thickened, but still moist; do not stir constantly. Remove from the pan immediately. Sprinkle with the black pepper and cheese.

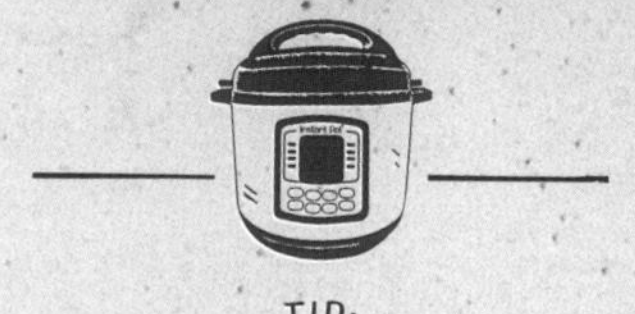

TIP:

If making more than 2 servings, you will need a large skillet.

SPICY HAM-AND-EGGS BENEDICT

SERVES: 4 | HANDS-ON: 17 MINUTES | UNDER PRESSURE: 2 MINUTES | QUICK PRESSURE RELEASE

If eggs Benedict is your go-to brunch order, easily re-create it at home with the help of your Instant Pot®. Although this recipe calls for frozen biscuits, you can also make a batch of Buttermilk Biscuits (page 46) and use them instead.

4 frozen biscuits
2 tablespoons butter, melted
3 tablespoons chopped fresh chives
1 (0.9-ounce) envelope hollandaise sauce mix
1 cup milk
1 tablespoon lemon juice
¾ cup chopped lean ham
¼ to ½ teaspoon cayenne pepper
4 large eggs
2 cups loosely packed arugula
1 small avocado, sliced
Black pepper

1. Bake the biscuits according to package directions.
2. Preheat the oven to 375°F.
3. Combine the melted butter and 1 tablespoon of the chives; split the biscuits, and brush with the butter mixture. Place the biscuits, buttered sides up, on a baking sheet. Bake at 375°F for 5 minutes or until toasted.
4. Cook the hollandaise sauce mix according to package directions, using the 1 cup milk and the 1 tablespoon lemon juice and omitting butter. Cook the ham, stirring occasionally, in a medium-size nonstick skillet over medium 3 to 4 minutes or until browned. Stir the ham and the cayenne pepper into the hollandaise sauce; keep warm.
5. Poach the eggs in the Instant Pot® according to the instructions on page 17.
6. While the eggs are poaching, place the bottom halves of the biscuits, buttered sides up, on each of 4 individual serving plates. Top evenly with the arugula and avocado. Carefully place the eggs on top of the avocado. Spoon hollandaise sauce evenly on top of each egg. Sprinkle with the remaining 2 tablespoons chives, and add the black pepper to taste. Top with the remaining biscuit halves, and serve immediately.

BUTTERMILK BISCUITS

MAKES: 8 TO 9 BISCUITS | HANDS-ON: 10 MINUTES | BAKE: 10 TO 12 MINUTES

Bake a batch of these biscuits to top Beef Pot Pie (page 78). Preheating your oven is key to tall, fluffy biscuits because the dough starts to rise as soon as it hits the heat. Freeze any leftovers and warm in the microwave, then crisp in the oven at 375°F for about 5 minutes.

2 cups all-purpose flour
2 teaspoons baking powder
1 teaspoon sugar
¾ teaspoon table salt
¼ teaspoon baking soda
¼ cup unsalted butter, cut in pieces
¾ cup buttermilk

1. Preheat the oven to 450°F.
2. Process the flour, baking powder, sugar, salt, and baking soda in a food processor until blended. Add the butter; process until the consistency of coarse meal. Add the buttermilk; pulse just until dry flour mixture is moistened.
3. Turn the dough out onto a floured surface, and pat to ½-inch thickness. Cut out biscuits using a floured 2½-inch cutter (do not twist the cutter). Place the biscuits, 2 inches apart, on an ungreased baking sheet.
4. Bake at 450°F for 10 to 12 minutes or until golden.

SKILLET CORNBREAD

SERVES: 8 | HANDS-ON: 10 MINUTES | BAKE: 38 MINUTES

Use your leftover Greek Yogurt whey (page 15) in this easy cornbread recipe, and serve with steaming bowls of Mexican Chicken Stew (page 125).

1¼ cups (about 5.6 ounces) all-purpose flour

1 cup plus 3 tablespoons plain white cornmeal

¼ cup sugar

1 tablespoon baking powder

1 teaspoon table salt

¼ teaspoon baking soda

2 ounces (¼ cup) butter, melted

⅔ cup Greek Yogurt whey (page 15)

⅓ cup Greek Yogurt (page 15)

2 large eggs

1. Preheat the oven to 400°F.

2. Lightly grease an 8-inch cast-iron skillet, and heat in the oven 5 minutes.

3. Meanwhile, weigh or lightly spoon the flour into dry measuring cups; level with a knife. Combine the flour, cornmeal, sugar, baking powder, salt, and baking soda in a bowl; whisk in the melted butter. Add the whey, yogurt, and eggs, stirring with a whisk just until smooth.

4. Pour the batter into the hot skillet. Bake at 400°F for 30 to 33 minutes or until golden brown.

6-QUART

PEASANT BREAD

SERVES: 16 | HANDS-ON: 25 MINUTES | PROOF: 1 HOUR, 30 MINUTES | BAKE: 35 MINUTES

- **1 cup Greek Yogurt whey (page 15) or water**
- **¼ cup stone-ground white, yellow, or speckled grits**
- **1½ teaspoons table salt**
- **2 tablespoons canola oil**
- **3 tablespoons honey**
- **1 package dry yeast (about 2¼ teaspoons)**
- **¼ cup warm water (100° to 110°F)**
- **6 tablespoons (about 1.7 ounces) whole-wheat flour**
- **¼ cup (about 1.1 ounces) stone-ground rye flour**
- **2 tablespoons raw sunflower seeds, chopped**
- **2¼ to 2⅓ cups (about 10.1 to 10.5 ounces) all-purpose flour**
- **Cooking spray**
- **1 egg white, beaten**
- **1 tablespoon water**
- **1 teaspoon each: poppy seeds or chia seeds, fennel seeds or caraway seeds, and sesame seeds**

1. Stir together the whey, grits, and salt in a small saucepan. Bring to a boil; reduce heat, cover, and simmer, stirring frequently, until thick (about 8 minutes). Remove from heat, and stir in the oil and honey. Let cool to room temperature. Transfer to the bowl of a heavy-duty electric stand mixer.

2. While grits cool, dissolve the yeast in the warm water in a 1-cup glass measuring cup; let stand 5 minutes. Stir the yeast mixture into the grits mixture. Add the whole-wheat flour and rye flour to the yeast mixture; beat at medium speed, using a dough hook attachment, 2 minutes. Scrape down the sides of the bowl, and add the sunflower seeds. Gradually add 2¼ cups of the all-purpose flour. Decrease the speed to low, and knead 8 minutes or until the dough is smooth and elastic but still slightly sticky. Turn the dough out onto a lightly floured surface. Shape the dough into a ball.

3. Coat the inner pot of a 6-quart Instant Pot® with cooking spray. Place the dough in the pot, turning to coat the top. Coat the top of the dough with cooking spray. Lock the lid; turn the Pressure Valve to "Sealing." Press YOGURT [Less], and let the dough rise for 1 hour or until doubled in bulk.

4. Punch down the dough, and turn out onto a lightly floured surface. Wash and dry the inner pot. Center and fit a 16-inch-long piece of parchment paper into the inner pot. Shape the dough into a 6-inch round; place on the parchment paper in the pot. Return the inner pot to the cooker.

5. Lock the lid; turn Pressure Valve to "Sealing." Press YOGURT [Less], and let the dough rise for 30 minutes.

6. While the dough proofs, preheat the oven to 375°F. Place a 5-quart cast-iron Dutch oven with cast-iron lid on the middle rack of the oven, and heat at least 30 minutes.

7. When the dough has risen enough, combine the egg white and the 1 tablespoon water in a small bowl. Gently brush the dough with the egg white mixture, and sprinkle with the seed mixture. Using a sharp knife, make 3 cuts in top of the loaf in a triangular pattern.

8. Transfer the Dutch oven from the oven to a heatproof surface. Remove the lid from the Instant Pot®. Gather the corners of the parchment paper, and transfer the loaf, along with the paper, to the Dutch oven. Carefully cover with the hot lid, and bake at 375°F for 25 minutes. Uncover, and bake 10 more minutes or until the bread is golden brown. Remove the loaf from the Dutch oven and from the parchment paper, and place on a wire rack. Cool completely before slicing.

NOTE: To bake in a loaf pan: After the first proofing, punch the dough down, and roll into a 14- x 7-inch rectangle. Roll up rectangle tightly, starting with a short edge, pressing firmly to eliminate air pockets; pinch seam and ends to seal. Place the dough, seam side down, in an 8- x 4-inch glass loaf pan coated with cooking spray. Cover and let rise in a warm place (85°F), free from drafts, about 30 minutes or until doubled in size. Preheat the oven to 350°F. Uncover the dough; brush with the egg mixture and sprinkle with desired seeds. Bake at 350°F for about 35 to 40 minutes or until bread is browned and sounds hollow when tapped. (If bread browns too quickly, tent loaf with foil after 25 minutes.) Remove the loaf from pan, and cool completely on a wire rack.

6-QUART

WHEAT 'N' HONEY DINNER ROLLS

MAKES: 2 DOZEN | HANDS-ON: 28 MINUTES | PROOF: 2 HOURS | BAKE: 15 MINUTES

Step up your grilling game and save half the dough to make homemade hamburger buns. You'll end up with one dozen rolls and 4 buns. The sesame seeds are optional but they do add a nice texture.

- **1 cup Greek Yogurt whey (page 15)**
- **½ cup Greek Yogurt (page 15)**
- **¼ cup canola oil**
- **¼ cup honey**
- **¾ cup white whole-wheat flour**
- **¼ cup plain toasted wheat germ**
- **1 package quick-rise yeast (about 2½ teaspoons)**
- **2¾ to 3¼ cups all-purpose flour**
- **1½ teaspoons table salt**
- **½ teaspoon baking soda**
- **Cooking spray**
- **1 large egg, beaten**
- **2 teaspoons water**
- **Sesame seeds (optional)**

1. Whisk together the whey and yogurt in a small saucepan until smooth. Cook over medium-low to 100° to 110°F. Remove from the heat; stir in the oil and honey. Combine the whole-wheat flour, wheat germ, and yeast in the bowl of a heavy-duty electric mixer fitted with the dough hook attachment. Add the whey mixture, and beat at medium speed for 2 minutes.

2. Combine 2¾ cups of the all-purpose flour, the salt, and baking soda in medium bowl. Add to the whole-wheat flour mixture. Beat at low speed for 8 minutes or until the dough is smooth and elastic, adding additional flour, up to ½ cup if necessary, to form a soft, smooth dough. Shape the dough into a ball with floured hands.

3. Coat the inner pot of a 6-quart Instant Pot® with cooking spray. Place the dough in the pot; coat dough with cooking spray. Lock the lid; turn Pressure Valve to "Venting." Press YOGURT [Less], and set the timer for 1 hour and 30 minutes or until dough doubles in bulk. Punch down the dough, and divide in half. Shape each half of the dough into 12 balls, and place in an 8-inch round cake pan coated with cooking spray. Combine the egg and 2 teaspoons water in a small bowl. Brush the tops of the rolls with the egg wash. Sprinkle with the sesame seeds, if desired. Cover and let rise in a warm (85°F) place, free from drafts, 30 minutes or until almost double in bulk.

4. Preheat the oven to 375°F.

5. Bake at 375°F for 15 to 17 minutes or until golden brown, shielding tops with aluminum foil, if necessary, during the last 2 minutes to prevent over browning. Remove the rolls from the pans, and let cool on wire racks.

TIP:

Dough may be shaped into 8 large balls to make hamburger buns. Place the balls on a large baking sheet lined with parchment paper; flatten slightly. Brush with egg wash, and, if desired, sprinkle with sesame seeds. Cover and let rise for 20 to 30 minutes. Bake at 375°F for 14 to 16 minutes. Cool completely on wire racks. Freeze up to 3 months.

6-QUART

FARM HOUSE YOGURT BREAD

MAKES: 1 LOAF | HANDS-ON: 20 MINUTES | PROOF: ABOUT 1 HOUR, 30 MINUTES
BAKE: 30 MINUTES

Greek Yogurt and whey (page 15) give this soft, airy bread a tangy taste similar to sourdough. You may substitute a metal loaf pan for the glass pan, but increase the oven temperature to 375°F. Since this bread is so moist and tender, slice it with a meat slicer or electric knife for the best results.

- **¼ cup warm water (100° to 110°F)**
- **1 package active dry yeast (about 2¼ teaspoons)**
- **Pinch of sugar**
- **Cooking spray**
- **2 tablespoons unsalted butter**
- **½ cup Greek Yogurt whey (page 15)**
- **½ cup Greek Yogurt (page 15), room temperature**
- **1 tablespoon sugar**
- **3 to 3¼ cups bread flour**
- **1 teaspoon table salt**
- **1 egg, beaten**
- **2 teaspoons water**
- **4 cups boiling water**

1. Stir together ¼ cup warm water, yeast, and pinch of sugar in a 1-cup measuring cup; let stand 10 minutes or until foamy.

2. Lightly coat the inner pot of a 6-quart Instant Pot® with cooking spray. Place the butter in a small saucepan. Cook over low heat just until melted. Whisk together the whey and yogurt until smooth; add to the butter. Cook over low to 100° to 110°F. Remove from the heat; add 1 tablespoon sugar, stirring until sugar dissolves.

3. Place 1 cup of the flour in the bowl of a heavy-duty electric mixer fitted with a dough hook attachment. Add the whey mixture, and beat at medium speed for 2 minutes.

4. Add the yeast mixture, 1¾ cups of the remaining flour, and the salt to the yogurt mixture. Beat at low speed for 8 to 10 minutes or until dough is smooth and elastic, adding additional flour, up to ½ cup if necessary, to form a soft, smooth dough. Turn dough out onto a lightly floured work surface. Shape the dough into a ball with floured hands.

5. Place the dough in the pot, smooth side up; coat dough with cooking spray. Lock the lid; turn Pressure Valve to "Venting." Press YOGURT [Less], set the timer for 1 hour, and let proof until dough is almost doubled in bulk. Punch down the dough.

6. On a lightly floured surface, roll out the dough into a 14- x 7-inch rectangle. Tightly roll up the dough, jelly-roll style, starting with the short side. Pinch the seam and ends to seal; place in an 8- x 4-inch glass loaf pan coated with cooking spray.

7. Combine the beaten egg and 2 teaspoons water in a small bowl. Brush the loaf with the egg wash. Place an 8- x 8-inch baking pan on a lower rack of the oven. Pour the boiling water into the pan. Set the bread on the middle rack above the pan. Close the oven door, and let rise for about 15 minutes or until almost doubled in bulk. Place the egg wash in the refrigerator while the dough proofs in the oven. Remove the dough from the oven, and brush with additional egg wash. Remove the pan of water from the oven.

8. Preheat the oven to 350°F.

9. Bake at 350°F for 30 minutes or until the loaf is golden brown and sounds hollow when tapped. Immediately remove the loaf from the pan; let cool completely on a wire rack before slicing.

TIPS:

The dough is very lively and can easily over proof, so watch closely. A good deal of rising will take place while the oven preheats and during the first few minutes of baking (known as "oven spring").

•••

This bread freezes well up to 3 months. Slice before freezing so that slices can be thawed, one or more at a time.

6-QUART

BUTTER-RUM BANANA BREAD

SERVES: 12 | HANDS-ON: 12 MINUTES | UNDER PRESSURE: 58 MINUTES
10-MINUTE NATURAL PRESSURE RELEASE

Rich butter and a dash of rum flavoring dress up a quick bread classic. Sift powdered sugar over the bread for extra sweetness.

Butter-flavored cooking spray
1½ cups all-purpose flour
1½ cups water
2 small very ripe bananas, peeled and cut into 1-inch pieces (see Tip)
2 tablespoons unsalted butter
½ cup Greek Yogurt (page 15)
¾ cup firmly packed light brown sugar
¾ teaspoon baking powder
¾ teaspoon baking soda
½ teaspoon table salt
½ teaspoon ground cinnamon
1 teaspoon vanilla extract
½ teaspoon rum flavoring
2 large eggs
½ cup toasted pecan halves

1. Coat a 6-cup nonstick Bundt pan with cooking spray. Dust the pan with 2 teaspoons of the flour, tapping pan to shake out excess. Pour the 1½ cups water into the inner pot of a 6-quart Instant Pot®.

2. Process the bananas and butter in a food processor until finely chopped, about 20 seconds. Add the remaining flour, the yogurt and remaining ingredients, except the pecan halves. Process 10 seconds. Scrape down the sides.

3. Add the pecan halves; pulse 3 times or just until chopped. Pour the batter into the prepared pan, smoothing the top. Tap the pan on a work surface to remove air bubbles. Cover just the top of the pan with aluminum foil coated with cooking spray, coated side down. Place the pan on the Steam Rack. Using the rack handles, gently lower the pan into the pot. Place the pot in the cooker.

4. Close the lid; turn Pressure Valve to "Sealing." PRESSURE COOK [High Pressure] 58 minutes. Allow a 10-minute Natural Pressure Release (page 10).

5. Turn the valve to "Venting" to release the remaining pressure. Lift the cake from the pot, using the rack handles. Remove the foil.

6. Let cool 5 minutes in the pan. Loosen the bread from the sides and center of the pan using a plastic knife or small spatula. Invert the bread onto a wire cooling rack; cool completely.

TIP:

The best banana flavor comes from bananas that are extremely ripe and somewhat soft. Do not use very large bananas in this recipe. When they are puréed, they should equal about 1 cup.

6-QUART

PUMPKIN BREAD

SERVES: 16 | HANDS-ON: 15 MINUTES | UNDER PRESSURE: 58 MINUTES
10-MINUTE NATURAL PRESSURE RELEASE

This tasty, moist bread is a delicious way to utilize the whey left from making Greek Yogurt (page 15). For even more fall flavor, serve with steaming mugs of Hot Spiced Cider (page 59).

Cooking spray
1¾ cups all-purpose flour
1½ cups water
1⅓ cups sugar
⅔ cup canned pumpkin
⅓ cup butter, softened
⅓ cup Greek Yogurt whey (page 15)
2 large eggs
1 teaspoon baking soda
½ teaspoon table salt
½ teaspoon ground cinnamon
½ teaspoon ground cloves
¼ teaspoon baking powder
⅓ cup walnut halves

1. Coat a 6-cup nonstick Bundt pan with cooking spray. Dust the pan with 2 teaspoons of the flour, tapping pan to shake out excess. Pour the 1½ cups water into the inner pot of a 6-quart Instant Pot®.

2. Process the sugar, pumpkin, and butter in a food processor until blended, about 20 seconds. Add the remaining flour, whey, and remaining ingredients, except the walnut halves. Process 10 seconds. Scrape down the sides.

3. Add the walnut halves; pulse 3 times or just until chopped. Spoon the batter into the prepared pan, smoothing the top. Tap the pan on a work surface to remove air bubbles. Cover the top of the pan with aluminum foil coated with cooking spray, coated side down. Place the pan on the Steam Rack. Using the rack handles, gently lower the pan into the pot. Place the pot in the cooker.

4. Close the lid; turn Pressure Valve to "Sealing." PRESSURE COOK [High Pressure] for 58 minutes. Allow a 10-minute Natural Pressure Release (page 10). Turn the valve to "Venting" to release the remaining pressure. Lift the cake from the pot, using the rack handles. Remove the foil. Let cool 5 minutes in the pan.

5. Loosen the bread from the sides and center of the pan using a plastic knife or small spatula. Invert the bread onto a wire cooling rack; cool completely.

BRAN-OAT MUFFINS WITH APRICOTS AND PECANS

MAKES: 1 DOZEN | HANDS-ON: 20 MINUTES | BAKE: 22 MINUTES

Take care to grate just the orange part of the rind, not the white pith, which is bitter. Soaking too long or processing the batter until smooth will destroy the pleasantly pebbly texture of the cereal nuggets in these orange-scented muffins, so do not over-process.

- **⅔ cup apricot nectar, unfiltered fresh-pressed apple cider, orange juice, or Greek yogurt whey**
- **½ cup Greek Yogurt whey (page 15)**
- **¼ cup canola oil**
- **1 tablespoon grated orange rind (about 1 large navel orange)**
- **1 large egg, beaten**
- **2 cups bran cereal nuggets (such as Bran Buds)**
- **1 cup uncooked regular oats**
- **¾ cup all-purpose flour**
- **½ cup sugar**
- **½ teaspoon baking soda**
- **¼ teaspoon table salt**
- **⅛ teaspoon ground nutmeg**
- **3 tablespoons coarsely chopped dried apricots or dried peaches**
- **2 tablespoons chopped toasted pecans**
- **Cooking spray**

1. Preheat oven to 375°F.
2. Stir together the nectar, whey, oil, orange rind, and egg in a medium bowl. Stir in the cereal nuggets, and let stand 10 minutes. (Do not over soak.)
3. Meanwhile, process the oats in a food processor about 20 seconds, or until finely ground.
4. Add the flour, sugar, baking soda, salt, and nutmeg to the oats. Process just until blended.
5. Add the cereal mixture, dried apricots, and toasted pecans; pulse 3 times or just until the dry ingredients are moistened. (Batter will be thick and slightly bumpy from the cereal.) Spoon the batter evenly into 12 (2½-inch) muffin cups coated with cooking spray. (Cups will be almost full.)
6. Bake at 375°F for 20 to 22 minutes or until golden brown. Gently remove from pans immediately. Let stand on a wire rack 3 minutes before serving. Serve warm.

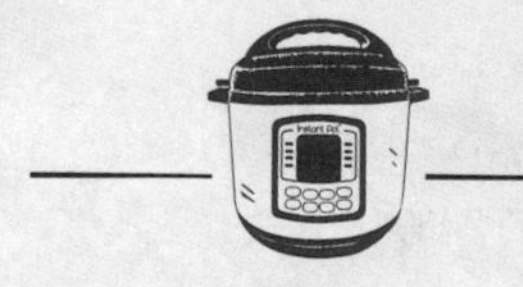

TIP:

Muffins may be frozen for up to 2 months. Microwave at HIGH just until thawed and warm; finish in a 375°F oven until the edges are crisp, about 5 minutes.

CARROT-POPPY SEED MUFFINS

MAKES: 1 DOZEN | HANDS-ON: 15 MINUTES | BAKE: 22 MINUTES

These kid-friendly muffins are a great way to sneak in extra veggies. You can use a box grater or food processor fitted with a shredding blade to shred the carrots. Switch up both the color and flavor by substituting shredded beets for the carrots and omitting the whey.

- **1½ cups (about 6.75 ounces) all-purpose flour**
- **¾ cup firmly packed dark brown sugar**
- **1 tablespoon poppy seeds**
- **1¼ teaspoons baking powder**
- **½ teaspoon baking soda**
- **½ teaspoon table salt**
- **2 large eggs, lightly beaten**
- **5 tablespoons olive oil**
- **1 tablespoon firmly packed grated orange rind**
- **2 cups shredded carrots (about 3 large)**
- **¾ cup Greek Yogurt whey (page 15)**
- **12 paper baking cups**

1. Preheat oven to 375°F.
2. Combine flour, brown sugar, and next 4 ingredients in a large bowl; stir with a whisk. Stir in the eggs, olive oil, and orange rind. Fold in the shredded carrots and whey. Place paper baking cups in a 12-cup muffin pan. Spoon batter into cups, filling two-thirds full.
3. Bake at 375°F for 20 to 22 minutes or until golden brown.

BEET-POPPY SEED MUFFINS

Switch up the color and flavor by using shredded beets in place of carrots. Prepare recipe as directed, substituting 1 large fresh beet, peeled and shredded (about 1½ cups), for carrots. Omit whey. (Do not squeeze juice from shredded beet.)

6-QUART

FRESH APPLE-PECAN COFFEE CAKE

SERVES: 8 | HANDS-ON: 12 MINUTES | UNDER PRESSURE: 55 MINUTES
10-MINUTE NATURAL PRESSURE RELEASE

Treat yourself to a generous slice of this spiced breakfast cake on a slow weekend morning. It pairs nicely with a Chai Latte (page 59).

Cooking spray
2 teaspoons all-purpose flour
1½ cups water
1½ cups all-purpose flour
½ teaspoon baking soda
¼ teaspoon table salt
¾ cup sugar
⅓ cup canola oil
1 teaspoon vanilla extract
2 large eggs
1½ cups chopped peeled apple
½ cup chopped pecans
Powdered sugar

1. Coat a 6-cup nonstick Bundt pan with the cooking spray; dust with the 2 teaspoons flour, tapping the pan to shake out excess. Pour the 1½ cups water into the inner pot of a 6-quart Instant Pot®.

2. Combine the 1½ cups flour, baking soda, and salt in a medium bowl. Combine the sugar, oil, vanilla, and eggs in large bowl; beat at medium speed with an electric mixer 2 full minutes. Add the flour mixture; stir by hand until blended and smooth. Gently stir in the chopped apple and pecans. Pour the batter into the prepared pan, smoothing the top. Tap the pan on a work surface to remove air bubbles. Cover just the top of the pan with aluminum foil coated with cooking spray, coated side down. Place the pan on the Steam Rack. Using the rack handles, gently lower the pan into the pot. Place the pot in the cooker.

3. Close the lid; turn Pressure Valve to "Sealing." PRESSURE COOK [High Pressure] for 55 minutes. Allow a 10-minute Natural Pressure Release (page 10). Turn the valve to "Venting" to release remaining pressure. Lift the cake from the pot, using the handles. Remove the foil. Let cool 10 minutes in the pan. Loosen the cake from the sides and center of the pan using a plastic knife or small spatula. Invert the cake onto a wire cooling rack; cool completely. Dust the cake with powdered sugar before serving.

TIP:

The crisp flavors of Braeburn, Fuji, and Gala apples are best for this cake.

6-QUART

FRENCH TOAST BREAKFAST PUDDING

SERVES: 6 TO 8 | HANDS-ON: 20 MINUTES | SLOW COOK: 3 HOURS

Yes, you can eat bread pudding for breakfast! Maple syrup adds just the right amount of sweetness and indulgent flavor. To toast the pecans, heat in a skillet over medium until browned and fragrant, about 2 to 5 minutes.

Cooking spray
16 ounces French bread, cut into 1-inch cubes
4 large eggs, lightly beaten
¼ cup packed brown sugar
1 teaspoon ground cinnamon
1 teaspoon vanilla extract
¼ teaspoon table salt
¼ teaspoon grated whole nutmeg
2 cups 2% reduced-fat milk
½ cup heavy cream
½ cup coarsely chopped toasted pecan halves
½ cup maple syrup

1. Remove the inner pot from a 6-quart Instant Pot®, and coat the pot with cooking spray. Place the bread cubes in the pot.

2. Combine the eggs, brown sugar, cinnamon, vanilla, salt, and nutmeg, in a large bowl. Add the milk and cream, stirring with a whisk until blended. Pour the milk mixture over the bread in the pot, stirring gently and pressing with a spoon to coat and submerge all the bread cubes.

3. Tear off a 10½-inch-long piece of aluminum foil; lay foil on top of the inner pot, gently smoothing it down the side of the pot. Trim the pointed corners even with the rest of the foil, and tightly tuck it in under the rim.

4. Cut 1 (1¼-inch-long) slit in the foil, about 1 inch from edge, with a thin, sharp knife. Cut a second 1¼-inch-long slit parallel to and about 1 inch to the inside of the first. Repeat this procedure 3 times, creating 2 concentric slits in the foil at intervals of 12, 3, 6, and 9 o'clock. Set the inner pot inside of the cooker.

5. Lock the lid; turn Pressure Valve "Venting." Press SLOW COOK [Normal], and cook for 3 hours. (A knife inserted in the center should come out clean.) Transfer the inner pot from the cooker to a wire rack. Uncover and let stand 10 minutes. Spoon into serving bowls. Sprinkle each serving with about 1 tablespoon of the pecans, and drizzle with 2 tablespoons of the maple syrup.

6-QUART

MULLED FRUIT PUNCH

MAKES: 9 CUPS | HANDS-ON: 5 MINUTES | UNDER PRESSURE: 5 MINUTES
15-MINUTE NATURAL PRESSURE RELEASE

The spirit of this hot punch lifts to your liking with the addition of a good quality fruity red wine. Start with 1 cup and add more to taste, up to 1 bottle. The flavor mellows after bringing to a simmer, so taste before adding more wine.

1 large navel orange
3 cups apple juice
2 cups 100% pomegranate-blueberry juice (such as POM Wonderful)
½ cup orange juice
6 large whole cloves
6 large whole allspice berries
3 (2-inch) cinnamon sticks
½ cup sugar
1 (750-milliliter) bottle Merlot, or to taste

1. Cut off the ends of the orange, and cut it crosswise into ¼-inch-thick slices. Cut the slices in half to create half-moon shapes. Place 6 half-moon slices in the inner pot of a 6-quart Instant Pot®. Cut the remaining half-moon slices in half again to create wedge shapes; set aside.

2. Add the apple juice, pomegranate-blueberry juice, orange juice, cloves, allspice berries, and cinnamon sticks to the pot. Lock the lid; turn Pressure Valve to "Sealing." PRESSURE COOK [High Pressure] for 5 minutes. Allow a 15-minute Natural Pressure Release (page 10). Turn the valve to "Venting" to release the remaining pressure. Turn off the cooker.

3. Stir in the sugar and, if desired, wine, beginning with 1 cup. Press SAUTÉ [Less]. Bring the mixture to a simmer, stirring occasionally. Adjust the wine amount, if desired, as the mixture simmers. Turn off the cooker. Remove and discard the spices and orange slices with a slotted spoon. Press KEEP WARM [Less]. Ladle into cups or mugs, and add 1 reserved orange wedge to each serving. Serve very warm.

TIP:

The longer the spices are left in the punch, the more intense the flavor. The orange slices tend to become bitter over time, so they are best removed soon after coming to a simmer.

6- OR 8-QUART

HOT SPICED CIDER

MAKES: 1 GALLON | HANDS ON: 5 MINUTES | UNDER PRESSURE: 15 MINUTES | NATURAL PRESSURE RELEASE

You can substitute unsweetened apple juice for the apple cider, but reduce the brown sugar to 3 tablespoons. Leave the Instant Pot® in KEEP WARM mode to keep the cider hot before serving.

1 (128-ounce) bottle unfiltered apple cider made from fresh apples
⅓ cup firmly packed light brown sugar
2 teaspoons whole cloves
1 teaspoon whole allspice berries
8 (3-inch) cinnamon sticks

Pour the apple cider into the inner pot of a 6- or 8-quart Instant Pot®. Add the brown sugar and remaining ingredients, stirring until the brown sugar dissolves. Lock the lid; turn Pressure Valve to "Sealing." PRESSURE COOK [High Pressure] for 15 minutes. Open the cooker using a complete Natural Pressure Release (page 7). Ladle cider mixture through a small sieve into mugs, and serve hot.

TIPS:

If desired, reserve the empty cider container. Cool the cider mixture; remove and discard half of the cinnamon sticks. Place the remaining cinnamon sticks in the empty container, and pour the cider, along with the cloves and allspice through a funnel into the container. Store in the refrigerator up to 1 month. To serve, shake chilled cider mixture well, and pour through a sieve into 1 or more mugs. Reheat in the microwave.

...

This recipe can also be made using the SLOW COOK [More] setting for 6 hours. (Turn the Pressure Valve to "Venting.")

6-QUART

CHAI LATTE

SERVES: 6 | HANDS-ON: 8 MINUTES | UNDER PRESSURE: 2 MINUTES | NATURAL PRESSURE RELEASE

Black pepper adds a bit of a bite to this creamy beverage. Whole milk yields a richer, creamier tea, but you may substitute lower fat milk, if desired.

2 family-size black tea bags or 8 regular-size black tea bags
5 cups water
2 cups whole milk
⅓ cup sugar
1¾ teaspoons ground cardamom
¾ teaspoon ground cinnamon
½ teaspoon ground ginger
½ teaspoon ground cloves
½ teaspoon freshly ground black pepper

Remove the paper tags from the tea bags, if present. Combine the water, milk, and tea bags in the inner pot of a 6-quart Instant Pot®. Whisk together the sugar and spices in a small bowl. Add the sugar mixture to the milk mixture, stirring until the sugar dissolves and the tea bags are wet. PRESSURE COOK [High Pressure] for 2 minutes. Allow a complete Natural Pressure Release (page 7). Remove the tea bags. Stir the tea well. Ladle into mugs through a fine-mesh sieve to remove the spice sediment. Serve hot.

TIP:

Cool leftover chai completely, strain, and store in a covered container in the refrigerator up to 5 days. Pour into 1 or more mugs, and reheat in the microwave.

1 Tablespoon

3

MEATS

6-QUART

CABERNET-BRAISED BEEF SHORT RIBS

SERVES: 6 | HANDS-ON: 10 MINUTES | UNDER PRESSURE: 52 MINUTES
QUICK PRESSURE RELEASE

A rich red wine sauce elevates these easy short ribs into a date-night worthy meal.

4 tablespoons all-purpose flour
2 pounds bone-in beef short ribs, trimmed
½ teaspoon table salt
½ teaspoon freshly ground black pepper
1 tablespoon olive oil
1½ cups (1-inch-thick) sliced celery
1 cup (1-inch-thick) sliced carrot
6 garlic cloves, sliced
2 (6-inch) rosemary sprigs
1 medium onion, cut into 8 wedges
2 tablespoons tomato paste
½ cup fat-free, lower-sodium beef broth
½ cup cabernet sauvignon or other dry red wine
¼ cup water
1 tablespoon cold water
3 cups hot cooked wide egg noodles
Garnish: chopped fresh parsley (optional)

1. Place 3 tablespoons of the flour in a shallow dish. Sprinkle the beef with salt and pepper; dredge in the flour. Remove the lid from a 6-quart Instant Pot®. Press SAUTÉ [Normal]. When the word "Hot" appears, swirl the oil in the inner pot. Add the beef to the pot; cook 8 minutes, browning on all sides. Remove the beef from pot, reserving 1 tablespoon drippings in pot.

2. Add the celery, carrot, garlic, rosemary, and onion to the drippings in the cooker; cook, stirring constantly, 4 minutes. Stir in the tomato paste. Add the broth, wine, and ¼ cup water to cooker, scraping with a wooden or plastic spatula to loosen browned bits from the bottom of the pot. Return the ribs to the pot. Turn off the cooker.

3. Lock the lid; turn Pressure Valve to "Sealing." PRESSURE COOK [High Pressure] for 52 minutes. Open the cooker using Quick Pressure Release (page 7).

4. Remove the ribs from the pot. Strain the cooking liquid through a fine sieve into a bowl; discard solids. Return the cooking liquid to the pot. With the lid off, press SAUTÉ [Normal]. Bring cooking liquid to a boil.

5. Stir together 1 tablespoon cold water and 1 tablespoon flour in a small bowl until smooth. Add the flour mixture to the cooking liquid, stirring with a whisk. Cook until mixture is slightly thick, about 5 minutes. Turn off the cooker. Serve ribs and noodles with the sauce. Garnish with the chopped parsley, if desired.

6-QUART

ITALIAN POT ROAST

SERVES: 6 | HANDS-ON: 12 MINUTES | UNDER PRESSURE: 55 MINUTES
NATURAL PRESSURE RELEASE

The Instant Pot® makes it easy to enjoy the slow-cooked flavor of pot roast on a busy weeknight. Toss the saucy meat with noodles; wide egg noodles work well.

- **1 (3- to 4-pound) boneless chuck roast, trimmed**
- **1 teaspoon freshly ground black pepper**
- **2 tablespoons olive oil**
- **1 large sweet onion, cut in half and sliced**
- **1 (8-ounce) package sliced mushrooms**
- **1 (14-ounce) can beef broth**
- **1 (8-ounce) can tomato sauce**
- **1 (1-ounce) envelope dry onion soup mix**
- **3 tablespoons tomato paste**
- **1 teaspoon dried Italian seasoning**
- **2 tablespoons cornstarch**
- **2 tablespoons water**

1. Sprinkle both sides of the roast with the pepper.

2. Remove the lid of a 6-quart Instant Pot®. Add the oil; press SAUTÉ [Normal]. When the oil is shimmering, add the roast to the inner pot, and cook 5 minutes on each side or until browned. Remove the roast from the pot.

3. Add the onion and mushrooms. Cook, stirring constantly, 5 minutes or until tender. Stir in the broth, tomato sauce, and onion soup mix, scraping bottom of pot with a wooden or plastic spatula until the bottom of the pot feels smooth.

4. Turn off the cooker. Return the roast to the pot, turning and nestling it into the broth mixture. Lock the lid; turn Pressure Valve to "Sealing." PRESSURE COOK [High Pressure] for 55 minutes.

5. Open the cooker using a Natural Pressure Release (page 7). Turn off the cooker. Remove the roast from the pot, and place on a cutting board; cut into large chunks, removing any large pieces of fat. Keep the roast warm.

6. Skim the fat from the cooking liquid. Add the tomato paste and Italian seasoning, stirring with a whisk. Combine the cornstarch and 2 tablespoons water; add to the cooking liquid, stirring with a whisk.

7. With the lid off, press SAUTÉ [Normal]. Bring the mixture to a boil, stirring frequently with a whisk. Cook 2 to 3 minutes or until thickened. Stir in the roast. Turn off the cooker. Let stand until thoroughly heated.

6-QUART

SUNDAY POT ROAST IN GRAVY

SERVES: 6 TO 8 | HANDS ON: 30 MINUTES | SLOW COOK: 12 HOURS

Browning the meat first is the key to this tender roast's rich flavor. Coffee and allspice enhance the meaty flavor while tapioca starch perfectly thickens the gravy right in the pot.

2 cups hot water
1 teaspoon instant coffee granules
2 teaspoons table salt
¼ teaspoon freshly ground black pepper
⅛ teaspoon ground allspice
1 large garlic clove, minced
Cooking spray
2 cups chopped onion
2 celery stalks, cut crosswise into ¼-inch slices
¼ cup quick-cooking tapioca
1 (4-pound) boneless chuck roast
1 tablespoon canola oil
Hot mashed potatoes

1. Stir together the water, coffee granules, salt, pepper, allspice, and garlic in a 2-cup glass measuring cup until coffee and salt dissolve. Set aside.

2. Coat the inner pot of a 6-quart Instant Pot® with cooking spray. Place the onion and celery in a single layer in the pot. Sprinkle the tapioca over the vegetables in an even layer. (Do not stir.) Trim the fat from the roast, and cut into large pieces, if necessary, to fit the pot.

3. Heat a large skillet over medium-high; swirl in the oil to coat the bottom of the skillet. Add the roast, and cook 5 minutes on each side until dark brown. Place the roast on top of the vegetables in the pot.

4. Stir the coffee mixture and add to the skillet, scraping to loosen browned bits; pour over the roast in the pot. (Do not stir.)

5. Lock the lid; turn Pressure Valve to "Venting." Cook on SLOW COOK [More] 12 hours or until the roast is very tender. Turn off the cooker. Transfer the roast to a serving plate. Stir the gravy until evenly thickened. Spoon some of the gravy over the roast. Pass the remaining gravy to spoon over the mashed potatoes.

TIPS:

To keep meats from sticking to stainless steel skillets, first heat the skillet over medium-high just until hot, then swirl in vegetable oil to coat the bottom of the pan. Add the meat, but do not try to turn it until the meat "releases itself" from the pan. If a slight tug with tongs is met with resistance, keep cooking until the meat easily releases. Because of its low smoke point, olive oil should be gently heated along with the skillet before adding the meat.

...

Extend leftover pot roast by using it in Beef Pot Pie (page 78) for an easy weeknight meal.

6-QUART

BEEF BOURGUIGNON

SERVES: 7 | HANDS-ON: 10 MINUTES | UNDER PRESSURE: 23 MINUTES
QUICK PRESSURE RELEASE

This classic French stew is delicious over noodles or mashed potatoes. Traditionally, Beef Bourguignon simmers for several hours, but the Instant Pot® cooks it in less than half an hour.

¼ cup all-purpose flour (about 1.1 ounces)
½ teaspoon table salt
½ teaspoon freshly ground black pepper
1½ pounds boneless chuck roast, trimmed and cut into 1-inch cubes
2 bacon slices, diced
½ cup dry red wine
1 (10½-ounce) can beef broth
3 cups baby carrots (about ¾ pound)
2 cups sliced shiitake mushroom caps (about ½ pound)
2 teaspoons dried thyme
6 shallots, halved (about ½ pound)
4 garlic cloves, thinly sliced
7 cups hot cooked medium egg noodles (about 5 cups uncooked pasta)
Garnish: thyme leaves (optional)

1. Combine the flour, salt, and pepper in a large zip-top plastic bag. Add the beef; seal and shake to coat.

2. Remove the lid of a 6-quart Instant Pot®. Place the bacon in the pot. Press SAUTÉ [Normal], and cook, stirring constantly, 30 seconds. Add half of the beef mixture to the cooker; cook 5 minutes, browning on all sides. Remove the beef and bacon from the cooker. Repeat the procedure with the remaining beef mixture. Turn off the cooker. Return the cooked beef and bacon to cooker. Stir in the wine and broth, scraping the pot with a wooden or plastic spatula to loosen browned bits. Add the carrots, mushrooms, thyme, shallots, and garlic.

3. Lock the lid; turn Pressure Valve to "Sealing." PRESSURE COOK [High Pressure] for 23 minutes. Turn off the cooker. Open the cooker using Quick Pressure Release (page 7). Serve the beef mixture over the noodles. Garnish with the thyme leaves, if desired.

TIP:

You may substitute crimini mushrooms for the shiitakes, if desired.

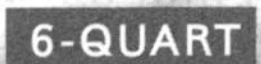

6-QUART

BEEF STROGANOFF

SERVES: 4 | HANDS-ON: 25 MINUTES | UNDER PRESSURE: 12 MINUTES
QUICK PRESSURE RELEASE

Egg noodles offer the classic taste of Beef Stroganoff, but you can serve with rice if you prefer.

¾ cup water
2 beef bouillon cubes
2 tablespoons unsalted butter
1½ cups sliced crimini mushrooms
1½ cups chopped onion
2 garlic cloves, minced
1¼ pounds London broil steak, cut across the grain into thin strips
¼ cup dry sherry
½ teaspoon freshly grated black pepper
2 tablespoons all-purpose flour
1 (10½-ounce) can cream of mushroom soup
⅓ cup sour cream
Hot cooked noodles or rice
Chopped fresh parsley

1. Combine ¾ cup water and the bouillon cubes in a 1-cup glass measuring cup. Microwave at HIGH 2 minutes. Stir until the bouillon dissolves. Set aside.

2. Place the butter in the inner pot of a 6-quart Instant Pot®. Press SAUTÉ [Normal]. When the butter melts, add the mushrooms and onion. Cook, stirring often, 3 minutes. Add the garlic; cook, stirring constantly, 30 seconds. Add the steak strips. Adjust heat to SAUTÉ [More]; cook, stirring often, until beef is browned. Stir in ½ cup of the bouillon mixture, ¼ cup sherry, and the pepper.

3. Lock the lid; turn Pressure Valve to "Sealing." PRESSURE COOK [High Pressure] for 12 minutes. Open the cooker using Quick Pressure Release (page7). Turn off the cooker.

4. Stir together the flour and the remaining ¼ cup bouillon mixture in a small bowl until smooth; stir into the beef mixture. Press SAUTÉ [Normal]; bring to a boil. Cook 5 minutes or until thickened. Add the soup, stirring until blended. Turn off the cooker. Remove the pot from the cooker. Stir in the sour cream. Serve over the hot cooked noodles or rice. Sprinkle with the parsley.

TIP:

For extra tender meat, make sure you cut across the grain.

6-QUART

CHEESY ONE-POT MOSTACCIOLI

SERVES: 6 | HANDS-ON: 20 MINUTES | UNDER PRESSURE: 5 MINUTES | QUICK PRESSURE RELEASE

If you like your pasta creamy and cheesy, this recipe is for you. Neufchâtel cheese has fewer calories than cream cheese and slightly more moisture, so it blends nicely into the rich sauce. Serve with a green salad or sautéed zucchini and your favorite crusty bread.

Cooking spray

1 pound lean ground beef (93/7)

1 tablespoon dried chopped onion

½ teaspoon garlic powder

½ teaspoon dried Italian seasoning

¼ teaspoon freshly grated black pepper

⅛ teaspoon ground red pepper

1 (24-ounce) jar marinara sauce with Burgundy (such as Bertoli Vineyard)

1 (14.5-ounce) can fire-roasted diced tomatoes with garlic, undrained

8 ounces uncooked mostaccioli pasta

1½ cups water

1⅓ cups 2% reduced-fat cottage cheese

3 ounces Neufchâtel cheese, softened

⅔ cup (2 ounces) freshly shredded Parmesan cheese

1 (8-ounce) package pre-shredded Italian 5-cheese blend

Chopped fresh Italian parsley

1. Coat the inner pot of a 6-quart Instant Pot® with cooking spray. Add the ground beef. Press SAUTÉ [Normal]; cook uncovered, stirring until the meat crumbles, is no longer pink, and the liquid is almost absorbed, about 5 minutes. Stir in the dried chopped onion, garlic powder, Italian seasoning, black pepper, and ground red pepper. Add the pasta sauce and tomatoes; stir well, scraping with a wooden or plastic spatula until the bottom of the pot feels smooth. Add the pasta and 1½ cups water; stir to coat and submerge pasta in the sauce mixture.

2. Lock the lid; turn Pressure Valve to "Sealing." PRESSURE COOK [High Pressure] for 5 minutes. Open the cooker using Quick Pressure Release (page 7).

3. While the pasta mixture cooks, process the cottage cheese, Neufchâtel cheese, and ⅓ cup of the Parmesan cheese in a food processor until smooth. Combine the remaining ⅓ cup Parmesan cheese and 1 cup of the Italian cheese blend in a bowl.

4. Stir the cottage cheese mixture into the pasta mixture in the pot. Stir in the Parmesan cheese mixture. Cover and let stand 5 minutes. Turn off the cooker. Uncover and let stand 5 minutes. Stir well.

5. Spoon the pasta mixture into large, shallow pasta bowls; sprinkle with the reserved Italian cheese blend and parsley.

6-QUART

NOT-QUITE-CLASSIC BOLOGNESE

SERVES: 8 | HANDS-ON: 25 MINUTES | SLOW COOK: 8 HOURS

Bolognese is a beloved slow-cook staple in many kitchens. Our reimagined recipe pairs ground turkey and sirloin together and introduces a dash of ground nutmeg.

Olive oil–flavored cooking spray
1 pound ground sirloin
1 pound lean ground turkey
1 tablespoon olive oil
1 cup diced onion
1 cup diced carrot
¾ cup diced celery
3 garlic cloves, minced
⅓ cup dry white wine
1 teaspoon table salt
¾ teaspoon freshly ground black pepper
½ teaspoon dried thyme
¼ teaspoon grated whole nutmeg
1 (28-ounce) can crushed San Marzano tomatoes, undrained
1 bay leaf
16 ounces uncooked spaghetti
¼ cup half-and-half
2 ounces grated fresh Parmigiano-Reggiano cheese (about ½ cup)

1. Coat a large cast-iron skillet with cooking spray. Add the beef and turkey to the skillet; cook over medium-high 7 minutes or until browned, stirring to crumble. Drain well.

2. Place the olive oil in the inner pot of a 6-quart Instant Pot®. Press SAUTÉ [Normal]. When the oil is shimmering, add the onion, carrot, and celery to the pot; cook, stirring constantly, 5 minutes or until the onions are translucent. Add the garlic; cook, stirring constantly, 30 seconds. Turn off the cooker.

3. Stir in the meat mixture, wine, salt, pepper, thyme, nutmeg, tomatoes, and bay leaf. Lock the lid; turn Pressure Valve to "Venting." SLOW COOK [Normal] for 8 hours.

4. During last 15 minutes of cooking, cook the pasta according to package directions; drain. Remove the lid of Instant Pot®, and stir the half-and-half into the sauce in the pot. Spoon sauce over the cooked pasta, and sprinkle with the cheese.

6-QUART

SWEDISH MEATBALLS

SERVES: 4 | HANDS-ON: 20 MINUTES | UNDER PRESSURE: 5 MINUTES
10-MINUTE NATURAL PRESSURE RELEASE

Swedish Meatballs are tender meatballs bathed in a creamy sauce. They are traditionally served with buttered boiled potatoes, but we liked them mashed. You can make your own breadcrumbs by pulsing day-old bread in the food processor until your desired crumb size is reached.

2 tablespoons olive oil
1 cup finely chopped onion
1 pound ground sirloin
½ cup plain dry breadcrumbs
1 large egg
½ teaspoon table salt
½ teaspoon freshly ground black pepper
2 tablespoons butter
1⅔ cups beef stock
2 tablespoons all-purpose flour
¼ teaspoon ground nutmeg
⅔ cup milk
2 tablespoons dry sherry
1 tablespoon chopped fresh parsley
Mashed potatoes

1. Remove the lid of a 6-quart Instant Pot®. Place 1 tablespoon of the olive oil in the inner pot; press SAUTÉ [Normal]. When the oil is shimmering, tilt the pot to evenly distribute it over the bottom of the pot. Add the onion and cook, stirring constantly, until golden. Turn off the cooker; remove the inner pot from the cooker. Transfer the onion from the pot to a large bowl, scraping the sides.

2. Add the beef, breadcrumbs, egg, salt, and ¼ teaspoon of the pepper to the onion in the bowl, mixing gently to combine. Shape the mixture into 24 balls.

3. Add the remaining 1 tablespoon olive oil to the inner pot; return the pot to the cooker. Press SAUTÉ [Normal]. Heat the oil, spreading it evenly over the bottom of the pot with a wooden or plastic spatula; add half of the meatballs to the pot. Cook, turning occasionally, until brown on all sides. (Meatballs will not be done.) As the meatballs brown, transfer them to a plate and replace them with the remaining meatballs, a few at a time, until all are browned. Turn off the cooker. Wipe the oily drippings from the cooker with a paper towel held with long tongs, leaving the fond on the bottom of the pot. Add the butter to the pot. As the butter melts, stir in the stock, scraping to loosen browned bits. Arrange the meatballs, in a single layer, in the stock.

4. Lock the lid; turn Pressure Valve to "Sealing." PRESSURE COOK [High Pressure] for 5 minutes. Allow a 10-minute Natural Pressure Release (page 10). Turn Pressure Valve to "Venting" to release any remaining pressure. Transfer the meatballs to a plate with a slotted spoon, reserving cooking liquid in the pot.

5. Place the flour, nutmeg, and the remaining ¼ teaspoon pepper in a bowl. Slowly whisk in the milk until smooth. Whisk the milk mixture and sherry into the cooking liquid in the pot. Press SAUTÉ [Normal]; cook uncovered, stirring occasionally, until the sauce simmers and thickens, about 5 minutes. Gently stir the meatballs into the sauce. Turn off the cooker, and let the meatball mixture stand 1 minute. Carefully pour the meatballs and sauce into a serving bowl; sprinkle with the parsley. Serve immediately with mashed potatoes.

NOTE: Do not substitute beef broth, which is not as flavorful and rich as beef stock.

TIP:

Fond is a French term referring to the rich, brown crust left after browning meat, which adds flavor to this dish. Do not let the fond burn or it will become bitter. If the fond is becoming too dark, remove the inner pot from the cooker to quickly control the heat. Be sure to loosen the fond from the bottom of the pot and stir it into the stock. If left on the bottom of the pot, the cooker may overheat and fail to pressurize.

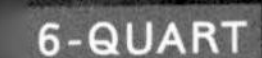

6-QUART

NANA'S SPAGHETTI AND MEATBALLS

ERVES: 4 TO 6 | HANDS-ON: 38 MINUTES | UNDER PRESSURE: 5 MINUTES
5-MINUTE NATURAL PRESSURE RELEASE

Placing the pasta strands in the pot on an angle, rather than parallel to each other, will help ensure that they don't clump together. Just be sure to thoroughly wet the pasta strands with the sauce and that all are submerged in the liquid.

- **1 large egg**
- **tablespoon chopped fresh parsley**
- **½ teaspoon table salt**
- **¼ teaspoon freshly ground pepper**
- **tablespoon grated Parmesan cheese**
- **3 garlic cloves, minced**
- **pound ground sirloin**
- **½ cup Italian-seasoned dry breadcrumbs**
- **tablespoon olive oil**
- **cup chopped onion**
- **½ cup chopped green bell pepper**
- **½ pound fresh mushrooms, finely chopped**
- **1 (6-ounce) can tomato paste**
- **1½ cups water**
- **3 (8-ounce) cans tomato sauce**
- **1 (14½-ounce) can diced tomatoes**
- **1 teaspoon sugar**
- **½ teaspoon dried Italian seasoning**
- **8 ounces spaghetti, broken in half**
- **3 tablespoons chopped fresh basil**
- **Additional fresh basil and grated Parmesan cheese (optional)**

. Whisk together the egg, parsley, salt, pepper, tablespoon Parmesan cheese, and 1 of the minced garlic cloves in a large bowl. Add the ground sirloin and breadcrumbs; mix gently until combined. Shape the mixture into 24 meatballs.

2. Place the olive oil in the inner pot of a 6-quart Instant Pot®. Press SAUTÉ [Normal]. When the oil is shimmering, add half of the meatballs to the pot. Cook, turning occasionally, until brown on all sides. As meatballs brown, transfer them to a plate, and replace them with the remaining meatballs, a few at a time, until all are browned. Add the onion and green pepper to the pot. Cook, stirring constantly, 3 minutes. Add the mushrooms; cook, stirring constantly, 3 minutes. Stir in the remaining 2 minced garlic cloves; cook, stirring constantly, 30 seconds. Stir in the tomato paste, scraping to remove the browned bits from the bottom of the pot. Gradually stir in the water, tomato sauce, tomatoes, sugar, and Italian seasoning. Gradually add the pasta, stirring to coat and separate the strands. (Make sure all the pasta is moistened and submerged in the liquid.) Place the meatballs in a single layer on top of the pasta mixture. Turn off the cooker.

3. Lock the lid; turn Pressure Valve to "Sealing." PRESSURE COOK [High Pressure] for 5 minutes. Allow a 5-minute Natural Pressure Release (page 10). Turn Pressure Valve to "Venting" to release any remaining pressure. Add the basil. Gently stir the mixture with a spaghetti server to separate the spaghetti and coat the meatballs with the sauce. Top each serving with basil and additional grated Parmesan cheese, if desired.

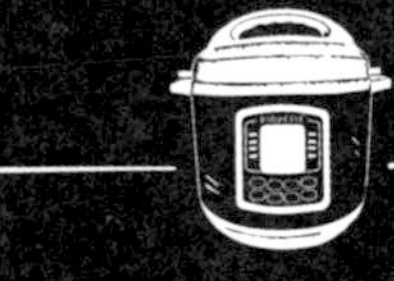

TIP:

Try using your food processor to finely chop the mushrooms.

8-QUART

GRILLADES AND CHEESY GRITS

SERVES: 8 | HANDS-ON: 27 MINUTES | UNDER PRESSURE: 8 MINUTES
NATURAL PRESSURE RELEASE

Very thinly-cut steak shortens prep time for this classic Cajun dish. Chipotle chile powder provides the characteristic heat in addition to smoky flavor.

GRILLADES

- 1 teaspoon table salt
- ¾ teaspoon chipotle chile powder
- 2 tablespoons canola oil
- 2 pounds Milanesa-cut top round steak, cut into ½-inch-wide strips
- ¾ cup chopped onion
- ⅔ cup chopped green bell pepper
- ⅓ cup chopped celery
- ½ teaspoon dried thyme
- 1 bay leaf
- 1 (14.5-ounce) can stewed tomatoes, undrained and chopped
- 2 tablespoons all-purpose flour
- 3 tablespoons water
- ¼ cup thinly sliced scallions (optional)

CHEESY GRITS

- 2 cups water
- 1 cup milk
- 1 cup drained canned yellow hominy
- ¾ cup regular yellow grits
- ½ teaspoon table salt
- 1 cup (4 ounces) shredded sharp Cheddar cheese
- 3 tablespoons butter, cut into pieces
- 2 tablespoons heavy cream

1. Make the Grillades: Combine the salt and chipotle chile powder in a small bowl. Heat a 12-inch skillet over high. Add 1 tablespoon of the oil, swirling to coat. Add half of the beef strips. Sprinkle with half of the chipotle chile mixture. Cook the beef 3 minutes, stirring occasionally, until browned. Transfer the beef to a plate. Repeat the procedure with the remaining oil, beef, and chipotle chile mixture. Stir in the onion, bell pepper, celery, thyme, bay leaf, and tomatoes, scraping the bottom of the skillet to loosen browned bits. Pour the beef mixture into the inner pot of an 8-quart Instant Pot®. Stir in the first half of the beef.

2. Lock the lid; turn Pressure Valve to "Sealing. PRESSURE COOK [High Pressure] for 8 minutes. Open the cooker using a complete Natural Pressure Release (page 7).

3. Make the Cheesy Grits: While the grillades cook, combine the 2 cups water, milk, hominy, grits, and salt in a 3-quart saucepan. Bring to a boil, stirring occasionally. Reduce the heat to low; cover and cook 20 minutes or until thickened, stirring often. Remove from the heat. Add the cheese and butter, stirring until melted. Stir in the cream. Cover and keep warm.

4. When the pressure is completely released, turn the cooker off. Combine the flour and the 3 tablespoons water, stirring until smooth; stir into the beef mixture in the pot. Press SAUTÉ [Normal], and bring the mixture to a boil, stirring constantly. Cook, stirring constantly, 2 minutes. Turn off the cooker. Let the grillades stand in the cooker for 3 more minutes, stirring occasionally. (Grillades will continue to simmer and thicken.)

5. Spoon the grits into large shallow bowls. Spoon the grillades over the grits. Sprinkle with the scallions, if desired.

TIP:

Use clean kitchen scissors to chop the tomatoes right in the can.

8-QUART

SWISS STEAK

SERVES: 6 | HANDS-ON: 20 MINUTES | UNDER PRESSURE: 20 MINUTES
NATURAL PRESSURE RELEASE

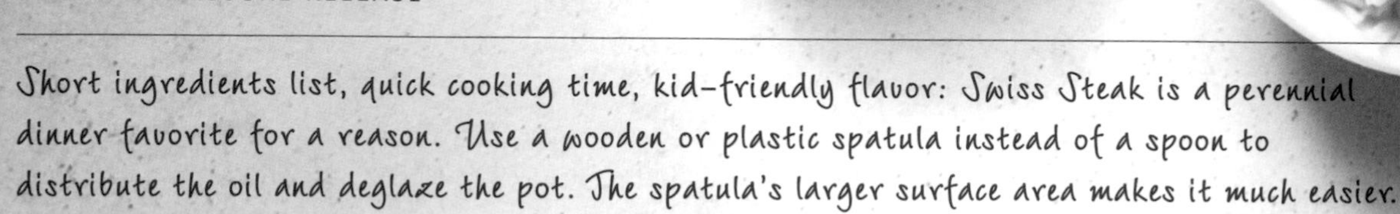
Short ingredients list, quick cooking time, kid-friendly flavor: Swiss Steak is a perennial dinner favorite for a reason. Use a wooden or plastic spatula instead of a spoon to distribute the oil and deglaze the pot. The spatula's larger surface area makes it much easier.

- **2 pounds London broil steak (1 inch thick), trimmed and cut crosswise into 6 pieces**
- **1 teaspoon table salt**
- **¼ teaspoon freshly ground black pepper**
- **¼ cup all-purpose flour**
- **2 tablespoons canola oil**
- **1 (8-ounce) package sliced crimini mushrooms**
- **¾ cup finely chopped onion**
- **⅔ cup finely chopped green bell pepper**
- **1 (14½-ounce) can diced tomatoes, undrained**
- **2 tablespoons all-purpose flour**
- **3 tablespoons water**
- **Hot cooked rice or mashed potatoes**
- **Fresh chopped parsley**

1. Sprinkle both sides of the steak pieces with the salt and pepper. Place the ¼ cup flour in a large zip-top plastic freezer bag; add the steak to the bag, one piece at a time. Seal or tightly hold the bag closed; shake to coat.

2. Remove the lid from an 8-quart Instant Pot®. Press SAUTÉ [Normal]. When inner pot is hot, swirl in the oil. (Distribute the oil evenly over the bottom of the pot with a wooden or plastic spatula before adding each steak piece.) Shake the excess flour off each steak piece, and add to the hot oil, carefully positioning each piece so that all can be added in a single layer. Cook 4 to 5 minutes on each side, or until dark brown, turning only once with long tongs. Turn off the cooker. Transfer the steak to a platter.

3. Add the mushrooms, onion, bell pepper, and tomatoes to the pot. Scrape the bottom of the pot with the spatula, scraping from the center to the edges until all of the fond is loosened into the tomato mixture and the bottom of the pot appears clean.

4. Nestle the steak into the tomato mixture, spooning the mixture on top so that the steak is on the bottom of the pot. Lock the lid; turn Pressure Valve to "Sealing." PRESSURE COOK [High Pressure] for 20 minutes. Open the cooker using Natural Pressure Release (page 7). Transfer steak to a serving platter. Turn off the cooker.

5. Stir together the 2 tablespoons flour and the 3 tablespoons water until smooth. Stir into cooking liquid in the pot. Press SAUTÉ [Normal], and bring the mixture to a boil. Cook uncovered, stirring often, until thickened, about 4 minutes. Turn off the cooker, and remove the pot from the cooker. Spoon some of the sauce over the steak. Serve over rice or mashed potatoes with remaining sauce. Sprinkle with the fresh chopped parsley.

6-QUART

SALISBURY STEAK WITH MUSHROOM-ONION GRAVY

SERVES: 4 | HANDS-ON: 20 MINUTES | UNDER PRESSURE: 4 MINUTES
10-MINUTE NATURAL PRESSURE RELEASE

Don't skip the Worcestershire sauce; just 2 tablespoons add a jolt of sweet, spicy, salty, and sour flavor that perks up this rich dish. Serve with Lemony Steamed Kale (page 181) and Wheat 'n' Honey Dinner Rolls (page 49) to sop up all the gravy goodness.

1 beef bouillon cube
1 cup water
2 tablespoons Worcestershire sauce
1½ teaspoons seasoned salt
½ teaspoon freshly ground black pepper
2 medium onions, sliced
1 large egg
¼ teaspoon ground allspice
1 pound ground chuck
⅓ cup quick-cooking oats
2 teaspoons olive oil
2 tablespoons butter
8 ounces sliced crimini mushrooms
4 large garlic cloves, minced
½ cup milk
2 tablespoons cornstarch
1 to 2 tablespoons dry sherry
Hot mashed potatoes

1. Combine the bouillon cube and the 1 cup water in a 1-cup glass measuring cup. Microwave at HIGH 2 minutes. Stir in 1 tablespoon of the Worcestershire sauce, ½ teaspoon of the seasoned salt, and ¼ teaspoon of the black pepper. Set aside.

2. Finely chop 1 to 2 onion slices to measure ½ cup. Separate remaining onion slices into rings. Whisk together the egg, remaining 1 tablespoon of the Worcestershire sauce, remaining 1 teaspoon of the seasoned salt, remaining ¼ teaspoon of the pepper, and the allspice in a large bowl. Add the ground chuck and oats.

3. Add the olive oil to the inner pot of a 6-quart Instant Pot®. Press SAUTÉ [Normal]. Evenly distribute the oil over the bottom of the pot with a wooden or plastic spatula. Add the ½ cup chopped onion. Cook, stirring constantly, 3 minutes. Turn off the cooker; remove the pot from the cooker, and add the onion to the meat mixture; stir gently until combined. Shape the mixture into 4 (4½-inch) slightly oblong patties.

4. Return the inner pot to the cooker; add the patties to the pot. Press SAUTÉ [Normal]; brown patties on both sides, about 1 to 2 minutes. Remove patties from the pot. Melt the butter in the pot. Add the reserved onion rings and the mushrooms. Cook, stirring constantly, 3 minutes. Turn off the cooker. Add the garlic; cook, stirring constantly, 30 seconds. Add the bouillon mixture to the onion mixture, stirring with a wooden or plastic spatula until the bottom of the pot feels smooth.

5. Nestle the patties into the mushroom mixture. Lock the lid; turn the Pressure Valve to "Sealing." PRESSURE COOK [High Pressure] for 4 minutes. Allow a 10-minute Natural Pressure Release (page 10). Turn Pressure Valve to release remaining pressure. Turn off the cooker. Transfer the patties to a plate, reserving the mushroom mixture in the pot; keep the patties warm.

6. Gradually add the milk to the cornstarch in a small bowl, whisking until smooth. Whisk the milk mixture into the mushroom mixture. Press SAUTÉ [Normal], and bring to a simmer, stirring often. Cook, stirring often, until the mixture thickens, about 2 minutes. Turn off the cooker. Stir in the sherry. Return the patties to the mushroom mixture. Cook just until thoroughly heated. Serve the patties with the Mushroom-Onion Gravy over the hot mashed potatoes.

6-QUART

BEEF POT PIE

SERVES: 4 | HANDS-ON: 18 MINUTES | UNDER PRESSURE: 3 MINUTES | QUICK PRESSURE RELEASE

Easily turn leftover Sunday Pot Roast in Gravy (page 67) into weeknight fare with a deconstructed pot pie. Flaky Buttermilk Biscuits (page 46) serve as a shortcut crust.

- **2 cups beef stock**
- **1 cup ½-inch cubed baking potato**
- **1 cup chopped onion**
- **⅔ cup sliced carrot**
- **⅔ cup sliced celery**
- **½ teaspoon table salt**
- **¼ teaspoon freshly ground black pepper**
- **¼ teaspoon dried oregano**
- **1 small bay leaf**
- **1 tablespoon butter**
- **2 teaspoons Worcestershire sauce**
- **4 teaspoons cornstarch**
- **2 tablespoons water**
- **2 cups ½-inch cubed Sunday Pot Roast in Gravy (page 67)**
- **¾ cup frozen petite green peas, thawed**
- **3 tablespoons Burgundy wine (optional)**
- **Buttermilk Biscuits (page 46), split and toasted**

1. Combine the beef stock, potato, onion, carrot, celery, salt, pepper, oregano, and bay leaf in the inner pot of a 6-quart Instant Pot®. Lock the lid; turn Pressure Valve to "Sealing." PRESSURE COOK [High Pressure] for 3 minutes. Open the cooker using Quick Pressure Release (page 7). Turn off the cooker.

2. Remove the bay leaf, and stir in the butter and Worcestershire sauce. Combine the cornstarch and 2 tablespoons water, stirring until smooth. Stir the cornstarch mixture into the vegetable mixture. Press SAUTÉ [Normal]; cook, stirring often, until the mixture boils and thickens. Stir in the cubed roast, peas, and, if desired, wine. Cook, uncovered, stirring occasionally until thoroughly heated, about 3 minutes. Turn off the cooker. Remove the pot from the cooker, and allow the meat mixture to cool slightly.

3. Spoon the meat mixture into bowls, and top with toasted biscuit halves, cut side down.

NOTE: Beef stock is more flavorful than beef broth and is preferred in this recipe.

TIP:

It will be easier to cut the pot roast into cubes if it is chilled first.

6-QUART

SUPER SIMPLE SLOPPY JOES

SERVES:8 | HANDS-ON: 8 MINUTES | SAUTÉ: 25 MINUTES

This simple, satisfying recipe shows off the Instant Pot®'s added convenience when space or kitchen accommodations are at a premium, like in an RV or college dorm. At home, try serving over Wheat 'n' Honey Dinner Rolls (page 49) shaped into hamburger buns.

Cooking spray
1½ pounds lean ground beef
1 (14½-ounce) can diced tomatoes, undrained
1¼ cups ketchup
½ cup bottled barbecue sauce
1 tablespoon Worcestershire sauce
8 hamburger buns, toasted

1. Remove the lid from a 6-quart Instant Pot®. Coat the pot with cooking spray. Add the ground beef. Press SAUTÉ [Normal]. Cook the ground beef, stirring until it crumbles and is no longer pink. Turn off the cooker. Drain the beef well. Return the beef to the pot. Wipe the rim of pot to remove any greasy residue. Return pot to the cooker.

2. Stir in the tomatoes, ketchup, barbecue sauce, and Worcestershire sauce. Press SAUTÉ [Normal]; bring to a simmer, and cook 15 minutes or until thickened, stirring often. Serve the mixture on toasted buns.

6-QUART

RED BEANS AND RICE

SERVES: 6 | HANDS-ON: 15 MINUTES | UNDER PRESSURE: 25 MINUTES
SLOW PRESSURE RELEASE

Unlike traditional Red Beans and Rice, the beans in this recipe are cooked separately and served over the rice. Ten garlic cloves sounds excessive, but one bite and you'll taste how much flavor they add.

- **1 pound dried red kidney beans**
- **8 cups water**
- **1 tablespoon olive oil**
- **1 pound andouille sausage, cut into ¾-inch pieces**
- **1½ cups chopped onion**
- **1½ cups chopped poblano chile**
- **1 cup diced celery**
- **2 tablespoons chopped fresh thyme**
- **½ teaspoon kosher salt**
- **10 garlic cloves, crushed**
- **1 (12-ounce) can beer**
- **4 cups unsalted chicken stock**
- **½ teaspoon ground red pepper**
- **¼ teaspoon freshly ground black pepper**
- **3 bay leaves**
- **½ cup thinly sliced scallions**
- **2 tablespoons cider vinegar**
- **4 cups hot cooked long-grain rice**

1. Sort and wash the beans; place in the inner pot of a 6-quart Instant Pot®. Add the 8 cups water. Lock the lid; PRESSURE COOK [High Pressure] for 25 minutes. Turn off the cooker. Open the cooker using Slow Pressure Release (page 10). Drain the beans; discard the cooking liquid.

2. Wash the pot, and dry thoroughly. Return pot to the cooker; add the oil. Press SAUTÉ [Normal]. When the oil is shimmering, add the sausage; cook, stirring often, 6 minutes or until browned. Add the onion, chile, celery, thyme, salt, and garlic; cook 8 minutes. Stir in the beer. When the mixture comes to a boil, cook 2 minutes, scraping the pot to loosen browned bits. Add the beans, stock, red pepper, black pepper, and bay leaves. Bring to a simmer; cook 10 minutes, stirring occasionally. Remove and discard the bay leaves. Stir in ¼ cup of the scallions and the vinegar. Serve over the rice; sprinkle with the remaining ¼ cup scallions.

6-QUART

FRUITED LAMB TAGINE

SERVES: 4 | HANDS-ON: 25 MINUTES | UNDER PRESSURE: 35 MINUTES
NATURAL PRESSURE RELEASE

The secret ingredient in this recipe is garam masala, a blend of Indian spices that are also found in North African, specifically Moroccan, dishes. Using a spice blend cuts down on the number of individual spices you have to purchase and measure.

1 cup dried pitted plums
1 cup dried apricots
Boiling water
2 pounds boneless leg of lamb, cut into ½-inch cubes
2 teaspoons garam masala
½ teaspoon ground turmeric
½ teaspoon table salt
¼ teaspoon black pepper
2 tablespoons olive oil
1 (14-ounce) can beef broth
1 (8-ounce) container refrigerated chopped onion
2 tablespoons all-purpose flour
¼ cup water
⅓ cup orange marmalade
Hot cooked couscous
Garnishes: chopped fresh cilantro, toasted slivered almonds (optional)

1. Place the dried plums and apricots in a medium bowl. Add boiling water to cover. Set aside.

2. Place the lamb in a large bowl. Combine the garam masala, turmeric, salt, and pepper; sprinkle over the lamb, rubbing until the lamb is evenly coated.

3. Remove the lid from a 6-quart Instant Pot®. Add the oil to the inner pot. Press SAUTÉ [Normal]. When the oil is shimmering, add the lamb; cook 2 minutes on each side or until browned. Add the broth and onion; cook, scraping with a wooden or plastic spatula until the bottom of the pot feels smooth.

4. Lock the lid; turn Pressure Valve to "Sealing." PRESSURE COOK [High Pressure] for 35 minutes. Allow a complete Natural Pressure Release (page 7). Turn off the cooker.

5. With lid off, press SAUTÉ [Normal]; bring lamb mixture to a boil. Combine the flour and ¼ cup water, stirring with a whisk until smooth; add to the lamb mixture, stirring constantly. Cook 5 minutes, stirring frequently, or until thickened. Stir in the marmalade.

6. Drain the dried fruit, and stir into the lamb mixture. Cook, stirring frequently, until thoroughly heated. Turn off the cooker. Serve over couscous. Garnish with the cilantro and almonds, if desired.

6-QUART

SAUCY CHIPOTLE BARBECUE PORK

SERVES: 8 | HANDS-ON: 15 MINUTES | UNDER PRESSURE: 75 MINUTES
NATURAL PRESSURE RELEASE

This spicy recipe cooks up an ample amount of sauce—a delicious bonus for barbecue lovers. Use it for dripping over a sandwich, as a dip for fries, or for dressing baked potatoes.

2 teaspoons dry mustard
1 teaspoon table salt
½ teaspoon cayenne pepper
1 (4-pound) boneless pork shoulder roast, cut in half (Boston butt)
2 tablespoons butter
1 (18-ounce) bottle spicy barbecue sauce
1 (12-ounce) bottle Baja chipotle marinade
½ cup water
1 large onion, chopped (about 2½ cups)
Garnish: sliced green onions (optional)

1. Rub the mustard, salt, and cayenne pepper over the pork. Remove the lid from a 6-quart Instant Pot®. Add the butter to the inner pot. Press SAUTÉ [Normal]. When the butter melts, add the pork; cook 10 minutes or until browned on all sides. Remove the pork from the pot.

2. Add the barbecue sauce, marinade, and ½ cup water, scraping with a wooden or plastic spatula until the bottom of the pot feels smooth. Stir in the onion, and return the roast to the pot.

3. Lock the lid; turn Pressure Valve to "Sealing." PRESSURE COOK [High Pressure] for 75 minutes. Open cooker using Natural Pressure Release (page 7). Garnish with the slice green onions, if desired.

6-QUART

BARBECUE PORK

SERVES: 6 | HANDS-ON: 10 MINUTES | SLOW COOK: 9 HOURS

Serve this saucy pork with buns and slaw, stuff a quesadilla, or spoon over Creamy Parmesan Grits (page 194). You can assemble the ingredients in the morning, slow cook, and enjoy barbecue for dinner.

Cooking spray
1 (3- to 4-pound) boneless pork shoulder roast (Boston butt), trimmed
1 (18-ounce) bottle barbecue sauce
1 (12-ounce) can cola soft drink

1. Coat the inner pot of a 6-quart Instant Pot® with cooking spray. Place the roast in the pot; pour the barbecue sauce and cola over the roast.

2. Lock the lid; turn Pressure Valve to "Venting." Press SLOW COOK [Normal]; cook 9 hours, adding additional time up to 11 hours, if necessary, until the meat shreds easily with a fork.

3. Transfer the pork to a cutting board; shred with 2 forks, removing any large pieces of fat. Skim the fat from the sauce, and stir in the shredded pork.

6-QUART

SWEET AND SMOKY RIBS

SERVES: 4 | HANDS-ON: 12 MINUTES | UNDER PRESSURE: 15 MINUTES
QUICK PRESSURE RELEASE | BAKE: 40 MINUTES

With the Instant Pot®, there's no need to tend a smoker or grill for hours. You can easily satisfy your craving for ribs, rain or shine. The dry rub also works well on steak and chicken, so store in an airtight container for another use.

Cooking spray
5 pounds (2 slabs) small pork spare ribs or baby back ribs
Smoky Dry Rub (recipe at right)
1 cup unfiltered fresh-pressed apple cider
½ teaspoon hickory liquid smoke (such as Wright's)
2 cups bottled barbecue sauce

1. Place a rack in an aluminum foil-lined sheet pan. Coat the rack with cooking spray, and set aside. To remove the membrane from the bone sides of the ribs, lift the edge of the membrane at 1 end with a table knife; firmly grasp the edge of the membrane with a dry paper towel, and pull, using even pressure. (Membrane should come off in 1 piece.) Cut the slabs in half. Rub 1 tablespoon of the Smoky Dry Rub over both sides of each slab half.

2. Combine the apple cider and liquid smoke in the inner pot of a 6-quart Instant Pot®. Place the Steam Rack in the pot. Arrange the ribs on the rack, in an upright manner, with the meat sides facing outward.

3. Lock the lid; turn Pressure Valve to "Sealing." PRESSURE COOK [High Pressure] for 15 minutes. Open the cooker using Quick Pressure Release (page 7).

4. Preheat the oven to 300°F with an oven rack centered in the top half of the oven.

5. Transfer the ribs, meat sides up, to a cutting board. Blot the moisture from the entire surface of the slabs with a paper towel, being careful not to wipe off the seasoning. Sprinkle additional Smoky Dry Rub (about ½ tablespoon) over the meaty side of each slab half. Place the slabs, meat side up, on the rack in the prepared pan.

6. Bake at 300°F for 20 minutes. Brush both sides of the slabs with the barbecue sauce. Bake 10 minutes. Brush the tops with the sauce, and bake an additional 10 minutes. Remove from the oven. Cut the slabs into individual ribs, and serve with additional sauce.

SMOKY DRY RUB

MAKES ½ CUP | HANDS-ON: 5 MINUTES

¼ cup firmly packed dark brown sugar
2 tablespoons smoked paprika
1 tablespoon kosher salt
2 teaspoons garlic salt
2 teaspoons chili powder
2 teaspoons smoked ground black pepper
1 teaspoon onion salt
1 teaspoon celery salt
1 teaspoon ground chipotle chile pepper
1 teaspoon ground cumin

Combine all ingredients, blending well. Use on pork or beef ribs, steaks, or chicken. Store in an airtight container at room temperature up to 1 month.

NOTE: We tested with McCormick Smokehouse Ground Black Pepper and Chipotle Chile Pepper.

TIP:

If using spare ribs, ask the butcher for spare ribs that have the "riblets," the portion of the bone and cartilage that attach to the breast bone, removed. They are smaller and will fit the Instant Pot®. Whole spare ribs are too large for the cooker.

6-QUART

CUMIN PORK AND POBLANO CORN

SERVES: 6 | HANDS-ON: 25 MINUTES | UNDER PRESSURE: 40 MINUTES
NATURAL PRESSURE RELEASE

Varying in heat, poblano chiles are large and dark green to brown. They work well with the sweet fresh corn in this dish. If fresh corn is not in season, you can substitute thawed frozen corn.

- **1 (2½-pound) bone-in pork shoulder (Boston butt) trimmed**
- **1½ tablespoons chili powder**
- **2 teaspoons ground cumin**
- **½ teaspoon table salt**
- **¾ teaspoon freshly ground black pepper**
- **2 tablespoons extra-virgin olive oil**
- **1½ cups water**
- **1½ cups fat-free, lower-sodium chicken broth**
- **1 tablespoon minced fresh garlic**
- **4 poblano chiles, seeded and chopped (about 3 cups)**
- **1 large red bell pepper, diced (about 1½ cups)**
- **4 cups fresh corn kernels (about 5 ears)**
- **¾ cup chopped fresh cilantro**
- **Lime wedges**

1. Pat the pork dry with paper towels. Combine the chili powder, cumin, ¼ teaspoon of the salt, and the black pepper in a medium bowl. Remove 1 tablespoon of the spice mixture; set aside. Add the pork to the remaining spice mixture in the bowl, turning to coat.

2. Place 1 tablespoon of the oil in the inner pot of a 6-quart Instant Pot®. Press SAUTÉ [Normal]. When the oil is shimmering, swirl to coat the bottom of the pot; add the pork, and cook 4 minutes, browning on all sides. Remove the pork from the pot; add 1½ cups water and the broth, scraping with a wooden or plastic spatula until the bottom of the pot feels clean. Return the pork to the pot. Turn off the cooker.

3. Lock the lid; turn Pressure Valve to "Sealing." PRESSURE COOK [High Pressure] for 40 minutes. Open the cooker using Natural Pressure Release (page 7). Remove the pork from the pot; separate the pork into bite-sized pieces.

4. Strain the cooking liquid through a fine sieve into a bowl; discard solids. Skim the fat off the cooking liquid; discard the fat. Return the skimmed liquid to the inner pot. Press SAUTÉ [More], and bring the mixture to a boil; boil until reduced to 2 cups. Pour the sauce into a bowl; cover and keep warm. Turn off the cooker.

5. Wash the inner pot and dry thoroughly. Return the pot to the cooker. Add the remaining 1 tablespoon oil to the pot. Press SAUTÉ [Normal]. When the oil is shimmering, swirl to coat the bottom of the pot. Add the reserved 1 tablespoon spice mixture, garlic, poblano chiles, and bell pepper. Cook, stirring constantly, 5 minutes or until crisp-tender. Stir in the corn, and cook 4 minutes or until thoroughly heated. Turn off the cooker. Stir in the remaining ¼ teaspoon salt and cilantro. Divide the vegetable mixture among 6 plates. Top with the pork and sauce; serve with the lime wedges.

Close
Instant Pot
www.InstantPot.com
Soup
Meat/Stew
Bean/Chili
Poultry
Slow Cook
Sauté
Low Pressure
High Pressure
Less
Normal
More
Pressure
Manual
Adjust
Timer
Rice
Multigrain
Porridge
Steam
Yogurt
Keep Warm/Cancel

6-QUART

◂ PORK CARNITAS TACOS

SERVES: 7 | HANDS-ON: 25 MINUTES | UNDER PRESSURE: 29 MINUTES
NATURAL PRESSURE RELEASE

For a lighter meal, swap lettuce cups for the corn tortillas.

1½ cups fresh orange juice
1 cup thinly sliced onion
5 teaspoons chipotle chile powder
1 tablespoon ground cumin
1 teaspoon kosher salt
6 garlic cloves, minced
3 pounds boneless pork shoulder (Boston butt), trimmed and cut into 2-inch pieces
14 (6-inch) corn tortillas
2½ cups chopped tomato
⅓ cup cilantro leaves
Lime wedges (optional)

1. Combine the orange juice, onion, chile powder, cumin, salt, and garlic in the inner pot of a 6-quart Instant Pot®. Add the pork, tossing to coat. Lock the lid; turn Pressure Valve to "Sealing." PRESSURE COOK [High Pressure] for 29 minutes. Open the cooker using Natural Pressure Release (page 7).

2. Remove the pork from cooker with a slotted spoon; shred with 2 forks to measure 4¾ cups meat. Remove and discard any chunks of fat. Spread pork in a single layer on a jelly-roll pan or broiler pan lined with foil.

3. Skim the fat from the cooking liquid; discard the fat. With the lid off, press SAUTE [Normal]. Bring cooking liquid to a boil. Cook, uncovered, 5 minutes or until slightly thick, stirring often.

4. Preheat the broiler.

5. Drizzle the pork with ¼ cup of the cooking liquid. Discard the remaining cooking liquid, or set aside for serving, if desired. Broil the pork 3 to 5 minutes or until the pork is browned and edges are crispy, turning occasionally.

6. Heat the tortillas in the microwave according to package directions. Spoon ⅓ cup shredded pork mixture onto each tortilla. Top each with about 3 tablespoons tomato and about 1½ teaspoons cilantro. Serve with the lime wedges, if desired.

6-QUART

JALAPEÑO-GLAZED PORK CHOPS AND RICE

SERVES: 6 | HANDS-ON: 25 MINUTES | UNDER PRESSURE: 23 MINUTES | SLOW PRESSURE RELEASE

Jalapeño jelly makes a quick, flavorful glaze for pork chops. Serve with Bacon and Onion-Dressed Green Beans (page 185) for a complete meal.

6 (8-ounce) bone-in pork chops (about ¾ inch thick)
½ teaspoon table salt
½ teaspoon freshly ground black pepper
1 tablespoon canola oil
2 cups uncooked brown basmati rice
1 cup chopped onion
2 garlic cloves, chopped
2½ cups water
2 cups fat-free, lower-sodium chicken broth
½ cup jalapeño pepper jelly
¼ cup sliced scallions

1. Sprinkle the pork chops with ¼ teaspoon of the salt and ¼ teaspoon of the pepper. Remove the lid from a 6-quart Instant Pot®. Press SAUTÉ [Normal]. When the word "Hot" appears, swirl in 1 teaspoon of the oil. Add 2 pork chops to the inner pot; cook 2 minutes on each side or until browned. Remove the pork from the pot; set aside. Repeat the procedure twice with the remaining pork chops. Add the remaining 2 teaspoons oil to the pot. Add the rice, onion, and garlic; cook, stirring constantly, 5 minutes or until the onion is tender. Stir in the remaining ¼ teaspoon salt, remaining ¼ teaspoon pepper, 2½ cups water, and the broth.

2. Lock the lid; turn Pressure Valve to "Sealing." PRESSURE COOK [High Pressure] for 19 minutes. Turn off the cooker. Open the cooker using a Slow Pressure Release (page 10).

3. Add the pork chops to the pot. Lock the lid; turn Pressure Valve to "Sealing." PRESSURE COOK [High Pressure] for 4 minutes. Open the cooker, using Slow Pressure Release (page 10). Turn off the cooker.

4. Remove the pork chops from the pot. Place the rice mixture on a serving platter; top with the pork chops. Place the jelly in a small microwave-safe bowl. Microwave at HIGH 30 to 60 seconds or until jelly melts. Brush the pork chops with the warm jelly, and sprinkle with the scallions.

6-QUART

BRAISED PORK LOIN WITH DRIED PLUMS

SERVES: 10 | HANDS-ON: 25 MINUTES | SLOW COOK: 7 HOURS

Dried plums, tender leeks, and a savory sauce dress up these pork loins.

1 (3¼-pound) boneless pork loin roast, trimmed
1½ teaspoons freshly ground black pepper
1 teaspoon table salt
1 teaspoon dry mustard
1 teaspoon dried sage
½ teaspoon dried thyme
1 tablespoon olive oil
2 cups sliced onion
1 cup finely chopped leek
1 cup finely chopped carrot
½ cup port or other sweet red wine
⅓ cup fat-free, lower-sodium chicken broth
⅓ cup water
1 cup pitted dried plums (about 20 dried plums)
2 bay leaves
2 tablespoons cornstarch
2 tablespoons water
Garnish: thyme leaves (optional)

1. Cut the pork in half crosswise. Combine the pepper, salt, dry mustard, sage, and thyme. Rub the seasoning mixture over the surface of the pork halves.

2. Heat a large Dutch oven over medium-high. Add the oil to pan; swirl to coat. Add the pork to the pan; cook 5 minutes, browning on all sides. Transfer the pork to the inner pot of a 6-quart Instant Pot®. Add the onion, leek, and carrot to the Dutch oven; cook, stirring constantly, 5 minutes or until vegetables are golden. Stir in the wine, broth, and ⅓ cup water, scraping the pan to loosen browned bits. Pour the onion mixture over the pork in the cooker; add the plums and bay leaves.

3. Lock the lid; turn Pressure Valve to "Venting." Press SLOW COOK [More]. Cook for 1 hour. Turn off the cooker. Press SLOW COOK [Normal]; cook 6 hours. (Cook additional time, if necessary, until pork is tender.)

4. Remove the pork from the pot; keep warm. Combine the cornstarch and 2 tablespoons water in a small bowl; stir well. Add the cornstarch mixture to the cooking liquid in the pot. Turn off the cooker.

5. Press SAUTÉ [Normal]. Bring mixture to a boil, and cook 2 minutes or until sauce is thick, stirring frequently. Discard bay leaves. Slice the pork, and serve with the sauce. Garnish with the thyme leaves, if desired.

6-QUART

PORK LOIN ROAST WITH ROSEMARY-PINEAPPLE SAUCE

SERVES: 6 | HANDS-ON: 15 MINUTES | UNDER PRESSURE: 20 MINUTES
QUICK PRESSURE RELEASE

The trick to preparing very lean cuts of meat that are juicy and succulent? Don't overcook them. Cutting the roast across the grain into thin slices also enhances tenderness.

- **1 (2-pound) boneless center-cut pork loin roast**
- **2 tablespoons olive oil**
- **1 teaspoon table salt**
- **½ teaspoon freshly ground black pepper**
- **¼ cup thawed unsweetened frozen pineapple juice concentrate**
- **¼ cup dry sherry**
- **¼ cup brown sugar**
- **2 tablespoons water**
- **1 tablespoon minced fresh rosemary**
- **2 large garlic cloves, minced**
- **½ cup Chicken Bone Broth (page 24) or chicken stock**
- **2 tablespoons cornstarch**

1. Remove the top fat and silver skin from the pork roast, if present. Rub the pork with 1 tablespoon of the olive oil. Combine the salt and pepper, and rub onto all sides of the roast.

2. Remove the lid from a 6-quart Instant Pot®. Add the remaining 1 tablespoon of the oil to the pot. Press SAUTÉ [Normal]. When the oil is shimmering, add the pork. Brown pork on all sides, about 3 minutes on each side.

3. While the pork is browning, stir together the juice concentrate, sherry, brown sugar, water, rosemary, and garlic in a bowl. Remove the browned pork from the pot. Turn off the cooker. Stir in the juice concentrate mixture, scraping the pot with a wooden or plastic spatula to loosen browned bits until the bottom of the pot appears clean.

4. Return the pork to the pot. Lock the lid; turn Pressure Valve to "Sealing." PRESSURE COOK [High Pressure] for 20 minutes. Perform a Quick Pressure Release (page 7), but do not remove the lid. Let the pork rest in the cooker 5 minutes. Turn off the cooker.

5. Transfer the pork to a cutting board. Cover and let rest 3 minutes.

6. Meanwhile, press SAUTÉ [Normal]. Bring the cooking liquid to a boil. Combine the broth, or stock, and cornstarch in a bowl, stirring until smooth. Stir the cornstarch mixture into the boiling cooking liquid. Cook, stirring constantly, 1 to 2 minutes or until the sauce thickens. Turn off the cooker. Cut the pork across the grain into thin slices and serve with the sauce.

NOTE: Do not use pork tenderloin in this recipe.

4

POULTRY & SEAFOOD

6-QUART

CHICKEN AND SMOKED SAUSAGE CASSOULET

SERVES: 6 TO 8 | HANDS-ON: 22 MINUTES | UNDER PRESSURE: 5 MINUTES
QUICK PRESSURE RELEASE

While you could buy a rotisserie chicken and canned beans, this recipe utilizes the more economical, home-cooked versions prepared in your Instant Pot®. To save time, purchase peeled and cubed butternut squash. Look for it in the produce or frozen vegetable aisle at the supermarket.

2 tablespoons olive oil
2 tablespoons butter
2 cups panko (Japanese-style breadcrumbs)
Cooking spray
½ pound smoked sausage, sliced
1 cup chopped onion
1 small butternut squash, peeled and cubed
1¾ cups broth, from Pressure Cooker Rotisserie-Style Chicken (page 26)
2 cups shredded Pressure Cooker Rotisserie-Style Chicken (page 26)
2 cups cooked dried cannellini beans (page 28)
1 (14½-ounce) can diced tomatoes with rosemary and oregano, undrained
½ teaspoon table salt
¼ teaspoon freshly ground pepper

1. Remove the lid from a 6-quart Instant Pot®. Place the oil and butter in the inner pot. Press SAUTÉ [Normal]. When the butter melts, add the panko, and cook, stirring often, 1 to 2 minutes or until the crumbs are golden brown. Turn off the cooker. Remove the crumbs from the pot and set aside.

2. Wipe the pot clean with a paper towel; coat with cooking spray. Press SAUTÉ [Normal]; add the sausage, and cook, stirring often, 4 minutes or until browned. Remove the sausage from the pot. Add the onion and squash. Cook, stirring constantly, 3 minutes. Turn off the cooker.

3. Add the broth, sausage, chicken, beans, tomatoes, salt, and pepper, scraping with a wooden or plastic spatula until the bottom of the pot feels smooth. Lock the lid; turn Pressure Valve to "Sealing." PRESSURE COOK [High Pressure] for 5 minutes.

4. Open the cooker using Quick Pressure Release (page 7). Turn off the cooker. Remove the inner pot from the cooker, and let stand 5 minutes. Spoon into shallow bowls; top evenly with the reserved crumbs, and serve immediately.

TIP:

You may substitute 1 (15.5-ounce) can cannellini beans, drained and rinsed, for the cooked dried beans and 1 (14-ounce) can chicken broth for the homemade broth, if desired.

GREEK PIZZA WITH CHICKEN AND ARTICHOKES

SERVES: 4 | HANDS-ON: 10 MINUTES | BAKE: 7 MINUTES

If you prefer a crispier crust, bake the pizza directly on the oven rack. Kalamata olives, marinated artichoke hearts, and tangy feta add Mediterranean flavor to this easy meal.

1 (16-ounce) package refrigerated pizza dough

6 ounces shredded mozzarella cheese, (about 1½ cups)

2 cups shredded Pressure Cooker Rotisserie-Style Chicken (page 26)

1 (7-ounce) jar roasted red bell peppers, drained and cut into strips

1 (6-ounce) jar marinated artichoke hearts, drained and coarsely chopped

10 pitted kalamata olives, thinly sliced

1½ tablespoons chopped fresh oregano

1 tablespoon olive oil

½ teaspoon freshly ground black pepper

4 ounces feta cheese, crumbled (about 1 cup)

1. Preheat the oven to 500°F.
2. On a floured surface, roll out the pizza dough to a 15-inch circle. Sprinkle ¾ cup of the mozzarella cheese onto the prepared pizza dough. Top evenly with the chicken.
3. Combine the roasted red bell peppers, artichoke hearts, olives, oregano, olive oil, and black pepper in a bowl; toss gently. Spoon the bell pepper mixture evenly over the chicken; sprinkle with remaining ¾ cup mozzarella cheese, and top with the feta cheese.
4. Bake at 500°F for 5 to 7 minutes or until browned and bubbly.

6-QUART

CHICKEN-AND-GREEN CHILE ENCHILADAS

SERVES: 4 TO 6 | HANDS-ON: 20 MINUTES | BAKE: 30 MINUTES

Transform leftover Pressure Cooker Rotisserie-Style Chicken (page 26) into a flavor fiesta. Green chiles give these cheesy enchiladas a mild, family-friendly flavor. To turn up the heat, try adding jalapeños.

1 tablespoon canola oil

1 cup chopped onion

1 teaspoon jarred minced garlic

3 (10-ounce) cans enchilada sauce

3½ cups chopped Pressure Cooker Rotisserie-Style Chicken (page 26)

2 (4.5-ounce) cans chopped green chiles, drained

1 (8-ounce) package pre-shredded Mexican 4-cheese blend

1 tablespoon chopped fresh cilantro

8 (10-inch) burrito-size flour tortillas

Cooking spray

1. Preheat the oven to 425°F.

2. Remove lid from a 6-quart Instant Pot®. Press SAUTÉ [Normal]. When the word "Hot" appears, swirl in the oil. Add the onion; cook, stirring constantly, 5 minutes or until tender. Add the garlic; cook, stirring constantly, 30 seconds. Stir in 1½ cups of the enchilada sauce, the chicken, and chiles. Turn off the cooker. When the pot has cooled slightly, stir in 1 cup of the cheese and cilantro. Remove the pot from the cooker.

3. Spoon about ½ cup of the chicken mixture down the center of each tortilla; roll up tortillas, and place, seam sides down, in a lightly greased 13- x 9-inch baking dish coated with cooking spray. Pour remaining enchilada sauce over tortillas. Sprinkle with remaining 1 cup cheese.

4. Cover and bake at 425°F for 20 minutes; uncover and bake 10 more minutes or until the cheese melts and is golden brown.

6-QUART

CHICKEN AND KAFFIR LIME CURRY

SERVES: 5 | HANDS-ON: 14 MINUTES | SLOW COOK: 1 HOUR

While you could sauté the chicken in the Instant Pot®, using a skillet with greater surface area allows you to cook all of the chicken at one time. Kaffir lime leaves are dark green and shiny on the top and pale and porous on the bottom. Look for them by the fresh herbs in your supermarket.

1¼ pounds skinless, boneless chicken breasts, cut into bite-sized pieces
1½ tablespoons cornstarch
2 teaspoons red curry powder
¼ teaspoon table salt
1 teaspoon olive oil
2 cups chicken stock (such as Kitchen Basics)
1 (13.66-ounce) can light coconut milk
6 kaffir lime leaves
4 cups hot cooked Jasmine Rice (page 20)
Sliced scallions (optional)
Chopped fresh cilantro (optional)

1. Sprinkle the chicken with 1 tablespoon of the cornstarch, 1 teaspoon of the curry powder, and the salt. Heat the oil in a large nonstick skillet over medium-high; swirl to coat. Add the chicken to the skillet; cook, stirring constantly, 5 to 6 minutes or until golden brown. Stir in ½ cup of the stock, scraping the pan to loosen browned bits. Transfer the chicken mixture to the inner pot of a 6-quart Instant Pot®.

2. Whisk together the remaining 1½ cups stock, remaining 1½ teaspoons cornstarch, remaining 1 teaspoon curry powder, and the coconut milk in a bowl. Stir the coconut milk mixture into the chicken mixture in the cooker. Add the kaffir lime leaves.

3. Lock the lid; turn Pressure Valve to "Venting." SLOW COOK [More] for 1 to 2 hours. Discard lime leaves.

4. Serve the chicken mixture over the rice; sprinkle with the scallions and cilantro, if desired.

6-QUART

PEANUT CHICKEN AND SUGAR SNAP PEAS WITH NOODLES

SERVES: 6 | HANDS-ON: 11 MINUTES | SLOW COOK: 2 HOURS, 30 MINUTES

Curb your takeout cravings with this satisfying noodle bowl that's full of tender chicken, sugar snap peas, and carrots. Make sure you use natural-style peanut butter as it contains much less sugar and will not sweeten the sauce. Crushed red pepper adds a spicy bite, but you can omit it if you'd like.

1½ pounds chicken breast tenders, cut into bite-sized pieces
3 tablespoons cornstarch
2 tablespoons teriyaki sauce
2 teaspoons minced fresh garlic
¼ teaspoon crushed red pepper
1 teaspoon dark sesame oil
2 cups fat-free, lower-sodium chicken broth
¼ cup natural-style peanut butter
2½ cups trimmed sugar snap peas
1 cup matchstick-cut carrots
1 (12-ounce) package spaghetti
½ cup sliced scallions
¼ cup chopped unsalted, dry-roasted peanuts
Lime wedges (optional)

1. Combine the chicken, 2 tablespoons of the cornstarch, 1 tablespoon of the teriyaki sauce, 1 teaspoon of the garlic, and red pepper in a bowl; toss well. Heat a large nonstick skillet over medium-high. Add the oil to the skillet; swirl to coat. Add the chicken mixture to the skillet; cook 6 minutes, browning on all sides. Stir in ½ cup of the broth, scraping the skillet to loosen browned bits. Transfer the chicken mixture to the inner pot of a 6-quart Instant Pot®.

2. Combine the remaining 1½ cups broth, peanut butter, remaining 1 tablespoon cornstarch, remaining 1 tablespoon teriyaki sauce, and remaining 1 teaspoon garlic in a bowl; pour over the chicken mixture.

3. Lock the lid; turn Pressure Valve to "Venting." SLOW COOK [More] for 2 hours. Stir in the peas and carrots; SLOW COOK [More] for 30 more minutes. (Peas should be crisp-tender.)

4. While the peas and carrots cook, cook the pasta according to package directions; drain. Add the cooked spaghetti to the chicken mixture; toss well. Sprinkle with the scallions and peanuts; serve with the lime wedges, if desired.

6-QUART

CHICKEN FRICASSEE

SERVES: 4 | HANDS-ON: 41 MINUTES | UNDER PRESSURE: 11 MINUTES
QUICK PRESSURE RELEASE

Somewhere between a sauté and a stew, fricassee is a classic one-pot French dish. This fricassee is swimming with sweet pearl onions and meaty mushrooms. To peel the onions, quickly dunk them in boiling water, drain them, and drop in a bowl of ice water. Once cool, cut off the root end and pinch the onion to slide the skin off.

- **4 chicken leg quarters (about 2½ pounds), skinned**
- **½ teaspoon kosher salt**
- **½ teaspoon freshly ground black pepper**
- **Twine**
- **3 thyme sprigs**
- **2 sage sprigs**
- **1 cup (about 4.5 ounces) all-purpose flour**
- **1 tablespoon olive oil**
- **1 tablespoon butter**
- **1 pound crimini mushrooms, quartered**
- **¾ cup dry white wine**
- **1¼ cups fat-free, lower-sodium chicken broth**
- **1 pound baby carrots**
- **10 ounces pearl onions, peeled**
- **1 tablespoon chopped fresh thyme**
- **1 tablespoon chopped fresh sage**

1. Pat the chicken dry with paper towels; sprinkle with the salt and pepper. Tie twine around the thyme and sage sprigs. Place the flour in a heavy-duty zip-top freezer bag. Add the chicken, 1 piece at time to the flour; hold the bag closed and shake until coated. Remove from the bag, shaking off excess. Place the oil and butter in the inner pot of a 6-quart Instant Pot®. Press SAUTÉ [Normal]. When the butter melts, spread the oil mixture over the bottom of the pot. Place 2 chicken leg quarters, flesh sides down, in the pot; cook 5 minutes or until browned. Remove the chicken from the pot; set aside, and keep warm. Spread the drippings over the bottom of the pot. Add the remaining 2 chicken leg quarters. Cook 5 minutes or until browned; remove from the pot, and keep warm.

2. Add the mushrooms to the pot. Cook, stirring often, 7 minutes or until liquid almost evaporates. Remove the mushrooms from the pot using a slotted spoon; set aside, and keep warm.

3. Add the wine to the cooker, scraping with a wooden or plastic spatula until the bottom of the pot feels smooth. Bring the wine mixture to a boil; cook 30 seconds. Add the chicken, herb sprigs, and broth. Turn off the cooker. Lock the lid; turn Pressure Valve to "Sealing." PRESSURE COOK [High Pressure] for 8 minutes. Turn off the cooker. Open the cooker using Quick Pressure Release (page 7).

4. Add the mushrooms, carrots, and onions to the pot. Lock the lid; turn Pressure Valve to "Sealing." PRESSURE COOK [High Pressure] for 3 minutes. Turn off the cooker. Open the cooker using Quick Pressure Release (page 7). Transfer the chicken and vegetables to a platter with a slotted spoon; keep warm.

5. Press SAUTÉ [More]. Bring cooking liquid to a boil, and cook until the cooking liquid is reduced to 1 cup (about 12 minutes), stirring occasionally. Remove herb sprigs; discard. Add the chopped thyme and chopped sage to the cooking liquid. Serve the chicken and vegetables with the cooking liquid.

6-QUART

CHICKEN KORMA

SERVES: 8 | HANDS-ON: 15 MINUTES | SLOW COOK: 7 HOURS

Spiced but not spicy, Chicken Korma leftovers make an excellent lunch.

- **2 pounds skinless, boneless chicken thighs, cut into bite-sized pieces**
- **2 cups coarsely chopped onion (1 onion)**
- **2 tablespoons minced peeled fresh ginger**
- **2 teaspoons curry powder**
- **1 teaspoon ground coriander**
- **½ teaspoon ground cumin**
- **½ teaspoon crushed red pepper**
- **4 garlic cloves, minced**
- **2 cups (½-inch) cubed peeled baking potato**
- **1 teaspoon table salt**
- **1 (14.5-ounce) can diced tomatoes, undrained**
- **2 bay leaves**
- **1 (3-inch) cinnamon stick**
- **½ cup plain fat-free yogurt**
- **4 cups hot cooked long-grain brown rice**
- **¼ cup chopped fresh cilantro**

1. Heat a large nonstick skillet over medium-high; add the chicken. Cook 8 minutes or until lightly browned, turning occasionally. Transfer the chicken to a 6-quart Instant Pot®. Add the onion to the skillet; cook, stirring constantly, 3 minutes. Add the ginger, curry powder, coriander, cumin, red pepper, and garlic; cook, stirring constantly, 2 minutes. Spoon the onion mixture over the chicken in the inner pot. Stir in the potato, salt, tomatoes, bay leaves, and cinnamon stick.

2. Lock the lid; turn Pressure Valve to "Venting." SLOW COOK [Normal] for 7 hours. Discard the bay leaves and cinnamon stick. Turn off the cooker. Let the chicken mixture stand 15 minutes. Stir in the yogurt. Serve the chicken mixture over the rice, and sprinkle with the cilantro.

6-QUART

CHICKEN WITH HONEY-LEMON LEEKS

SERVES: 4 | HANDS-ON: 20 MINUTES | UNDER PRESSURE: 12 MINUTES | NATURAL PRESSURE RELEASE

A generous squeeze of lemon juice adds brightness to the rich caramelized leeks. Leeks have a habit of carrying dirt in their many layers, so dunk the slices in a bowl of water, swishing so that the dirt sinks to the bottom. Scoop the slices out with a slotted spoon to remove excess water.

- **8 bone-in, skinless chicken thighs (about 2 pounds)**
- **¾ teaspoon kosher salt**
- **½ teaspoon freshly ground black pepper**
- **1 tablespoon grated lemon rind**
- **2 tablespoons olive oil**
- **1 cup chicken broth**
- **4 cups thinly sliced leek (about 3 large)**
- **3 tablespoons fresh lemon juice**
- **2 teaspoons honey**
- **2 tablespoons chopped fresh parsley or chives (optional)**
- **Lemon wedges (optional)**

1. Sprinkle the chicken evenly with ½ teaspoon of the salt and the pepper. Massage the lemon rind into the chicken. Remove the lid from a 6-quart Instant Pot®. Place 1 tablespoon of the olive oil in the inner pot. Press SAUTÉ [Normal]. Heat until the oil is shimmering; spread over the bottom of the pot. Add the chicken to the pot in batches. Cook 3 minutes on each side or until browned. Transfer the browned chicken to a platter. Turn off the cooker. Add the chicken broth to the pot, scraping with a wooden or plastic spatula until the bottom of the pot feels smooth. Insert the Steam Rack, with the handles in the up position, into the pot in the broth. Place the chicken in the pot on top of the rack.

2. Lock the lid; turn Pressure Valve to "Sealing." PRESSURE COOK [High Pressure] for 12 minutes. Open the cooker using a Natural Pressure Release (page 7). Transfer the chicken to a platter; keep warm. Turn off the cooker.

3. While the chicken cooks, add the remaining 1 tablespoon oil to a large nonstick skillet; swirl to coat. Add the leek and remaining ¼ teaspoon salt; cook 15 minutes or until the leek begins to brown, stirring often. Stir in the lemon juice and honey. Top the chicken with the leek mixture. If desired, sprinkle with the fresh parsley or chives, and serve with the lemon wedges.

6-QUART

CHICKEN PAPRIKASH

SERVES: 6 | HANDS-ON: 25 MINUTES | SLOW COOK: 4 HOURS

Serve this slow-cooked chicken over egg noodles, rice, or mashed potatoes.

- **6 skinless, boneless chicken thighs (about 1¾ pounds), trimmed**
- **½ teaspoon table salt**
- **½ teaspoon freshly ground black pepper**
- **3 tablespoons white rice flour**
- **1 tablespoon canola oil**
- **2 cups chopped onion**
- **1 cup chopped red bell pepper**
- **½ cup matchstick-cut carrots**
- **3 garlic cloves, minced**
- **Cooking spray**
- **1 (8-ounce) package presliced mushrooms**
- **1¼ cups fat-free, lower-sodium chicken broth**
- **2 tablespoons Hungarian sweet paprika**
- **½ cup reduced-fat sour cream**
- **1 tablespoon chopped fresh parsley**

1. Sprinkle the chicken with ¼ teaspoon of the salt and ¼ teaspoon of the black pepper. Place the flour in a shallow dish; dredge chicken in flour, reserving any remaining flour. Heat a large well-seasoned cast-iron skillet over medium-high. Add the oil to the skillet; swirl to coat. Add the chicken; cook 3 minutes on each side or until golden brown. Transfer the chicken to the inner pot of a 6-quart Instant Pot®.

2. Add the onion, bell pepper, carrots, and garlic to the skillet; coat the vegetables with the cooking spray. Cook, stirring constantly, 6 minutes or just until tender. Transfer the onion mixture to the pot.

3. Coat the mushrooms with the cooking spray, and add to the skillet. Cook, stirring constantly, 5 minutes or until browned. Transfer the mushrooms to the pot.

4. Combine the reserved flour, remaining ¼ teaspoon salt, remaining ¼ teaspoon black pepper, broth, and paprika in a bowl; stir with a whisk. Add the broth mixture to the pot. Lock the lid; turn the Pressure Valve to "Venting." SLOW COOK [Normal] for 4 hours.

5. Remove the chicken from the cooker, and place on a serving platter. Skim the fat from surface of the cooking liquid. Stir the sour cream into the cooking liquid. Serve the sauce with the chicken, and sprinkle with the parsley.

Instant Pot

6-QUART

COQ AU VIN

SERVES: 4 TO 6 | HANDS-ON: 30 MINUTES | UNDER PRESSURE: 12 MINUTES
QUICK PRESSURE RELEASE

The Instant Pot® makes preparing this traditional French dish of chicken in red wine much quicker. Crimini mushrooms are sometimes called baby bella mushrooms because they are young portobellas. Their firm texture holds up well in soups, stews, and liquid-heavy dishes like Coq au Vin.

6 bone-in chicken thighs, about 2¾ pounds
½ teaspoon table salt
¼ teaspoon freshly ground black pepper
Cooking spray
¼ pound (4 slices) hickory smoked bacon slices, cut crosswise into ¼-inch pieces
⅔ cup finely chopped shallot (about 1 large shallot)
1 large garlic clove, minced
½ (14.4-ounce) package (about 2 cups) frozen pearl onions
1 (8-ounce) package sliced crimini mushrooms
2 cups Burgundy wine
½ teaspoon dried thyme
1 large bay leaf
¼ cup Cognac or brandy (optional)
½ cup Chicken Bone Broth (page 24) or chicken stock
¼ cup all-purpose flour
2 tablespoons butter
Mashed potatoes
Chopped fresh Italian parsley

1. Trim excess fat and extra skin from the chicken; pat dry. Sprinkle with the salt and pepper, and set aside. Remove the lid from a 6-quart Instant Pot®. Coat the inner pot with the cooking spray; add the bacon. Press SAUTÉ [Normal]. Cook, stirring often with a wooden or plastic spatula, until crisp. Transfer the bacon from the pot to a paper towel–lined plate with a slotted spoon, reserving 2 tablespoons drippings in the pot.

2. Add the chicken to the drippings, skin side down; cook for 4 minutes on each side or until browned. Transfer to a large bowl. Add the shallot to the pot. Cook, stirring constantly, 1 minute. Add the garlic; cook, stirring constantly, 30 seconds. Add the onions and mushrooms. Cook, stirring constantly, 2 minutes. Add the wine, thyme, bay leaf, and, if desired, Cognac or brandy, scraping the pot with a wooden or plastic spatula to loosen browned bits until the bottom of the pot feels smooth. Nestle the chicken into the vegetable mixture, skin side up. Turn off the pot.

3. Lock the lid; turn Pressure Valve to "Sealing." PRESSURE COOK [High Pressure] for 12 minutes. Open the cooker using Quick Pressure Release (page 7). Turn off the cooker. Transfer the chicken, vegetables, and bacon to a large bowl with a slotted spoon.

4. Gradually whisk the ½ cup chicken broth or stock into the flour until smooth. Press SAUTÉ [Normal]. Whisk the broth mixture and butter into the wine mixture. Bring to a boil. Cook, stirring often, until reduced slightly and thickened, about 5 minutes. Remove the bay leaf. Return the chicken, vegetables, and bacon to the wine mixture. Cook until thoroughly heated. Turn off the cooker. Serve with the mashed potatoes. Sprinkle with the parsley.

6-QUART

SPICY CHICKEN CACCIATORE ▸

SERVES: 8 | HANDS-ON: 16 MINUTES | SLOW COOK: 4 HOURS, 30 MINUTES

Prechopped onions save you some tears and a few minutes of prep time. Transform leftovers into soup by shredding the chicken and combining the sauce with chicken stock, diced zucchini, and carrots.

½ cup (about 2.2 ounces) all-purpose flour
8 skinless, boneless chicken thighs (about 2 pounds)
1 tablespoon olive oil
2 cups chopped red bell pepper
2 (8-ounce) containers refrigerated prechopped onion (about 3 cups)
6 garlic cloves, minced
½ cup dry red wine
½ cup canned tomato purée
2 tablespoons capers, drained
1 ½ teaspoons crushed red pepper
1 teaspoon dried oregano
1 teaspoon freshly ground black pepper
¾ teaspoon table salt
1 (14.5-ounce) can unsalted diced tomatoes, undrained
¼ cup chopped fresh parsley
Hot cooked pasta

1. Place the flour in a shallow dish. Dredge the chicken in the flour, turning to coat; shake off and discard excess flour.

2. Heat a large nonstick skillet over medium-high heat. Add the oil to pan; swirl to coat. Add half of the chicken; cook 3 to 4 minutes on each side or until browned. Transfer the chicken to the inner pot of a 6-quart Instant Pot®. Repeat the procedure with the remaining chicken.

3. Add the bell pepper, onion, and garlic to the skillet. Cook, stirring constantly, 4 minutes. Stir in the wine. Cook 2 minutes, scraping skillet to loosen browned bits. Stir in the tomato purée. Pour the bell pepper mixture over the chicken in the pot. Add the capers, red pepper, oregano, black pepper, salt, and tomatoes to the pot.

4. Lock the lid; turn Pressure Valve to "Sealing." SLOW COOK [Normal] for 4 hours and 30 minutes. Sprinkle with the parsley before serving. Serve over pasta.

6-QUART

SPICY ASIAN CHICKEN THIGHS

SERVES: 8 | HANDS-ON: 15 MINUTES | UNDER PRESSURE: 17 MINUTES | QUICK PRESSURE RELEASE

8 bone-in chicken thighs (about 1¾ pounds), skinned
1 cup water
½ cup hoisin sauce
¼ cup rice vinegar
1 tablespoon brown sugar
2 tablespoons minced peeled fresh ginger
1 tablespoon minced fresh garlic
2 tablespoons sambal oelek (ground fresh chile paste)
2 tablespoons fresh lime juice
1 tablespoon dark sesame oil
Cooking spray
¼ cup thinly sliced scallions
¼ cup cilantro leaves
Lime wedges (optional)

1. Pat chicken dry with a paper towel. Combine the 1 cup water, hoisin sauce, vinegar, brown sugar, ginger, garlic, chile paste, lime juice, and sesame oil in a large bowl. Add the chicken, turning to coat. Place the chicken mixture in the inner pot of a 6-quart Instant Pot®. Lock the lid; turn Pressure Valve to "Sealing." PRESSURE COOK [High Pressure] for 17 minutes. Turn off the cooker. Open the cooker using Quick Pressure Release (page 7).

2. While the chicken mixture cooks, preheat broiler.

3. Line a jelly-roll pan with aluminum foil; coat the foil with the cooking spray. Remove the chicken from the pot with tongs, and place on the prepared pan. Broil the chicken 3 minutes on each side or until crisp and lightly browned.

4. While the chicken broils, press SAUTÉ [Normal]. Bring the cooking liquid to a boil; cook, uncovered, 5 minutes or until slightly thick, stirring occasionally.

5. Sprinkle the chicken with the scallions and cilantro; serve with the sauce and, if desired, the lime wedges.

TIP:

Finish these chicken thighs under the broiler to ensure a crispy outside and a juicy inside.

3-QUART

EASY CHICKEN AND DUMPLINGS

SERVES: 2 OR 3 | HANDS-ON: 16 MINUTES | UNDER PRESSURE: 12 MINUTES
SLOW COOK: 18 MINUTES | 5-MINUTE QUICK PRESSURE RELEASE

If you don't have any Chicken Bone Broth (page 24), commercial chicken stock is the next best thing, followed by chicken broth. Add a pinch of Italian seasoning to the latter two for extra flavor.

CHICKEN

2 boneless, skinless chicken breast halves (6 ounces each)

2 cups Chicken Bone Broth (page 24) or chicken stock

2 small carrots, sliced

1 medium celery stalk, chopped

⅛ teaspoon freshly grated black pepper

½ cup frozen petite green peas

DUMPLINGS

1 cup all-purpose flour

2 teaspoons baking powder

½ teaspoon table salt

½ cup milk

2 tablespoons canola oil

Chopped fresh Italian parsley (optional)

1. Make the Chicken: Combine all of the chicken ingredients, except the peas, in the inner pot of a 3-quart Instant Pot®. Lock the lid; turn Pressure Valve to "Sealing." PRESSURE COOK [High Pressure] for 12 minutes. Allow a 5-Minute Quick Pressure Release (page 10). Turn the valve to release remaining pressure. Turn off the cooker.

2. Transfer the chicken to a plate; let cool slightly.

3. Make the Dumplings: Whisk together the flour, baking powder, and salt in a medium bowl. Combine the milk and oil; add to the flour mixture, stirring until blended.

4. With the lid off, press SAUTÉ [More], and bring the broth to a boil. Cut the chicken into bite-size pieces. Add the chicken and the peas to the broth. Place the Steam Rack on top of the chicken mixture; return to a boil. Drop the batter by serving spoonfuls, in 6 portions, onto the rack. Turn off the cooker.

5. Lock the lid; turn the Pressure Valve to "Venting." Press SLOW COOK [More]; cook, without removing the lid, 18 minutes or until a wooden pick inserted in the center of dumplings comes out clean.

6. Carefully, transfer the dumplings to a plate with a large slotted spoon. Remove the rack from the cooker with tongs. Stir the chicken mixture; ladle into large shallow bowls. Top with the dumplings, and, if desired, sprinkle with the chopped parsley. Serve immediately.

NOTE: You may substitute 1 (14½-ounce) can fat-free, low-sodium chicken broth for the broth or stock.

TIPS:

Even on the highest slow cook setting, the Instant Pot® barely simmers the broth, which is necessary so as not to tear the dumplings apart like vigorous boiling would.

▪▪▪

The glass lid accessory is particularly handy for cooking the dumplings in this recipe, because you can keep the pot covered and still monitor the dumplings as they cook.

8-QUART

CHICKEN MIREPOIX

SERVES: 6 | HANDS-ON: 25 MINUTES
UNDER PRESSURE: 11 MINUTES | QUICK PRESSURE RELEASE

Mirepoix is a French cooking term for the combination of onion, carrots, and celery, which form an unusually flavorful seasoning trio in this homey chicken dish.

1 (5-pound) whole chicken
2 teaspoons table salt
½ cup all-purpose flour
¼ teaspoon freshly ground black pepper
3 tablespoons canola oil
1½ cups chopped onion
1½ cups water
3 cups sliced celery
3 cups ½-inch-thick sliced carrot
1 cup chopped green bell pepper
Freshly ground black pepper (optional)

1. Remove the giblets from the chicken. Cut the chicken into serving pieces (breast halves, drumsticks, and thighs), reserving the giblets, back, and wings for another use. Trim excess skin and fat. Rinse and pat the chicken pieces dry with paper towels. Sprinkle the chicken with 1 teaspoon of the salt.

2. Combine the flour, pepper, and remaining 1 teaspoon salt in a large heavy-duty zip-top plastic bag. Add the chicken, a couple of pieces at a time, to the bag. Seal the bag, and shake to coat.

3. Remove the lid from an 8-quart Instant Pot®. Press SAUTÉ [Normal]. When the inner pot is hot, swirl in the oil to coat the bottom of the pot. Shake excess flour from the chicken, and add to the hot oil; brown chicken 5 minutes on each side. Remove the chicken from the pot. Add the onion; cook, stirring often, until the onion is tender, about 5 minutes. Add the 1½ cups water, stirring and scraping with a wooden or plastic spatula to loosen browned bits from the bottom of the pot; return the chicken to the pot. Lock the lid; turn Pressure Valve to "Sealing." PRESSURE COOK [High Pressure] for 9 minutes. Open the cooker using Quick Pressure Release (page 7).

4. Add the celery, carrot, and bell pepper to the pot. Lock the lid; turn Pressure Valve to "Sealing." PRESSURE COOK [High Pressure] for 2 minutes. Turn off the cooker. Open the cooker using Quick Pressure Release (page 7). Transfer the chicken and vegetables to a platter. Cover and keep warm. With the lid off, press SAUTÉ [More], and bring the cooking liquid to a boil. Cook, uncovered, 10 minutes or until juices are slightly thickened and reduced to about 1½ cups, stirring and scraping the bottom of the pot occasionally. Add additional freshly ground pepper to taste, if desired. Serve the chicken and vegetables with the cooking liquid.

NOTE: You may substitute 2 leg quarters and 2 bone-in breast halves totaling 2¾ pounds for the whole chicken, if desired.

TIP:

Freeze the giblets, wings, and backs of chicken to use in making broth.

6-QUART

CHICKEN WITH RICH LEMON-HERB SAUCE

SERVES:4 | HANDS-ON: 15 MINUTES | UNDER PRESSURE: 25 MINUTES
NATURAL PRESSURE RELEASE

Don't skip the last step—whisking the flour mixture into the cooking liquid thickens the sauce and brings the flavors together.

- **2 teaspoons chopped fresh thyme**
- **2 teaspoons paprika**
- **1 teaspoon chopped fresh dill**
- **1 teaspoon table salt**
- **½ teaspoon freshly ground black pepper**
- **1 pound red potatoes (about 12), cut into 1-inch pieces**
- **8 ounces green beans, trimmed and cut into 2-inch pieces**
- **1 small onion, cut into 8 wedges**
- **2 tablespoons minced fresh garlic**
- **1 tablespoon olive oil**
- **1 (3½-pound) roasting chicken, skinned**
- **1 cup water**
- **3 tablespoons fresh lemon juice**
- **1 tablespoon all-purpose flour**
- **1 tablespoon cold water**

1. Combine the thyme, paprika, dill, salt, and pepper in a small bowl. Combine the potatoes, green beans, onion, and 1 tablespoon of the garlic in a large bowl; drizzle with the oil and sprinkle with 2½ teaspoons of the spice mixture, tossing to coat.

2. Remove and discard the giblets and neck from the chicken. Trim the excess fat. Sprinkle the chicken with the remaining spice mixture; rub with the remaining 1 tablespoon garlic.

3. Pour the 1 cup water into the inner pot of a 6-quart Instant Pot®. Add the potato mixture; place the chicken on top of the potato mixture. Drizzle the lemon juice over the chicken.

4. Lock the lid; turn Pressure Valve to "Sealing." PRESSURE COOK [High Pressure] for 25 minutes. Turn off the cooker. Open the cooker using Natural Pressure Release (page 7).

5. Carefully transfer the chicken to a platter. Remove the vegetables with a slotted spoon, and place around the chicken on the platter. Skim the fat from the surface of the cooking liquid; discard. Whisk together the flour and the 1 tablespoon cold water until smooth. Press SAUTÉ [Normal]. Whisk the flour mixture into the cooking liquid. Bring to a simmer; cook 5 minutes or until slightly thick, stirring occasionally. Serve the chicken and vegetables with the sauce.

6-QUART

CHINESE BARBECUE–STYLE WINGS

MAKES: 4 TO 6 APPETIZER SERVINGS | HANDS-ON: 20 MINUTES
UNDER PRESSURE: 5 MINUTES | 5-MINUTE NATURAL PRESSURE RELEASE

You can also use this method to make Buffalo wings in the Instant Pot®. Just substitute Buffalo sauce for the sauce in this recipe, and omit the rice and scallions.

Cooking spray
1 cup water
1 tablespoon hickory liquid smoke (such as Wright's)
3½ to 4 pounds chicken wing drumettes and wing portions
½ cup hoisin sauce
3 tablespoon light brown sugar
3 tablespoons soy sauce
3 tablespoons chili sauce
2 tablespoons grated peeled fresh ginger
2 tablespoons rice vinegar
1 tablespoon dry sherry
1 teaspoon dark sesame oil
¾ teaspoon Chinese five-spice powder
½ teaspoon hickory liquid smoke (such as Wright's)
2 large garlic cloves, pressed
Cooked Jasmine Rice (page 20; optional)
Thin scallions, trimmed (optional)

1. Place a cooling rack in an aluminum foil-lined sheet pan; coat the rack with the cooking spray. Pour the 1 cup water into the inner pot of a 6-quart Instant Pot®. Stir in the liquid smoke. Place the Steam Rack in the pot with the handles in the up position.

2. Place the wings in the pot. Lock the lid; turn Pressure Valve to "Sealing." PRESSURE COOK [High Pressure] for 5 minutes. Allow a 5-minute Natural Pressure Release (page 10). Turn the Pressure Valve to "Venting" to release the remaining pressure.

3. While the wings cook and the pressure releases naturally, preheat the broiler to high. Whisk together the hoisin sauce and remaining ingredients, except rice and scallions, in a 2-cup glass measuring cup.

4. Drain the wings, and place, one layer at a time, in a large bowl, blotting each layer dry with paper towels. Pour half of the sauce mixture over the wings, turning the wings to coat. Place the coated wings, skin side down, in a single layer on the rack in the prepared pan, reserving the sauce in the bowl.

5. Broil 7 minutes on each side or until desired crispness. Brush the wings with some of the remaining sauce. Serve immediately with the remaining sauce, and if desired, rice and scallions.

6-QUART

POLYNESIAN TURKEY LOAF

SERVES: 4 | HANDS-ON: 15 MINUTES | UNDER PRESSURE: 20 MINUTES
10-MINUTE NATURAL PRESSURE RELEASE

Ground turkey, a combination of both light and dark meat, has more moisture than turkey breast meat alone. It makes this loaf moist, yet firm enough to cut into slices. Omit the Polynesian Sauce, and make the loaf ahead to use in Turkey Loaf Sandwiches (page 156) or Josie's Special Scramble (page 44).

TURKEY LOAF

2 cups water

1 large egg

1 large garlic clove, minced

1 tablespoon minced fresh parsley

½ teaspoon table salt

¼ teaspoon freshly ground black pepper

⅛ teaspoon ground poultry seasoning

⅓ cup thinly sliced scallions (white and green parts)

1 pound ground turkey (light and dark meat)

⅓ cup Italian-seasoned dry bread crumbs

Cooking spray

POLYNESIAN SAUCE

1 (20-ounce) can pineapple tidbits in juice

¼ cup firmly packed light brown sugar

1 tablespoon cornstarch

2 teaspoons ketchup

¼ teaspoon grated lemon rind

1 tablespoon fresh lemon juice

1. Pour the 2 cups of water into the inner pot of a 6-quart Instant Pot®.

2. Make the Turkey Loaf: Whisk the egg in a large bowl. Whisk in the garlic, parsley, salt, pepper, poultry seasoning, and scallions. Add the turkey and bread crumbs; mix well using your fingers.

3. Fold a piece of aluminum foil into a 16- x 7-inch sling. Coat the foil with the cooking spray. Shape the turkey mixture into a 7- x 4-inch oval loaf in the center of the sling, parallel to the long side. Grasping the ends of the sling, lift the turkey loaf onto the Steam Rack, perpendicular to the handles. Lower the rack into the pot using the handles, making sure the ends of the foil are below the rim of the pot.

4. Lock the lid; turn Pressure Valve to "Sealing." PRESSURE COOK [High Pressure] for 20 minutes. Allow a 10-Minute Natural Pressure Release (page 10). Turn off the cooker, and turn the Pressure Valve to "Venting" to release remaining pressure. Remove the turkey loaf from the cooker using the rack handles, tilting the rack to pour accumulated liquid into the pot. Place the turkey loaf on a plate, and fold the foil over the loaf to cover and keep warm. Pour the water and drippings mixture from the pot; return the pot to the cooker.

5. Make the Polynesian Sauce: While the turkey loaf cooks, drain the pineapple to measure ¾ cup juice and 1 cup tidbits. Reserve the remaining pineapple tidbits and juice for another use. Whisk the brown sugar and cornstarch into the measured juice. Whisk in the ketchup. Pour the juice mixture into the inner pot.

6. Press SAUTÉ [Normal]; cook uncovered, whisking constantly, until the sauce boils and thickens, about 2 minutes. Turn off the cooker. Whisk in the lemon rind, and lemon juice. Add the reserved pineapple, stirring just until thoroughly heated. Cut the turkey loaf into slices, and pass the sauce to spoon over the slices.

TIP:

If you're short on time, omit the Polynesian Sauce and stir fresh orange rind to taste into whole-berry cranberry sauce. Serve with the turkey loaf.

6-QUART

CRAWFISH ÉTOUFFÉE

SERVES: 5 | HANDS-ON: 28 MINUTES | UNDER PRESSURE: 2 MINUTES
QUICK PRESSURE RELEASE

Mise en place is a French term that refers to having all your ingredients and equipment prepared and in order before starting a recipe. It's the best approach here because the roux is likely to scorch if the vegetables are not ready to add immediately when called for.

¾ cup butter, cut into pieces
½ cup all-purpose flour
1¼ cups chopped green pepper
1 cup thinly sliced celery
⅔ cup chopped scallions
1 tablespoon tomato paste
1¾ cups Chicken Bone Broth (page 24) or chicken stock
1½ cups water
3 tablespoons chopped fresh parsley
½ teaspoon table salt
¼ teaspoon freshly ground black pepper
¼ teaspoon ground chipotle chile
1 small bay leaf
1½ pounds cooked peeled and deveined crawfish tail meat, drained
Hot cooked rice

1. Remove the lid from a 6-quart Instant Pot®. Add the butter to the inner pot. Press SAUTÉ [Normal]. When butter has melted, stir in the flour. Cook, stirring constantly, until the roux is caramel colored, about 5 minutes. Add the green pepper, celery, scallions, and tomato paste; cook, stirring constantly, 5 minutes. Turn off the cooker.

2. Add the bone broth, 1½ cups water, parsley, salt, black pepper, ground chipotle chile, and bay leaf, scraping with a wooden or plastic spatula until the bottom of the pot feels smooth. Lock the lid; PRESSURE COOK [High Pressure] for 2 minutes. Open the cooker using Quick Pressure Release (page 7). Turn off the cooker.

3. Press SAUTÉ [Normal]. Add the crawfish; cook, stirring constantly, 5 minutes, scraping with a wooden spatula to loosen brown bits from the bottom of the pot. Turn off the cooker; immediately transfer the inner pot to a heatproof surface. Remove the bay leaf, and serve over the rice.

6-QUART

SHRIMP SCAMPI

SERVES: 4 | HANDS-ON: 18 MINUTES | UNDER PRESSURE: 0 MINUTES
5-MINUTE NATURAL PRESSURE RELEASE

Tossing in the zest just before serving adds a burst of fresh lemon flavor.

1 large lemon, yielding 2 to 3 teaspoons of zest
3 cups water
8 ounces uncooked linguine, broken in half
1½ pounds unpeeled large shrimp (26 to 30 count)
6 tablespoons butter
4 large garlic cloves, pressed
¾ teaspoon table salt
¼ teaspoon freshly ground black pepper
¼ cup minced fresh parsley

1. Grate the zest from the lemon. Squeeze the juice from the lemon to measure 3 tablespoons. Set zest and juice aside.

2. Pour the 3 cups water into the inner pot of a 6-quart Instant Pot®. Add 1 handful of the broken pasta. Lift the pasta slightly with your fingers and let it fall back into the water to wet all strands. Repeat the procedure, adding another handful of pasta perpendicular to the first. Continue adding and wetting the pasta, 1 handful at a time, until all is added; press to submerge all strands in the water. Lock the lid; turn Pressure Valve to "Sealing." Press PRESSURE COOK [High Pressure]; set time for 0 minutes.

3. While the pasta cooks, peel and devein the shrimp. When the pressure cook time is up, allow a 5-minute Natural Pressure Release (page 10). Immediately turn the Pressure Valve to "Venting" to release the remaining pressure. Turn off the cooker.

4. Immediately drain the pasta, and rinse under cold running water to stop the cooking process; drain well, and place in a large serving bowl. Stir with a pasta fork to separate the strands. Wash and dry the inner pot, and return it to the cooker.

5. Add the butter to the pot. Press SAUTÉ [Normal]. When the butter melts, add the shrimp and the garlic, stirring to coat the shrimp with butter. Cook, stirring constantly, 3 minutes. Stir in the reserved 3 tablespoons lemon juice, salt, and pepper. Turn off the cooker. Return the pasta to the pot; toss with the shrimp mixture until thoroughly heated. Remove the inner pot from the Instant Pot® and set on a heatproof surface. Sprinkle the shrimp mixture with the lemon zest and parsley. Toss well, and return to the bowl. Serve immediately.

6-QUART

SWEET-AND-SOUR SHRIMP

SERVES: 4 | HANDS-ON: 17 MINUTES | UNDER PRESSURE: 1 MINUTE | QUICK PRESSURE RELEASE

Since the shrimp and vegetables cook so quickly, stay close by and quickly release the pressure when the steaming time is up so the residual heat won't overcook them.

- **1 cup water**
- **1 (8-ounce) can pineapple chunks in juice**
- **⅓ cup firmly packed light brown sugar**
- **4 teaspoons cornstarch**
- **2 tablespoons low-sodium soy sauce**
- **¼ teaspoon garlic powder**
- **¼ teaspoon ground ginger**
- **⅛ teaspoon black pepper**
- **⅛ teaspoon crushed red pepper (optional)**
- **1 cup ¼-inch sliced carrots**
- **1 large red bell pepper, cut into 1-inch squares**
- **1 pound peeled and deveined large shrimp (26 to 30 count)**
- **4 scallions (both white and green parts), cut into 1-inch pieces**
- **1 tablespoon white vinegar**
- **2 tablespoons dry sherry**
- **White Basmati Rice (page 20)**

1. Place a collapsible vegetable steamer with a center post in the inner pot of a 6-quart Instant Pot®. Add the 1 cup water to the pot.

2. Drain the pineapple chunks, reserving the juice and pineapple. Add water, if necessary, to the juice to measure ½ cup. Whisk the brown sugar, cornstarch, soy sauce, garlic powder, ginger, black pepper, and, if desired, crushed red pepper into the juice mixture. Set aside.

3. Layer the carrots, bell pepper, shrimp, and scallions on top of the vegetable steamer in that order. Lock the lid. STEAM [High Pressure] for 1 minute. Open the cooker using the Quick Pressure Release (page 7). Turn off the cooker. Remove the vegetable steamer, using the center post, and set it on a plate. Pour the water from the pot, and return the pot to the cooker.

4. Add the pineapple juice mixture to the pot. Press SAUTÉ [Normal]. Bring to a boil; cook, whisking constantly, until thickened, about 1 minute. Stir in the vinegar and sherry. Add the shrimp, vegetables, and pineapple chunks to the sauce, stirring to coat. Turn off the cooker; remove the inner pot from the cooker to prevent overcooking. Serve immediately with the rice.

5

SOUPS, STEWS & CHILI

3- OR 6-QUART

BOSTON CLAM CHOWDER

MAKES: 6 CUPS | HANDS-ON: 10 MINUTES | UNDER PRESSURE: 5 MINUTES
QUICK PRESSURE RELEASE

This is "the creamy one." It's so easy to transport yourself to the seaport with this quick version of the famous chowder.

2 (6.5-ounce) cans minced clams
Cooking spray
3 bacon slices, cut crosswise into ¼-inch pieces
1½ cups water
3 small potatoes, peeled and cubed
½ cup chopped onion
1½ stalks celery, finely chopped
3 chicken bouillon cubes
¼ teaspoon freshly ground black pepper
⅛ teaspoon dried thyme, crushed
1 bay leaf
2 cups milk
3 tablespoons all-purpose flour

1. Drain the clams, reserving the clams and juice. Add water to the clam juice, if necessary, to measure 1 cup.

2. Remove the lid from a 3-quart or 6-quart Instant Pot®. Coat the inner pot with the cooking spray. Add the bacon, and press SAUTÉ [Normal]; cook, stirring often, until crisp, about 5 minutes. Turn off the cooker. Remove the bacon with a slotted spoon, and drain on paper towels, reserving the drippings in the pot. Add the 1½ cups of water, stirring and scraping to loosen the brown bits from the bottom of the pot. Stir the clam juice, potatoes, onion, and celery, bouillon cubes, pepper, thyme, and bay leaf into the vegetable mixture.

3. Lock the lid; turn Pressure Valve to "Sealing." PRESSURE COOK [High Pressure] for 5 minutes. Open the cooker using Quick Pressure Release (page 7). Turn off the cooker.

4. Gradually stir about ¼ cup of the milk into the flour until smooth. Stir flour mixture into the vegetable mixture in the pot; stir in the remaining milk. Press SAUTÉ [Normal], and cook uncovered, until soup simmers and thickens, stirring often, about 5 minutes. Turn off the cooker. Stir in the reserved clams, and let stand until thoroughly heated. Remove the inner pot from the cooker. Remove the bay leaf, ladle the chowder into bowls, and top with the crumbled bacon.

6-QUART

CINCINNATI TURKEY CHILI

SERVES: 4 | HANDS-ON: 16 MINUTES | UNDER PRESSURE: 5 MINUTES | QUICK PRESSURE RELEASE

Cooking spray
8 ounces lean ground turkey
½ cups refrigerated prechopped onion
1 cup chopped green bell pepper
1 tablespoon jarred minced garlic
1 tablespoon chili powder
2 tablespoons tomato paste
1 teaspoon ground cumin
1 teaspoon dried oregano
¼ teaspoon ground cinnamon
⅛ teaspoon ground allspice
½ cup fat-free, less-sodium chicken broth
1 (15-ounce) can kidney beans, drained and rinsed
1 (14.5-ounce) can diced tomatoes, undrained
4 ounces uncooked spaghetti, broken in half
2½ tablespoons chopped semisweet chocolate
¼ teaspoon table salt
3 ounces sharp Cheddar cheese, shredded (about ¾ cup)

1. Remove the lid from a 6-quart Instant Pot®. Coat the inner pot with the cooking spray. Add the turkey, and press SAUTÉ [Normal]. Cook 3 minutes or until beginning to brown, stirring to crumble with a wooden or plastic spatula. Add 1 cup of the onion, bell pepper, and garlic; cook, stirring constantly, 3 minutes. Turn off the cooker. Add the chili powder, tomato paste, cumin, oregano, cinnamon, and allspice; stir for 1 minute. Add the broth, beans, and tomatoes, scraping with the spatula until the bottom of the pot feels smooth.

2. Lock the lid; turn Pressure Valve to "Sealing." PRESSURE COOK [High Pressure] for 5 minutes.

3. While the chili cooks, cook pasta according to package directions. Drain; set aside.

4. When the pressure cooking time is up, turn off the cooker. Open the lid using Quick Pressure Release (page 7). Remove the pot from the cooker; stir in the chocolate and salt. Serve the chili over the spaghetti; top with remaining ½ cup onion and cheese.

NOTE: You can substitute 2 cups cooked, soaked red kidney beans (page 29) for the canned beans.

6-QUART

◂ SPICED TURKEY-CHICKPEA CHILI

SERVES: 8 | HANDS-ON: 8 MINUTES | SLOW COOK: 8 HOURS

- **1 cup chopped orange bell pepper**
- **2 cups fat-free, lower-sodium chicken broth**
- **½ cup dry white wine**
- **¼ cup minced seeded jalapeño chile**
- **1 teaspoon chili powder**
- **½ teaspoon Berbere seasoning**
- **½ teaspoon ground turmeric**
- **¼ teaspoon ground red pepper**
- **¼ teaspoon ground cinnamon**
- **1 pound lean ground turkey**
- **1 (14.5-ounce) can diced tomatoes, drained**
- **¾ pound dried chickpeas (garbanzo beans)**
- **1 (8-ounce) can lower-sodium tomato sauce**
- **3 large garlic cloves, minced**
- **½ teaspoon table salt**
- **Sour cream (optional)**
- **Chopped fresh cilantro (optional)**

1. Combine all ingredients, except the salt, sour cream, and cilantro, in the inner pot of a 6-quart Instant Pot®. Lock the lid; turn Pressure Valve to "Venting." SLOW COOK [Normal] for 8 hours. Cook additional time, if necessary, until the peas are tender. Add the salt, and stir well to crumble the turkey.

2. Ladle the chili into 8 bowls, and top with the sour cream and cilantro, if desired.

6-QUART

WHITE CHICKEN CHILI

SERVES: 8 | HANDS-ON: 35 MINUTES | UNDER PRESSURE: 45 MINUTES
10-MINUTE NATURAL PRESSURE RELEASE AND QUICK PRESSURE RELEASE

- **2 cups dried Great Northern beans**
- **3 tablespoons olive oil**
- **1 teaspoon table salt**
- **5 cups water**
- **2 pounds skinless, boneless chicken breast, cut into ½-inch pieces**
- **2 cups finely chopped onion**
- **2 garlic cloves, minced**
- **2 teaspoons ground cumin**
- **1 teaspoon ground coriander**
- **½ teaspoon dried oregano**
- **2 (4.5-ounce) cans chopped green chiles, undrained**
- **1 (14-ounce) can fat-free, less-sodium chicken broth**
- **½ teaspoon hot pepper sauce**
- **4 ounces Monterey Jack cheese, shredded (about 1 cup)**
- **½ cup chopped fresh cilantro**
- **½ cup chopped green onions**

1. Sort and wash the beans; drain. Combine the beans, 1 tablespoon of the oil, salt, and 5 cups water in the inner pot of a 6-quart Instant Pot®.

2. Lock the lid; turn Pressure Valve to "Sealing." PRESSURE COOK [High Pressure] for 35 minutes. Allow a 10-minute Natural Pressure Release (page10). Turn Pressure Valve to "Venting" to release remaining pressure. Drain the beans, reserving 1 cup of the cooking liquid.

3. Wash and thoroughly dry the inner pot, and return it to the cooker. Press SAUTÉ [Normal]. When the word "Hot" appears, swirl in 1 tablespoon of the oil. Add half of the chicken. Cook, without stirring, 1 to 2 minutes or until chicken begins to sizzle and releases from pot. Continue to cook 5 minutes, stirring occasionally with a wooden or plastic spatula. Remove the chicken from the pot. Repeat the procedure with the remaining 1 tablespoon oil and remaining half of chicken. Add the onion; cook, stirring constantly, 5 minutes or until tender. Add the garlic; cook, stirring constantly, 30 seconds. Stir in the cumin, coriander, and oregano; cook, stirring constantly, 1 minute. Stir in the chiles. Cook, stirring constantly, until the liquid almost evaporates. Turn off the cooker.

4. Add the reserved cooking liquid, beans, broth, and chicken, scraping with the spatula until the bottom of the pot feels smooth.

5. Lock the lid; turn Pressure Valve to "Sealing." PRESSURE COOK [High Pressure] for 10 minutes. Open the cooker, using Quick Pressure Release (page 7). Stir in the hot sauce. Ladle 1 cup of the chili into each of 8 bowls; sprinkle each serving with 2 tablespoons of the cheese, 1 tablespoon cilantro, and 1 tablespoon green onions.

Instant Pot
Duo Plus
Meat Stew
Cake
Egg
Slow Cook
Sauté
Pressure Level
Keep Warm
Delay Start
Cancel
Rice
Multigrain
Porridge
Steam
Sterilize
Yogurt
Pressure Cook
www.instantPot.com

6-QUART

HUNGARIAN BEEF STEW

SERVES: 6 | HANDS-ON: 25 MINUTES | UNDER PRESSURE: 30 MINUTES
10-MINUTE NATURAL PRESSURE RELEASE AND QUICK PRESSURE RELEASE

1½ pounds lean boneless chuck roast, trimmed and cut into 1-inch pieces
¾ teaspoon table salt
½ teaspoon freshly ground black pepper
2 tablespoons olive oil
2 medium onions, chopped
1 tablespoon paprika
1 teaspoon caraway seeds
3 garlic cloves, minced
1 cup dry red wine
1¾ cups water
1½ cups unsalted beef stock
1 pound fingerling potatoes, cut into 1-inch chunks
3 carrots, coarsely chopped
2 red bell peppers, sliced
2 tablespoons all-purpose flour

1. Sprinkle the beef with ½ teaspoon of the salt and ¼ teaspoon of the pepper.

2. Place the oil in the inner pot of a 6-quart Instant Pot®. Press SAUTÉ [Normal]. When the oil is shimmering, spread it over the bottom of the pot with a wooden or plastic spatula, and add half of the beef to the pot; cook 5 minutes, or until dark brown, stirring occasionally. Transfer the beef to a plate with a slotted spoon. Repeat the procedure with the remaining beef. (If the bottom of the pot is getting too brown, it may be necessary to reduce the heat to SAUTÉ [Less]. Do not let the fond become charred.)

3. Add the onions; cook, stirring constantly with the spatula, 5 minutes or until softened. Add the paprika, caraway seeds, and garlic; cook 1 minute, stirring. Add the wine; cook 2 minutes, scraping with the spatula until the bottom of the pot feels smooth. Stir in 1½ cups of the water, the remaining ¼ teaspoon salt, the remaining ¼ teaspoon pepper, stock, and beef, with the accumulated juices.

4. Lock the lid; turn Pressure Valve to "Sealing." PRESSURE COOK [High Pressure] for 25 minutes. Allow a 10-minute Natural Pressure Release (page 10). Turn the valve to "Venting" to release remaining pressure.

5. Add the potatoes, carrots, and peppers to the pot. Lock the lid; turn the Pressure Valve to "Sealing." PRESSURE COOK [High Pressure] for 5 minutes. Open the cooker using Quick Pressure Release (page 7). Turn off the cooker.

6. Gradually add the remaining ¼ cup water to the flour, stirring until smooth; add to the stew, stirring constantly. Press SAUTÉ [Normal]. Cook, stirring often, 5 minutes or until the stew boils and thickens slightly.

6-QUART

MEXICAN CHICKEN STEW

SERVES: 8 | HANDS-ON: 5 MINUTES | UNDER PRESSURE: 23 MINUTES | QUICK PRESSURE RELEASE

3 pounds chicken pieces, skinned
2 cups thinly sliced onion
¾ teaspoon table salt
½ teaspoon coarsely ground black pepper
3 (14.5-ounce) cans fat-free, lower-sodium chicken broth
4 garlic cloves, crushed
3 bell peppers, seeded and chopped
1 bay leaf
1 (15-ounce) can golden or white hominy, drained
2 tablespoons ground guajillo chile powder
1½ teaspoons dried oregano
½ cup roasted unsalted pumpkinseed kernels
¼ cup chopped fresh cilantro
¼ cup sliced radishes
¼ cup sliced scallions
½ cup crumbled queso fresco

1. Remove excess fat from the chicken pieces. Combine the chicken, onion, salt, pepper, broth, garlic, bell peppers, and bay leaf in the inner pot of a 6-quart Instant Pot®. Lock the lid; turn Pressure Valve to "Sealing." PRESSURE COOK [High Pressure] for 23 minutes. Open the cooker using Quick Pressure Release (page 7). Turn off the cooker. Remove the chicken from the broth mixture; cool slightly. Remove the chicken from the bones; cut chicken into bite-sized pieces. Discard bones.

2. Strain the stock through a sieve over a bowl; discard solids. Return the pot to the cooker; return the stock to the pot. Stir in the chicken, hominy, chile powder, and oregano. Press SAUTÉ [Normal]. Cook 5 minutes or until thoroughly heated. Skim the fat from surface of broth; discard.

3. Ladle the stew into 8 bowls; top each serving evenly with pumpkinseed kernels, cilantro, radishes, scallions, and queso fresco.

6-QUART

◂ POTATO, CORN, AND CHICKEN STEW

SERVES: 9 | HANDS-ON: 15 MINUTES | UNDER PRESSURE: 23 MINUTES | QUICK PRESSURE RELEASE

3½ cups fat-free, lower-sodium chicken broth
1½ cups fresh corn kernels (about 3 ears)
2 tablespoons olive oil
4 pounds bone-in chicken thighs, skinned (about 12 thighs)
½ cup chopped onion
½ cup thinly sliced carrot
1½ cups water
2½ cups finely shredded peeled baking potato
2½ cups cubed peeled Yukon gold or red potato
1½ teaspoons chopped fresh oregano
1 teaspoon chopped fresh thyme
¼ cup chopped fresh cilantro
1 tablespoon fresh lime juice
¼ teaspoon table salt
½ teaspoon hot pepper sauce (such as Tabasco)
¼ teaspoon freshly ground black pepper
¾ cup cubed peeled avocado
4½ teaspoons capers

1. Place 1 cup of the broth and ½ cup of the corn in a food processor; process until the corn is puréed.

2. Place 1 tablespoon of the oil in the inner pot of a 6-quart Instant Pot®. Press SAUTÉ [Normal]. When the oil is shimmering, add half of the chicken; cook 5 minutes, browning on both sides. Remove the chicken from the cooker. Repeat the procedure with the remaining half of the chicken; remove the chicken from the cooker. Carefully remove the pot from the cooker. Remove the drippings from the pot.

3. Return the pot to the cooker. Add the remaining 1 tablespoon of the oil to the cooker. Add the onion and carrot; cook, stirring constantly, 2 minutes. Stir in the 1½ cups water, potatoes, oregano, and thyme. Stir in the puréed corn mixture, remaining 2½ cups broth, and remaining 1 cup corn. Return the chicken thighs to the cooker. Turn off the cooker.

4. Lock the lid; turn the Pressure Valve to "Sealing." PRESSURE COOK [High Pressure] for 23 minutes. Open the cooker using Quick Pressure Release (page 7). Turn off the cooker. Remove the chicken from the cooker; cool slightly.

5. Remove the bones from the chicken; discard the bones. Shred the chicken into bite-sized pieces. Return the shredded chicken to the cooker. Stir in the cilantro, lime juice, salt, pepper sauce, and pepper. Press SAUTÉ [Normal]; cook, uncovered, 5 minutes, or until thoroughly heated, stirring often. Turn off the cooker. Ladle the stew into 9 bowls; top with the avocado and capers.

6-QUART

SUMMER BRUNSWICK STEW

SERVES: 10 | HANDS-ON: 20 MINUTES | UNDER PRESSURE: 5 MINUTES | QUICK PRESSURE RELEASE

2 tablespoons olive oil
1 large sweet onion, diced
2 garlic cloves, minced
6 cups chicken broth
2 cups diced peeled tomatoes
2 cups fresh lady peas or butter peas
2 cups fresh corn kernels (about 4 ears)
1 pound Yukon Gold potatoes, peeled and cut into ½-inch cubes (about 2 cups)
1 pound pulled barbecued pork (without sauce)
1 to 1½ cups barbecue sauce
Table salt and black pepper

1. Place the oil in the inner pot of a 6-quart Instant Pot®. Press SAUTÉ [Normal]. When the oil is shimmering, add the onion, and cook, stirring constantly with a wooden or plastic spatula, 5 minutes or until tender. Add the garlic; cook, stirring constantly, 30 seconds. Turn off the cooker. Add the broth, scraping with the spatula until the bottom of the pot feels smooth.

2. Stir in the tomatoes, peas, corn, and potatoes. Lock the lid; turn Pressure Valve to "Sealing." PRESSURE COOK [High Pressure] for 5 minutes. Open the cooker, using Quick Pressure Release (page 7). Add the pork and 1 cup of the barbecue sauce. Turn off the cooker.

3. With the lid off, press SAUTÉ [Normal]; cook 3 to 5 minutes or until thoroughly heated, stirring often. Stir in up to ½ cup additional barbecue sauce to taste, if desired. Season with the salt and black pepper to taste. Turn off the cooker.

NOTE: You may substitute 1 (14.5-ounce) can diced tomatoes for the diced fresh ones.

6-QUART

LENTIL STEW WITH HAM AND GREENS

SERVES: 5 | HANDS-ON: 17 MINUTES | UNDER PRESSURE: 20 MINUTES
QUICK PRESSURE RELEASE

Serve with thick slices of Peasant Bread (page 48), slathered with butter.

- **1 cup dried lentils**
- **1½ tablespoons olive oil**
- **1 cup chopped onion**
- **3 garlic cloves, minced**
- **4½ cups fat-free, less-sodium chicken broth**
- **3 cups chopped collard greens or Swiss chard**
- **1½ cups ½-inch cubed baking potato**
- **1 cup chopped smoked ham**
- **½ cup chopped carrot**
- **1 (14.5-ounce) can diced tomatoes, drained**
- **1 teaspoon dried basil**
- **½ teaspoon dried thyme**
- **½ teaspoon black pepper**
- **2 bay leaves**
- **3 tablespoons chopped fresh parsley**

1. Sort and wash the lentils; drain. Add the olive oil to the inner pot of a 6-quart Instant Pot®. Press SAUTÉ [Normal]. When the oil is shimmering, add the onion and garlic; cook, stirring constantly, 3 minutes. Stir in the broth and lentils. Turn off the cooker.

2. Lock the lid; turn Pressure Valve to "Sealing." PRESSURE COOK [High Pressure] for 15 minutes. Open cooker using Quick Pressure Release (page 7).

3. Add the collard greens, stirring to wilt slightly. Stir in the potato and remaining ingredients, except the parsley. Lock the lid; turn Pressure Valve to "Sealing." PRESSURE COOK [High Pressure] for 5 minutes. Open the cooker using Quick Pressure Release (page 7). Discard the bay leaves. Sprinkle with the parsley.

6-QUART

CALDO TLALPEÑO

SERVES: 4 TO 6 | HANDS-ON: 12 MINUTES | UNDER PRESSURE: 3 MINUTES | QUICK PRESSURE RELEASE

The heat from the chipotle peppers, the crisp radishes, and the slight tang from a squeeze of lime juice makes this spicy soup an excellent choice for hot summer days. An added plus: The Instant Pot® won't heat up your kitchen.

- 1 tablespoon olive oil
- 1 cup ¼-inch diced onion
- 1 cup ¼-inch diced carrots
- 3 large garlic cloves, minced
- 1 (14½-ounce) can diced tomatoes
- 2 large chipotle chiles in adobo, minced
- 4½ cups Chicken Bone Broth (page 24)
- 1½ cups drained cooked chickpeas (garbanzo beans; page 28)
- ½ teaspoon dried Italian seasoning
- ½ teaspoon table salt
- 3 cups shredded cooked, boneless, skinless chicken (page 25)
- ⅓ cup chopped fresh cilantro
- 1½ cups cubed queso fresco
- ⅓ cup thinly sliced radishes
- 1 medium avocado, sliced
- Lime wedges
- Tortilla chips

1. Place the olive oil in the inner pot of a 6-quart Instant Pot®. Press SAUTÉ [Normal]. When the oil is hot, add the onion and carrots. Cook, stirring constantly, just until the onion begins to soften. Turn off the cooker. Add the garlic; cook, stirring constantly, 30 seconds. Add the tomatoes and chipotle chiles, scraping with a wooden or plastic spatula until the bottom of the pot feels smooth. Stir in the bone broth, chickpeas, Italian seasoning, and salt.
2. Lock the lid; turn Pressure Valve to "Sealing." PRESSURE COOK [High Pressure] for 3 minutes. Open the cooker using Quick Pressure Release (page 7). Stir in the chicken and cilantro. Turn off the cooker. Let stand until thoroughly heated.
3. Ladle the soup into large shallow bowls. Sprinkle with the cheese and radishes. Top with the avocado slices just before serving. Add a lime wedge to each serving to squeeze into the soup. Serve with tortilla chips.

NOTE: You may substitute commercial chicken stock for the bone broth and 1 (15-ounce) can garbanzo beans, drained, for the cooked beans.

3- OR 6-QUART

MULLIGATAWNY SOUP

SERVES: 4 | HANDS-ON: 15 MINUTES | SAUTÉ: 18 MINUTES

Mulligatawny originated in India and was made popular in England during the British Raj. Today there are many styles of the curried soup, including this hearty chicken version.

- **2 tablespoons butter**
- **1 cup chopped onion (1 small)**
- **¼ cup all-purpose flour**
- **2 tablespoons curry powder**
- **¼ teaspoon ground coriander**
- **¼ teaspoon ground cloves**
- **5 cups Chicken Bone Broth (page 24) or chicken stock**
- **¼ cup sweetened flaked coconut**
- **2½ cups cubed Cooked Chicken Breast (page 25)**
- **2 tablespoons fresh lemon juice**
- **Salt and freshly ground pepper**
- **2 cups Jasmine Rice (page 20)**
- **Sweetened flaked coconut**
- **4 lemon wedges**
- **4 naan breads (Indian flatbread)**

1. Remove the lid from a 3- or 6-quart Instant Pot®. Add the butter to the inner pot. Press SAUTÉ [Normal]; cook until the butter melts. Add the onion; cook, stirring constantly, 3 minutes. Turn off the cooker. Stir in the flour until blended. Stir in the curry powder, coriander, and cloves. Gradually add in the broth, stirring constantly. Add the ¼ cup coconut. Increase the heat to SAUTÉ [More]. Bring to a boil, stirring constantly; cook, stirring often, until thickened, about 3 minutes. Reduce the heat to SAUTÉ [Less], and cook 10 minutes, stirring occasionally.

2. Stir in the chicken and 2 tablespoons lemon juice. Cook until thoroughly heated, about 2 minutes. Turn off the cooker. Stir in the salt and pepper to taste. Place about ½ cup of the rice in each of 4 large bowls. Ladle the soup evenly over the rice. Sprinkle each serving with additional flaked coconut. Serve with 1 lemon wedge to squeeze into the soup and 1 naan bread.

6-QUART

CREAMY CHICKEN-VEGETABLE SOUP

MAKES: 2 QUARTS | HANDS-ON: 20 MINUTES | UNDER PRESSURE: 5 MINUTES | QUICK PRESSURE RELEASE

While you could substitute chicken stock in this flavorful soup, bone broth adds much more richness, nutrition, and flavor.

- **2 tablespoons canola oil**
- **1 cup chopped onion**
- **½ cup thinly sliced carrot**
- **½ cup thinly sliced celery**
- **4 cups Chicken Bone Broth (page 24)**
- **1 cup cubed unpeeled baking potato**
- **2 tablespoons chopped fresh parsley**
- **1 teaspoon curry powder**
- **½ teaspoon poultry seasoning**
- **¼ teaspoon table salt**
- **Dash of ground red pepper**
- **Dash of freshly ground black pepper**
- **1 (10½-ounce) can cream of chicken soup, undiluted**
- **½ cup milk**
- **2 cups cubed cooked chicken breast (page 25)**
- **3 cups loosely packed chopped fresh spinach**
- **Freshly ground black pepper (optional)**

1. Remove the lid of a 6-quart Instant Pot®. Press SAUTÉ [Normal]. When the pot is hot, swirl in the oil. Add the onion, carrot, and celery; cook, stirring often, 7minutes. Add the broth, potato, parsley, curry powder, poultry seasoning, salt, ground red pepper, and black pepper.

2. Lock the lid; turn Pressure Valve to "Sealing." PRESSURE COOK [High Pressure] for 5 minutes. Open the cooker using Quick Pressure Release (page 7). Turn off the cooker.

3. Whisk together the cream of chicken soup and milk in a bowl until blended. Stir the milk mixture into the soup in the pot until blended. Stir in the chicken. Press SAUTÉ [Normal], and cook uncovered, until thoroughly heated, about 3 minutes. Turn off the cooker. Add the spinach; stir constantly until wilted, about 3 minutes. Serve the soup with additional black pepper, if desired.

6-QUART

CHICKEN-BARLEY SOUP

SERVES: 6 | HANDS-ON: 10 MINUTES | UNDER PRESSURE: 19 MINUTES
NATURAL PRESSURE RELEASE

Barley is a good source of iron and fiber, with a slight nutty sweetness. Because pearl barley releases starch as it cooks, it is a helpful thickener for soups and stews.

- 3 cups unsalted chicken stock
- 2 cups water
- 2 cups diced carrot
- 1 cup diced peeled Yukon gold or red potato
- 1 cup diced onion
- ¾ cup sliced celery
- ½ cup uncooked pearl barley
- 1 tablespoon chopped fresh oregano
- ½ teaspoon table salt
- ½ teaspoon freshly ground black pepper
- 1 bay leaf
- 2 cups shredded skinless, boneless Pressure Cooker Rotisserie-Style Chicken (page 26)
- Additional chopped fresh oregano (optional)
- Additional freshly ground black pepper (optional)

1. Combine all ingredients, except the chicken, in the inner pot of a 6-quart Instant Pot®. Lock the lid; turn Pressure Valve to "Sealing." PRESSURE COOK [High Pressure] for 19 minutes. Open the cooker using Natural Pressure Release (page 7). Turn off the cooker. Remove and discard the bay leaf.

2. Add the chicken to the pot. Press SAUTÉ [Normal]; cook, uncovered, 3 minutes or until thoroughly heated, stirring occasionally. Ladle the soup into 6 bowls. Sprinkle with additional oregano and pepper, if desired.

NOTE: You can substitute store-bought rotisserie chicken if desired.

6-QUART

SPICY CHICKEN AND BUTTERNUT SQUASH TORTILLA SOUP

SERVES: 6 | HANDS-ON: 18 MINUTES | SLOW COOK: 10 HOURS

Stirring tortilla strips into the soup helps thicken the broth and adds an earthy flavor.

1½ pounds bone-in chicken thighs, skinned (about 4 thighs)

1 tablespoon salt-free southwest chipotle seasoning (such as Mrs. Dash)

½ teaspoon kosher salt

1 teaspoon olive oil

2 cups thinly sliced celery stalks and leaves

1½ cups chopped red onion

⅓ cup thinly sliced jalapeño chile

1 tablespoon minced fresh garlic

1 teaspoon ground cumin

1 (32-ounce) carton chicken stock (such as Kitchen Basics)

3 cups cubed peeled butternut squash

2 bay leaves

6 (6-inch) corn tortillas

Cooking spray

⅛ teaspoon ground red pepper

Sliced jalapeño chile (optional)

1. Sprinkle the chicken with the seasoning and salt. Add the oil to the inner pot of a 6-quart Instant Pot®. Press SAUTÉ [Normal]. When the oil is shimmering, add the chicken to the pot; cook 5 minutes, browning on all sides. Remove the chicken from the pot. Add the celery, onion, and jalapeño to drippings; cook 4 minutes, stirring constantly with a wooden or plastic spatula. Add the garlic and cumin; cook, stirring constantly, 30 seconds. Stir in 1 cup of the stock, scraping with the spatula until the bottom of the pot feels smooth. Stir in the remaining stock, squash, and bay leaves; add the chicken. Turn off the cooker.

2. Lock the lid; turn Pressure Valve to "Venting." SLOW COOK [Normal] for 10 hours. Remove the chicken from the pot with a slotted spoon; cool slightly. Remove and discard the bay leaves.

3. While the chicken cools, cut the tortillas in half; cut the tortilla halves crosswise into thin strips to measure 1¾ cups. Heat a large well-seasoned cast-iron skillet over medium-high heat. Coat the tortilla strips with the cooking spray, and sprinkle with the red pepper. Add the tortilla strips to the skillet; cook 5 to 6 minutes or until crisp, stirring frequently. Remove from heat.

4. Remove and discard the bones from the chicken; cut the meat into bite-sized pieces. Return the chicken meat to the pot; stir in half of the tortilla strips. Ladle the soup into 6 bowls; top with the remaining tortilla strips and, if desired, jalapeño slices.

6-QUART

WHITE BEAN, TURKEY SAUSAGE, AND TORTELLINI SOUP

SERVES: 12 | HANDS-ON: 10 MINUTES | UNDER PRESSURE: 29 MINUTES
NATURAL PRESSURE RELEASE

Prepared tortellini, found in the dairy section of your supermarket, is a smart dinner shortcut. This soup freshens them up with turkey Italian sausage, fennel, and pesto.

1 pound dried navy beans
1 tablespoon canola oil
1 pound mild turkey Italian sausage, casings removed
4½ cups water
3½ cups fat-free, lower-sodium chicken broth
1 cup chopped fennel bulb
1 teaspoon chopped fresh oregano
1½ cups diced red bell pepper
1 (9-ounce) package fresh three-cheese tortellini
3 cups arugula
¼ cup refrigerated reduced-fat pesto

1. Sort and wash the beans; set aside. Remove the lid from a 6-quart Instant Pot®. Press SAUTÉ [Normal]. When the word "Hot" appears, swirl in the oil. Add the sausage, and cook 6 minutes or until browned, stirring to crumble with a wooden or plastic spatula. Turn off the cooker. Drain the sausage, discarding the drippings; set the sausage aside.

2. Add the 4½ cups water and the broth to the pot, scraping cooker with the spatula until the bottom of the pot feels smooth. Add the beans, fennel, and oregano to the pot. Lock the lid; turn Pressure Valve to "Sealing." PRESSSURE COOK [High Pressure] for 29 minutes. Open the cooker using Natural Pressure Release (page 7). Turn off the cooker.

3. With the lid off, press SAUTÉ [Normal]. Bring the soup to a boil; stir in the cooked sausage, bell pepper, and tortellini. Simmer 7 minutes or until the tortellini is done. Ladle the soup into 12 bowls; top with the arugula and pesto.

6-QUART

VEGETABLE BEEF SOUP

SERVES: 12 | HANDS-ON: 25 MINUTES | UNDER PRESSURE: 25 MINUTES
NATURAL PRESSURE RELEASE

If you prefer the taste of spinach in your soup, substitute it for the kale.

1 cup dried navy beans
1 tablespoon olive oil
½ pound boneless chuck eye roast, trimmed and cut into ½-inch cubes
1½ cups chopped onion
1¼ cups sliced carrot
1 cup chopped celery
4 cups lower-sodium beef broth
3 cups water
½ cup uncooked pearl barley
1 teaspoon thyme leaves
¼ teaspoon table salt
1 (14.5-ounce) can diced tomatoes with basil, garlic, and oregano, undrained
4 cups thinly sliced kale
1 teaspoon balsamic vinegar
6 teaspoons shredded fresh Parmesan cheese

1. Sort and wash the beans. Place the oil in the inner pot of a 6-quart Instant Pot®. Press SAUTÉ [Normal]. When the oil is shimmering, add the beef; cook 3 to 4 minutes or until browned, stirring occasionally with a wooden or plastic spatula. Add the onion, carrot, and celery; cook 7 minutes or until vegetables are lightly browned, stirring frequently. Stir in the beans, broth, 3 cups water, barley, thyme, salt, and tomatoes, scraping with the spatula until the bottom of the pot feels smooth. Turn off the cooker.

2. Lock the lid; turn Pressure Valve to "Sealing." PRESSURE COOK [High Pressure] for 25 minutes. Open the cooker using Natural Pressure Release (page 7).

3. Add the kale and vinegar, stirring until the kale wilts. Ladle the soup into 12 bowls; sprinkle with the cheese.

6-QUART

CAPITOL HILL SOUP

MAKES: 2 QUARTS | HANDS-ON: 18 MINUTES | UNDER PRESSURE: 10 TO 15 MINUTES
SOAK: AT LEAST 8 HOURS | 10-MINUTE NATURAL PRESSURE RELEASE

A similar hearty bean soup has been on the Senate restaurant's daily menu since at least 1903. Try our version and see for yourself why this inexpensive, simple soup has such staying power.

1 pound dried navy beans
Water for soaking
1 tablespoon olive oil
½ cup chopped onion
2 carrots, coarsely chopped
1 large garlic clove, minced
8 ounces cubed cooked ham
6 cups water
1 teaspoon table salt
½ teaspoon freshly ground black pepper
½ teaspoon hickory liquid smoke (such as Wright's)
2 large bay leaves

1. Sort and the wash the beans; place in the inner pot of a 6-quart Instant Pot®. Cover with water to 2 inches above beans. Lock the lid; turn the Pressure valve to "Sealing" or "Venting", and let soak 8 hours or overnight. Drain the beans, discarding the soaking water.

2. Wash the inner pot; dry thoroughly, and return to the cooker. Press SAUTÉ [Normal]. Heat the olive oil in the pot. Add the onion and carrots. Cook, stirring constantly, 3 minutes. Add the garlic; cook, stirring constantly, 30 seconds. Add the ham; cook, 3 minutes, stirring occasionally. Stir in the drained beans, 6 cups water, salt, pepper, liquid smoke, and bay leaves.

3. Lock the lid; turn Pressure Valve to "Sealing." PRESSURE COOK [High Pressure] for 10 to 15 minutes. Allow a 10-minute Natural Pressure Release (page 10). Turn the valve to "Venting" to release the remaining pressure. Turn off the cooker.

4. Transfer about 2 cups of the soup from the pot to a blender or food processor; process until smooth, and return to the pot. Stir well. Press SAUTÉ [Normal]; bring to a boil. Cook 10 minutes, stirring often with a wooden or plastic spatula to prevent the soup from sticking to the bottom of the pot. (Soup thickens as it cooks.) Remove the bay leaves before serving.

6-QUART

NEW YEAR'S DAY SOUP

MAKES: 3 QUARTS | HANDS-ON: 15 MINUTES | UNDER PRESSURE: 10 MINUTES
SLOW PRESSURE RELEASE AND 5-MINUTE NATURAL PRESSURE RELEASE

According to tradition, or perhaps superstition, eating black-eyed peas and leafy greens on New Year's Day will bring you good luck for the coming year. Whether true or not, this soup offers a welcome break from rich holiday fare.

2 cups dried black-eyed peas, sorted, washed, and drained
4 cups water
2 tablespoons olive oil
1 cup chopped onion
½ cup chopped green bell pepper
2 large garlic cloves
6 cups Chicken Bone Broth (page 24) or chicken stock
8 ounces cubed cooked ham
1 teaspoon table salt
½ teaspoon hickory liquid smoke (such as Wright's)
¼ teaspoon freshly ground black pepper
⅛ teaspoon crushed red pepper
6 cups firmly packed torn kale leaves

1. Place the drained peas and the 4 cups water in the inner pot of a 6-quart Instant Pot®. Lock the lid; turn Pressure Valve to "Sealing." PRESSURE COOK [High Pressure] for 2 minutes. Open the cooker using a Slow Pressure Release (page 10). Drain the peas; rinse and drain.

2. Wash the inner pot; dry thoroughly, and return to the cooker. Press SAUTÉ [Normal]. Add the oil. When the oil is hot, add the onion and bell pepper. Cook, stirring constantly, 3 minutes. Add the garlic; cook, stirring constantly, 30 seconds. Add the broth, or stock, scraping the pot with a wooden or plastic spatula to loosen browned bits until the bottom of the pot feels smooth. Stir in the drained peas, ham, salt, liquid smoke, and peppers.

3. Lock the lid; turn Pressure Valve to "Sealing." PRESSURE COOK [High Pressure] for 8 minutes. Allow a 5-minute Natural Pressure Release (page 10). Turn the valve to "Venting" to release the remaining pressure. Turn off the cooker. Press SAUTÉ [Normal]. Add the kale. Cook, stirring often, 5 minutes or until the kale is tender. Turn off the cooker. Ladle the soup into bowls, and serve hot.

6-QUART

SMOKED PORK AND SPLIT PEA SOUP

SERVES: 8 | HANDS-ON: 22 MINUTES | SLOW COOK: 10 HOURS

If you have one, an immersion blender is handy for puréeing this soup.

1 pound green split peas
6 whole allspice
3 cardamom pods
1 star anise
1 cup chopped onion
1 cup finely chopped carrot
7 cups water
¼ cup fresh orange juice
¼ cup dry sherry
1 teaspoon dried thyme
1 teaspoon freshly ground black pepper
½ teaspoon table salt
½ teaspoon ground cumin
3 garlic cloves, chopped
1 ham hock (about ½ pound)
1 bay leaf
15 ounces smoked pork chops, trimmed and diced (about 2 cups)
1 teaspoon grated orange rind

1. Sort and wash the peas; place in a large Dutch oven.

2. Place the allspice, cardamom pods, and star anise on a double layer of cheesecloth. Gather the edges of the cheesecloth together; tie securely, and place in the inner pot of a 6-quart Instant Pot®. Add the peas, onion, carrot, 7 cups water, orange juice, sherry, thyme, pepper, salt, ground cumin, garlic, ham hock, and bay leaf. Lock the lid; turn Pressure Valve to "Venting." SLOW COOK [Normal] for 6 hours.

3. Add the diced pork. Lock the lid; turn Pressure Valve to "Venting." SLOW COOK [Normal] for 4 hours. Cook additional time, if necessary, until the peas and pork are tender.

4. Discard the bay leaf, spice bag, and ham hock. Use an immersion blender to blend until smooth, or place half of the soup mixture in a blender. Remove the center piece of the blender lid (to allow steam to escape); secure the blender lid on the blender. Place a clean towel over the opening in the blender lid (to avoid splatters). Blend until smooth. Return the puréed mixture to the remaining soup in the pot. Stir in the orange rind before serving. Ladle the soup into 8 bowls.

6-QUART

SPANISH CHICKPEA SOUP

SERVES: 6 | HANDS-ON: 10 MINUTES | UNDER PRESSURE: 45 MINUTES
NATURAL PRESSURE RELEASE

Dried chickpeas are typically soaked overnight and then simmered for up to 2 1/2 hours to become tender. Here, they go into the Instant Pot® dry and come out tender without soaking in just under an hour.

- **8 ounces dried chickpeas (garbanzo beans)**
- **1 tablespoon olive oil**
- **1½ cups chopped onion**
- **4 ounces dry-cured Spanish chorizo, diced**
- **5 garlic cloves, minced**
- **3½ cups water**
- **2½ cups fat-free, lower-sodium chicken broth**
- **2 bay leaves**
- **4 cups baby spinach**
- **1 tablespoon sherry vinegar**
- **½ teaspoon freshly ground black pepper**
- **⅜ teaspoon kosher salt**
- **¼ teaspoon crushed red pepper**

1. Sort and wash the chickpeas. Place the olive oil in the inner pot of a 6-quart Instant Pot®. Press SAUTÉ [Normal]. When the oil is shimmering, add the onion; cook, stirring constantly with a wooden or plastic spatula, 3 minutes. Add the chorizo and garlic; cook, stirring constantly, 2 minutes. Add the chickpeas, water, broth, and bay leaves to the pot, scraping with the spatula until the bottom of the pot feels smooth. Turn off the cooker.

2. Lock the lid; turn Pressure Valve to "Sealing." PRESSURE COOK [High Pressure] for 45 minutes. Open the cooker using Natural Pressure Release (page 7).

3. Remove the bay leaves; discard. Add the spinach and remaining ingredients, stirring just until the spinach wilts. Turn off the cooker. Ladle the soup into 6 bowls. Serve immediately.

6-QUART

◂ SPICY BLACK BEAN SOUP WITH CHORIZO

SERVES: 8 | HANDS-ON: 10 MINUTES | UNDER PRESSURE: 10 MINUTES | SOAK: AT LEAST 8 HOURS
10-MINUTE NATURAL PRESSURE RELEASE

- 1 pound dried black beans
- Water for soaking
- 2 cups chopped onion
- 1 cup chopped Cubanelle peppers or green bell peppers
- 4 cups fat-free, lower-sodium chicken broth
- 2 cups water
- ¼ cup minced jalapeño pepper
- 2 teaspoons Spanish smoked paprika
- 1 teaspoon ground cumin
- 1 teaspoon dried oregano
- ½ teaspoon table salt
- ½ teaspoon hot pepper sauce (such as Tabasco)
- 3 ounces dry-cured Spanish chorizo, diced
- 4 garlic cloves, minced
- 1 bay leaf
- Sour cream (optional)
- Diced onion (optional)
- Chopped fresh cilantro (optional)

1. Sort and wash the beans; place the beans in the inner pot of a 6-quart Instant Pot®. Cover with water to 2 inches above the beans. Lock the lid; turn Pressure Valve to "Sealing" or "Venting", and let soak 8 hours or overnight. Drain the beans, discarding the soaking water.

2. Combine the drained beans, chopped onion, and remaining ingredients, except the sour cream, diced onion, and cilantro, in the pot. Lock the lid; turn Pressure Valve to "Sealing." PRESSURE COOK [High Pressure] for 10 minutes. Allow a 10-Minute Natural Pressure Release (page 10). Turn the valve to "Venting" to release remaining pressure. Turn off the cooker. Discard the bay leaf. Partially mash the beans with a potato masher. Ladle the soup into 8 bowls. Serve with the sour cream, diced onion, and cilantro, if desired.

6-QUART

TUSCAN WHITE BEAN SOUP WITH PROSCIUTTO

SERVES: 4 | HANDS-ON: 15 MINUTES | UNDER PRESSURE: 3 MINUTES | QUICK PRESSURE RELEASE

- 1 tablespoon olive oil
- ½ cup chopped prosciutto or ham (about 2 ounces)
- 1 cup chopped onion
- ¾ cup chopped celery
- ¾ cup chopped carrot
- 1 garlic clove, minced
- ¾ cup water
- 2 (19-ounce) cans cannellini beans or other white beans, undrained
- 2 bay leaves
- 1 (15.75-ounce) can fat-free, less-sodium chicken broth
- 2 tablespoons minced fresh parsley
- 2 tablespoons sherry (optional)
- ¼ teaspoon black pepper

1. Place the oil in the inner pot of a 6-quart Instant Pot®. Press SAUTÉ [Normal]. When the oil is shimmering, add the prosciutto; cook, stirring constantly with a wooden or plastic spatula, 2 minutes. Add the onion, celery, carrot, and garlic; cook, stirring constantly, 2 minutes. Stir in the ¾ cup water, cannellini beans, bay leaves, and broth, scraping with the spatula until the bottom of the pot feels smooth. Turn off the cooker.

2. Lock the lid; turn Pressure Valve to "Sealing." PRESSURE COOK [High Pressure] for 3 minutes. Open cooker using Quick Pressure Release (page 7). Turn off the cooker.

3. Stir in the parsley, sherry, and black pepper; let stand 1 minute. Discard the bay leaves.

NOTE: You may substitute 4 cups cooked soaked cannellini beans or Great Northern beans (page 29) and ½ cup bean cooking liquid or water for the canned beans.

6-QUART

BUTTERNUT SQUASH SOUP

SERVES: 6 | HANDS-ON: 11 MINUTES | UNDER PRESSURE: 5 MINUTES | QUICK PRESSURE RELEASE

A hint of curry powder gives this soup a distinctive flavor. It makes a great holiday dinner starter.

2 (14½-ounce) cans less-sodium chicken broth

1 small Granny Smith apple, peeled and cubed

4 cups cubed peeled butternut squash

1 cup chopped onion

1 teaspoon sugar

½ teaspoon table salt

½ teaspoon curry powder

⅛ teaspoon freshly ground black pepper

1 (5-ounce) can evaporated milk

Toasted squash seeds (optional)

1. Combine the broth, apple, squash, onion, sugar, salt, curry powder, and pepper in the inner pot of a 6-quart Instant Pot®. Lock the lid; turn Pressure Valve to "Sealing." PRESSURE COOK [High Pressure] for 5 minutes. Open the cooker using Quick Pressure Release (page 7). Turn off the cooker.

2. Process the soup using an immersion blender until smooth. Stir in the milk. Press SAUTÉ [Normal]; cook, stirring constantly, 1 to 2 minutes or just until thoroughly heated. Do not boil. Sprinkle with the toasted squash seeds, if desired.

TIP:

To toast the squash seeds, place cleaned seeds on a jelly-roll pan coated with cooking spray. Bake at 350°F for 10 to 12 minutes, stirring once.

6-QUART

CAULIFLOWER SOUP WITH SHIITAKES

SERVES: 4 | HANDS-ON: 10 MINUTES | UNDER PRESSURE: 4 MINUTES | QUICK PRESSURE RELEASE

The meaty taste of shiitake mushrooms makes them the perfect topping for creamy cauliflower soup.

2 tablespoons olive oil

¾ cup thinly sliced leeks, white and light green parts only

⅜ teaspoon kosher salt

4 cups coarsely chopped cauliflower florets (about 1 medium head)

1½ cups unsalted chicken stock (such as Swanson)

¾ cup water

2 teaspoons chopped fresh thyme

¼ cup 2% reduced-fat milk

1½ teaspoons butter

¼ teaspoon white pepper

1 (3.5-ounce) package shiitake mushroom caps

1 teaspoon lower-sodium Worcestershire sauce

1 teaspoon sherry vinegar

2 teaspoons chopped fresh parsley

1. Place 1 tablespoon of the olive oil in the inner pot of a 6-quart Instant Pot®. Press SAUTÉ [Normal]; add the leeks, and cook, stirring constantly, 1 minute. Add ⅛ teaspoon of the salt. Cook 5 minutes or until leeks are softened, stirring occasionally. Add the cauliflower, 1 cup and 6 tablespoons of the stock, ¾ cup water, and thyme. Turn off the cooker.

2. Lock the lid; turn Pressure Valve to "Sealing." PRESSURE COOK [High Pressure] for 4 minutes. Open the cooker using Quick Pressure Release (page 7). Turn off the cooker. Remove the pot from the cooker.

3. Place the cauliflower mixture, in batches, in a blender. Remove the center piece of the blender lid (to allow steam to escape); secure the blender lid on the blender. Place a clean towel over the opening in the blender lid (to avoid splatters). Blend until smooth. Return the soup to the pot. Stir in the remaining ¼ teaspoon salt, milk, butter, and pepper. Return the pot to the cooker. Press KEEP WARM.

4. While the soup cooks, thinly slice the mushroom caps. Heat a large skillet over medium-high. Add the remaining 1 tablespoon oil to the pan, and swirl to coat. Add the mushrooms; sauté 6 minutes or until browned. Add the remaining 2 tablespoons stock, Worcestershire sauce, and sherry vinegar. Cook 1 minute or until liquid is reduced and syrupy.

5. Ladle the soup evenly into 4 bowls. Top each serving with the mushroom mixture. Sprinkle evenly with the parsley.

6-QUART

◂ MINESTRONE SOUP

SERVES: 8 | HANDS-ON: 15 MINUTES | UNDER PRESSURE: 6 MINUTES | QUICK PRESSURE RELEASE

2 tablespoons olive oil

1 medium onion, chopped (about 1¼ cups)

3 tablespoons minced fresh or 1 tablespoon dried parsley

1 large garlic clove, minced

3 (14.5-ounce) cans fat-free, lower-sodium chicken broth

1 (16-ounce) can pinto beans, undrained

4 medium tomatoes, peeled and coarsely chopped (about 4 cups)

2 medium celery stalks, sliced (about 1 cup)

2 medium carrots, sliced (about 1 cup)

1 medium zucchini, halved lengthwise and sliced (about 2 cups)

½ cup uncooked elbow macaroni

2 teaspoons dried basil, crushed

½ teaspoon table salt

½ teaspoon dried Italian seasoning

⅛ teaspoon dried crushed red pepper

5 cups packed coarsely chopped stemmed kale leaves

Freshly grated Parmesan cheese

1. Place the oil in the inner pot of a 6-quart Instant Pot®. Press SAUTÉ [Normal]. When the oil is shimmering, add the onion. Cook, stirring often, 5 minutes or until the onion is tender but not brown. Add the parsley and garlic. Cook, stirring constantly, 30 seconds. Immediately add the chicken broth and beans.

2. Stir in the tomatoes, celery, carrots, zucchini, macaroni, basil, salt, Italian seasoning, and crushed red pepper. Turn off the cooker. Lock the lid; turn Pressure Valve to "Sealing." PRESSURE COOK [High Pressure] for 6 minutes. Open the cooker using Quick Pressure Release (page 7).

3. Press SAUTÉ [Normal]. Add the kale, stirring often, 2 to 3 minutes or until the soup just comes to a boil and the kale wilts. Turn off the cooker.

4. Ladle soup into 8 bowls; sprinkle with Parmesan cheese.

TIP:

To easily prepare the kale, fold the leaves in half lengthwise. Cut out the ribs, and roll up several leaves together. Cut the leaf roll in half lengthwise and then crosswise into 1-inch pieces. Rinse the kale in 3 washings of cold water, draining between washings, and finish with a whirl in a salad spinner to remove sandy grit.

6-QUART

RED PEPPER SOUP WITH GOUDA

SERVES: 6 | HANDS-ON: 10 MINUTES | UNDER PRESSURE: 6 MINUTES | NATURAL PRESSURE RELEASE

4 red bell peppers (about 1½ pounds), halved

1 tablespoon canola oil

1 cup diced onion

½ cup sliced carrot

½ cup sliced celery

½ teaspoon garlic powder

1 (14.5-ounce) can organic vegetable broth

1 (15.5-ounce) can unsalted navy beans, rinsed and drained

1 chipotle chile, canned in adobo sauce

1 teaspoon adobo sauce

1 cup half-and-half

1 ounce Gouda cheese, shredded (about ¼ cup)

1. Thinly slice 3 of the bell pepper halves, and chop 2 of the bell pepper halves; set aside the remaining bell pepper halves and chopped bell pepper. Remove the lid from a 6-quart Instant Pot®. Press SAUTÉ [Normal]. When the word "Hot" appears, swirl in the oil. Add the sliced bell pepper to the inner pot; cook, stirring constantly, 5 minutes or until browned. Turn off the cooker.

2. Stir in the remaining 3 bell pepper halves, onion, carrot, celery, garlic powder, broth, beans, chipotle chile, and adobo sauce. Lock the lid; turn the Pressure Valve to "Sealing." PRESSURE COOK [High Pressure] for 6 minutes. Open the cooker using Natural Pressure Release (page 7). Turn off the cooker. Remove the pot from the cooker; cool the soup 15 minutes.

3. Place half of the pepper mixture in a blender. Remove center piece of blender lid (to allow steam to escape); secure the blender lid on the blender. Place a clean towel over opening in the blender lid (to avoid splatters). Blend until smooth. Pour into a large bowl. Repeat the procedure with the remaining pepper mixture. Return the puréed mixture to the pot. Return the pot to the cooker. Stir in the half-and-half. Press SAUTÉ [Normal]. Cook, uncovered, 2 to 3 minutes or until thoroughly heated, stirring occasionally. Ladle the soup into 6 bowls; sprinkle with the cheese and chopped bell pepper.

6- OR 8-QUART

STONE SOUP

MAKES: 3 QUARTS | HANDS-ON: 20 MINUTES | UNDER PRESSURE: 5 MINUTES
QUICK PRESSURE RELEASE

Legend says a village learned to share long ago when a mysterious visitor asked them to contribute ingredients to his "stone soup." A variety of crowd-pleasing vegetables, minus the stones, makes this soup perfect for sharing with loved ones.

- 2 quarts Chicken Bone Broth (page 24)
- 1 (14½-ounce) can diced tomatoes with basil, garlic, and oregano
- 2 medium carrots, peeled and sliced
- 2 celery stalks, chopped
- 2 small potatoes, cubed
- 1 medium onion, finely chopped
- 1 medium turnip, peeled and cubed
- 1½ cups coarsely chopped green cabbage
- 1 cup 1-inch fresh or frozen green bean pieces
- ¾ cup fresh or frozen sliced okra
- ⅓ cup quick-cooking barley
- ½ teaspoon freshly ground black pepper
- ⅛ teaspoon crushed dried red pepper

Stir together all ingredients in the inner pot of a 6-quart or 8-quart Instant Pot®. Lock the lid; turn the Pressure Valve to "Sealing." PRESSURE COOK [High Pressure] for 5 minutes. Open the cooker using Quick Pressure Release (page 7).

NOTE: 1 (32-ounce) container chicken stock plus 1½ cups water may be substituted for the bone broth and 1 cup fresh cauliflower florets may be substituted for the turnip.

6-QUART

WILD MUSHROOM SOUP

SERVES: 12 | HANDS-ON: 30 MINUTES | SLOW COOK: 5 HOURS

Marsala, a fortified wine from Sicily, gives this soup wonderful flavor. Feel free to substitute sherry for a similar effect.

2 cups boiling water
1¼ cups dried porcini mushrooms (about 1½ ounces)
2 cups water
1 tablespoon cornstarch
2 teaspoons gluten-free reduced-sodium tamari soy sauce
½ teaspoon table salt
½ teaspoon freshly ground black pepper
2 tablespoons olive oil
2 cups sliced shallots (about 8 ounces)
1 garlic clove, minced
1 cup dry Marsala or Madeira
2 teaspoons chopped fresh thyme
3 pounds assorted mushrooms (such as crimini, portobello, shiitake, and button), sliced
Garnish: chopped fresh parsley (optional)

1. Pour the 2 cups boiling water over the porcini mushrooms. Let stand 20 minutes. Drain the porcini mushrooms in a colander over a bowl, reserving the mushroom broth and mushrooms. Strain the mushroom broth through a cheesecloth-lined colander into a bowl; discard sediment. Add the 2 cups water, cornstarch, soy sauce, salt, and pepper to the mushroom broth; set aside.

2. Place the oil in the inner pot of a 6-quart Instant Pot®. Press SAUTÉ [Normal]. When the oil is shimmering, add the shallots and garlic; cook, stirring constantly, 4 to 5 minutes or until shallots are soft. Stir in the Marsala. When the mixture comes to a boil, cook 30 seconds. Turn off the cooker.

3. Add the porcini mushrooms, broth mixture, thyme, and sliced mushrooms. Lock the lid; turn Pressure Valve to "Venting." SLOW COOK [More] for 5 hours. Ladle the soup into 12 bowls. Garnish with the parsley, if desired.

6

SANDWICHES & SALADS

CURRIED EGG SALAD SANDWICHES ▸

SERVES: 4 | HANDS-ON: 10 MINUTES

Greek yogurt replaces mayonnaise in this sandwich, but with the extra spice, you won't miss it.

- **8 Hard-Cooked Eggs (page 16), peeled and chopped**
- **½ cup plain Greek Yogurt (page 15)**
- **½ cup chopped red bell pepper**
- **1 teaspoon curry powder**
- **½ teaspoon table salt**
- **½ teaspoon black pepper**
- **2 cups fresh baby spinach**
- **8 slices rye bread, toasted**
- **4 oranges, cut into wedges (optional)**
- **Potato chips (optional)**

1. Combine the eggs, yogurt, bell pepper, curry powder, salt, and pepper in a medium bowl; stir well.
2. Place the spinach on 4 rye bread toast slices, top evenly with the egg salad, and cover with the remaining bread slices. Serve with the orange wedges and potato chips, if desired.

6-QUART

BUFFALO CHICKEN SANDWICHES

SERVES: 6 | HANDS-ON: 15 MINUTES | UNDER PRESSURE: 12 MINUTES | QUICK PRESSURE RELEASE

Enjoy all the flavors of chicken wings sandwiched between two toasted buns or rolls. Adjust the heat level to your liking with your choice of sauce.

- **4 skinned and boned chicken breast halves**
- **¼ teaspoon table salt**
- **⅛ teaspoon freshly ground black pepper**
- **1 tablespoon olive oil**
- **1 (14-ounce) bottle Buffalo wing sauce**
- **2 small celery stalks**
- **¾ cup matchstick carrots**
- **1 tablespoon thinly sliced red onion**
- **⅓ cup refrigerated blue cheese dressing**
- **6 bakery-style buns or kaiser rolls, lightly toasted**

1. Sprinkle the chicken with salt and pepper.
2. Remove the lid from a 6-quart Instant Pot®. Press SAUTÉ [Normal]. Place the oil in the inner pot. When the oil is shimmering, spread it over the bottom of the pot, and add the chicken. Cook 2 minutes on each side, or until lightly browned. Turn off the cooker.
3. Reserve 2 tablespoons of the wing sauce. Pour the remaining sauce over the chicken. Lock the lid; turn Pressure Valve to "Sealing." PRESSURE COOK [High Pressure] for 12 minutes.
4. While the chicken cooks, slice celery crosswise to measure ¾ cup. Combine reserved 2 tablespoons of the wing sauce, celery, carrots, onion, and dressing; toss to coat.
5. Open the Instant Pot®, using Quick Pressure Release (page 7). Transfer the chicken to a bowl, reserving the cooking liquid; shred the chicken with 2 forks or an electric mixer, and toss with ½ cup cooking liquid. Serve the shredded chicken mixture on buns; top with the carrot slaw.

6-QUART

TANGY ITALIAN BEEF SANDWICHES ▸

SERVES: 8 | HANDS-ON: 15 MINUTES | SLOW COOK: 10 HOURS

Thanks to the Instant Pot®, the beef slowly braises until it practically falls to shreds. Although great on sandwiches, it's also delicious over a baked potato topped with sour cream.

3 banana peppers
Cooking spray
2¼ pounds chuck roast, trimmed and halved
½ cup white vinegar
1 tablespoon onion powder
1 tablespoon garlic powder
1½ teaspoons crushed red pepper
½ teaspoon kosher salt
½ teaspoon freshly ground black pepper
7 bottled pepperoncini peppers, chopped
8 hamburger buns, toasted

1. Preheat the broiler.
2. Arrange the peppers on a baking sheet coated with cooking spray. Broil 6 minutes or until blackened in spots, turning occasionally.
3. Remove the lid from a 6-quart Instant Pot®. Press SAUTÉ [Normal]. When the word "Hot" appears, coat the inner pot with the cooking spray. Add the beef; cook 5 minutes, turning to brown on all sides. Remove the beef from the pot.
4. Add the peppers to the pot; stir in the vinegar, onion powder, garlic powder, and red pepper. Stir in ¼ teaspoon of the salt, black pepper, and chopped pepperoncini. Return the beef to the pot.
5. Lock the lid; turn Pressure Valve to "Venting." SLOW COOK [More] for 10 hours or until beef is very tender.
6. Remove the beef from the cooker; shred with 2 forks. Stir the beef and remaining ¼ teaspoon salt into the cooking liquid. Divide the beef mixture evenly among the hamburger buns, using a slotted spoon. Serve any extra sauce for dipping.

6-QUART

FRENCH DIP SANDWICHES

SERVES: 12 | HANDS-ON: 12 MINUTES | UNDER PRESSURE: 55 MINUTES
NATURAL PRESSURE RELEASE

Substitute smaller rolls to make bite-size sandwiches and serve as a hearty appetizer.

1 (3½- to 4-pound) boneless chuck roast, trimmed and cut in half
2 cups water
½ cup soy sauce
1 beef bouillon cube
1 bay leaf
3 to 4 peppercorns, crushed
1 teaspoon dried rosemary, crushed
1 teaspoon dried thyme
1 teaspoon garlic powder
12 French sandwich rolls, split and toasted

1. Place the roast in the inner pot of a 6-quart Instant Pot®. Combine the 2 cups water, soy sauce, bouillon cube, bay leaf, peppercorns, rosemary, thyme, and garlic powder; pour over the roast.
2. Lock the lid; turn Pressure Valve to "Sealing." PRESSURE COOK [High Pressure] for 55 minutes. Open cooker using Natural Pressure Release (page 7). Turn off the cooker.
3. Remove the roast, reserving the broth; shred the roast with 2 forks. Divide the shredded meat evenly among the rolls, and serve with the reserved broth for dipping.

TURKEY LOAF SANDWICH

SERVES: 1 OR MORE | HANDS-ON: 3 MINUTES

This tasty sandwich is the perfect way to enjoy leftover Polynesian Turkey Loaf (page 114). In fact, it is so good you may want to prepare the Polynesian Turkey Loaf without the sauce and use it just for sandwiches. An entire turkey loaf will make about 4 sandwiches.

FOR 1 SANDWICH

- **2 tablespoons whole berry cranberry sauce**
- **1 teaspoon Dijon mustard**
- **2 (⅓-inch-thick) slices cold Polynesian Turkey Loaf (page 114)**
- **1 sweet Hawaiian hamburger bun, split and toasted**
- **1 small kale leaf or ⅓ cup packed baby arugula leaves**

Stir together the cranberry sauce and mustard in a small bowl until blended. Place the turkey loaf slices in a single layer on the cut side of the bottom bun half. Top with the cranberry sauce mixture and the kale leaf or arugula. Cover with the bun top, and serve immediately.

6-QUART

HOT GERMAN POTATO SALAD

SERVES: 6 | HANDS-ON: 18 MINUTES | UNDER PRESSURE: 2 MINUTES | QUICK PRESSURE RELEASE

Because this potato salad comes together so quickly, it's helpful to have all the dressing ingredients measured and ready to add in rapid succession.

- **1½ cups water**
- **2 pounds small red potatoes, peeled**
- **6 tablespoons white wine vinegar**
- **Cooking spray**
- **½ cup finely chopped red onion**
- **4 ounces turkey kielbasa, diced**
- **½ cup fat-free, less-sodium chicken broth**
- **3 bacon slices, cooked and crumbled**
- **1 teaspoon caraway seeds**
- **½ teaspoon table salt**
- **¼ teaspoon freshly ground black pepper**
- **½ cup minced fresh parsley**

1. Open a collapsible vegetable steamer, and place it in the inner pot of a 6-quart Instant Pot®. Pour the 1½ cups water into the pot.

2. Cut the potatoes in half lengthwise; cut crosswise into ¼-inch-thick slices. Add the potatoes to the steamer.

3. Lock the lid; turn Pressure Valve to "Sealing." PRESSURE COOK [High Pressure] for 2 minutes. Open the cooker using Quick Pressure Release (page 7).

4. Place the potatoes in a large bowl; cool slightly and sprinkle with 2 tablespoons of the vinegar.

5. While the potatoes cool slightly, wash and dry the pot, and return it to the cooker. With the lid off, press SAUTÉ [Normal]. Coat the pot with the cooking spray, and add the onion and kielbasa. Cook, stirring constantly, 3 minutes or until the onion is tender. Add the remaining ¼ cup vinegar, broth, and bacon; cook, stirring constantly, 1 minute. Stir in the caraway seeds, salt, and pepper.

6. Pour the vinegar mixture over the potato slices; toss gently. Sprinkle with the parsley. Serve immediately.

6-QUART

PICNIC POTATO SALAD

SERVES: 5 | HANDS-ON: 15 MINUTES | UNDER PRESSURE: 4 MINUTES | QUICK PRESSURE RELEASE

With the Instant Pot®, you can have room temperature potato salad ready in less than 30 minutes.

- **1½ cups water**
- **2 pounds Yukon Gold potatoes, peeled and cut into 1-inch cubes**
- **2 large eggs**
- **½ cup mayonnaise**
- **¼ cup diced celery**
- **¼ cup sour cream**
- **2 tablespoons finely chopped sweet onion**
- **2 tablespoons sweet pickle relish**
- **1½ teaspoons spicy brown mustard**
- **½ teaspoon table salt**
- **⅜ teaspoon freshly ground pepper**

1. Open a collapsible vegetable steamer, and place it in the inner pot of a 6-quart Instant Pot®. Pour the 1½ cups water into the pot. Add the potatoes to the steamer, and place the eggs, about 2 inches apart and away from sides of pot, directly on top of the potatoes.

2. Lock the lid; turn Pressure Valve to "Sealing." PRESSURE COOK [High Pressure] for 4 minutes. Open the cooker using Quick Pressure Release (page 7). Place the eggs in a bowl of ice-cold water, and transfer the potatoes to a bowl; cool completely.

3. While the potatoes and eggs cool, combine the mayonnaise, celery, sour cream, sweet onion, relish, mustard, salt, and pepper in a bowl, stirring well. When the eggs and potato are cool, peel the eggs, and place the potatoes in a large bowl. Grate the eggs into the mayonnaise mixture. Stir to combine, and add to the potatoes, stirring gently. Serve immediately, or cover and chill 12 hours.

6-QUART

EDAMAME, CHICKEN, AND RICE SALAD

SERVES: 8 | HANDS-ON: 9 MINUTES | UNDER PRESSURE: 10 MINUTES
5-MINUTE NATURAL PRESSURE RELEASE

Cooking the chicken in a single layer allows the chicken to brown and not stew. The browned bits left behind help season the rice.

- **2 tablespoons canola oil**
- **1 pound skinless, boneless chicken breasts, cut into bite-sized pieces**
- **1 cup uncooked long-grain brown rice**
- **5 cups water**
- **¾ cup diced red onion**
- **3 cups small broccoli florets**
- **1½ cups diced red bell pepper**
- **1 cup chopped peanuts, toasted**
- **½ cup frozen shelled edamame, thawed**
- **⅓ cup lower-sodium soy sauce**
- **⅓ cup rice vinegar**
- **¼ cup chopped fresh cilantro**
- **1½ tablespoons sugar**
- **1 tablespoon grated peeled fresh ginger**
- **½ teaspoon table salt**

1. Remove the lid from a 6-quart Instant Pot®. Press SAUTÉ [Normal]. When the word "Hot" appears, swirl in 1 tablespoon of the oil. Add the chicken to the pot in a single layer, and cook 6 minutes, stirring often, until done. Remove the chicken from the pot; set aside.

2. Add the remaining 1 tablespoon oil, rice, and 5 cups water to the pot, scraping with a wooden or plastic spatula until the bottom of the pot feels smooth. Turn off the cooker.

3. Lock the lid; turn Pressure Valve to "Sealing." PRESSURE COOK [High Pressure] for 10 minutes. Allow a 5-Minute Natural Pressure Release (page 10). Turn Pressure Valve to "Venting" to release the remaining pressure. Turn off the cooker.

4. Place the onion in a medium bowl. Add cold water to cover; let stand 10 minutes. Drain.

5. Stir the broccoli into the cooked rice mixture in the pot; let stand 30 seconds. Drain the broccoli mixture through a fine sieve; rinse with cold water, and drain well.

6. Place the broccoli mixture in a large bowl. Add the chicken, onion, bell pepper, and remaining ingredients, tossing gently.

FARMER SALAD

SERVES: 8 | HANDS-ON: 18 MINUTES

Peppery arugula and tender greens build the base of this easy salad. Choose whichever level of doneness you prefer for the eggs; both soft-cooked and hard-cooked work well.

- 8 thick bacon slices, cooked and crumbled
- 8 cups loosely packed baby arugula
- 4 cups trimmed frisée
- 2 cups thinly sliced radicchio
- 2 cups brioche or challah bread cubes, toasted
- 1 ounce Parmesan cheese, shaved (about ½ cup)
- 8 soft-cooked or hard-cooked large eggs (page 16), peeled
- Parmesan Vinaigrette

Toss together the bacon, arugula, frisée, radicchio, brioche, and cheese. Divide the mixture among 8 plates or shallow bowls. Top each with 1 egg, broken or halved. Serve with Parmesan Vinaigrette.

PARMESAN VINAIGRETTE

MAKES 1½ CUPS | HANDS-ON: 8 MINUTES

- 5 ounces Parmesan cheese, grated (about 1¼ cups)
- ½ cup red wine vinegar
- 4 anchovy fillets
- 1 teaspoon grated lemon rind
- 1 tablespoon fresh lemon juice
- 1 garlic clove, pressed
- 1 teaspoon Dijon mustard
- 1 teaspoon Worcestershire sauce
- ½ cup olive oil
- Table salt and black pepper

Process the cheese, vinegar, anchovy fillets, lemon rind and juice, garlic, mustard, and Worcestershire sauce in a blender or food processor until smooth. Add the olive oil in a slow, steady stream, processing until smooth. Season with salt and black pepper to taste.

6-QUART

LEMON, WHEAT BERRY, AND CHICKPEA SALAD

SERVES: 10 | HANDS-ON: 10 MINUTES | UNDER PRESSURE: 35 MINUTES
NATURAL PRESSURE RELEASE

Look for wheat berries in the grain or bulk section of your supermarket.

- 8 ounces dried chickpeas (garbanzo beans)
- 8 ounces uncooked wheat berries (hard winter wheat)
- 8 cups water
- ¼ cup extra-virgin olive oil
- 1½ cups frozen green peas
- 1½ cups diced English cucumber
- 1 cup sliced bottled roasted red bell pepper
- ¾ cup diced red onion
- 2 teaspoons grated lemon rind
- ¼ cup fresh lemon juice
- 2 teaspoons dried dill
- ¼ teaspoon freshly ground black pepper
- 4 ounces crumbled feta cheese (about 1 cup)
- 1¼ teaspoons table salt

1. Sort and wash the chickpeas. Combine the chickpeas, wheat berries, 8 cups water, and 1 tablespoon of the oil in the inner pot of a 6-quart Instant Pot®. Lock the lid; turn Pressure Valve to "Sealing." PRESSURE COOK [High Pressure] for 35 minutes. Open the cooker using Natural Pressure Release (page 7).

2. While the cooker stands, combine the remaining 3 tablespoons oil, peas, cucumber, bell pepper, onion, lemon rind and juice, dill, and pepper. Drain the chickpea mixture through a fine sieve. Rinse with cold water; drain well. Add the chickpea mixture to the bowl; toss well. Stir in the feta cheese and salt. Serve immediately, or cover and chill.

1 TBSP - 15 ml
1 tablespoon

7

MEATLESS MAINS

6-QUART

INDIAN-SPICED LENTILS

SERVES: 4 | HANDS-ON: 8 MINUTES | SLOW COOK: 5 HOURS

The peppery taste of du Puy lentils pairs well with this medley of spices, including coriander, cumin, and cardamom. Fresh ginger adds a bright flavor that isn't found in the ground variety. Wipe any leftover ginger root dry, and store in a plastic bag in the crisper drawer of your fridge.

- **1½ cups dried du Puy lentils**
- **1 cup finely diced onion**
- **6 cups water**
- **3 tablespoons chopped peeled fresh ginger**
- **2 teaspoons ground cumin**
- **2 teaspoons ground coriander**
- **1 teaspoon ground cinnamon**
- **1 teaspoon ground cardamom**
- **1 teaspoon ground turmeric**
- **¾ teaspoon table salt**
- **¼ teaspoon ground cloves**
- **¼ teaspoon ground red pepper**
- **3 garlic cloves, minced**
- **2 jalapeño chiles, minced**
- **Brown Basmati Rice (page 20) for serving**

Combine all ingredients except rice in the inner pot of a 6-quart Instant Pot®. Lock the lid; turn the Pressure Valve to "Venting." SLOW COOK [Normal] for 5 hours. Serve with rice.

6-QUART

CHICKPEA TIKKA MASALA

SERVES: 6 | HANDS-ON: 10 MINUTES | UNDER PRESSURE: 40 MINUTES
NATURAL PRESSURE RELEASE

Dried chickpeas are a quick and easy (and wallet-friendly) swap for the traditional protein in chicken tikka masala. If you prefer, serve spoonfuls of the chickpea mixture over jasmine rice (page 20) instead of the couscous called for here.

- **8 ounces dried chickpeas (garbanzo beans)**
- **2 tablespoons canola oil**
- **1½ cups diced onion**
- **1½ cups diced carrot**
- **1½ teaspoons curry powder**
- **1 teaspoon ground cumin**
- **¼ teaspoon ground red pepper**
- **4 cups water**
- **1 cup frozen petite green peas**
- **½ cup chopped fresh cilantro**
- **1 tablespoon grated peeled fresh ginger**
- **1 teaspoon sugar**
- **¾ teaspoon table salt**
- **1 (14.5-ounce) can diced tomatoes, undrained**
- **1 (13.5-ounce) can light coconut milk**
- **¾ cup uncooked whole-wheat couscous**
- **1 lime, cut into 6 wedges**

1. Sort and wash the chickpeas; drain. Remove the lid from a 6-quart Instant Pot®. Press SAUTÉ [Normal]. When the word "Hot" appears, swirl in 1 tablespoon of the oil. Add the onion; cook, stirring frequently, 4 minutes or until browned. Add the remaining 1 tablespoon oil, carrot, curry powder, cumin, and red pepper; cook 30 seconds, stirring constantly. Stir in the chickpeas and 2¾ cups of the water to the pot. Turn off the cooker.

2. Lock the lid; turn the Pressure Valve to "Sealing." PRESSURE COOK [High Pressure] for 40 minutes. Turn off the cooker. Open the cooker using Natural Pressure Release (page 7). Stir in the green peas, cilantro, ginger, sugar, salt, tomatoes, and coconut milk. Press SAUTÉ [Normal]. Cook, uncovered, 5 minutes or until thoroughly heated, stirring often.

3. While the chickpeas cook, bring the remaining 1¼ cups water to a boil in a medium saucepan. Remove from the heat, and stir in couscous. Cover and let stand 5 minutes. Fluff with a fork. Divide the couscous among 6 shallow bowls; top with the chickpea mixture, and serve with lime wedges.

6-QUART

THYME-SCENTED WHITE BEAN CASSOULET

SERVES 6 | HANDS-ON: 15 MINUTES | SLOW COOK: 9 HOURS

Butter-tossed breadcrumbs stirred in at the end give this cozy dish a robust stew-like consistency. Look for small-to-medium-sized parsnips; they are sweeter than the larger varieties.

- 1 tablespoon olive oil
- 1½ cups chopped onion
- 1½ cups (½-inch-thick) slices diagonally cut carrot
- 1 cup (½-inch-thick) slices diagonally cut parsnip
- 2 garlic cloves, minced
- 3 cups cooked Great Northern beans (page 29)
- ¾ cup vegetable broth
- ½ teaspoon dried thyme
- ¼ teaspoon table salt
- 1¼ teaspoons freshly ground black pepper
- 1 (28-ounce) can diced tomatoes, undrained
- 1 bay leaf
- ¼ cup dry breadcrumbs
- 1 ounce grated fresh Parmesan cheese (about ¼ cup)
- 2 tablespoons butter, melted
- 2 links frozen meatless Italian sausage, thawed and chopped
- 2 tablespoons chopped fresh parsley

1. Add the olive oil to the inner pot of a 6-quart Instant Pot®. Press SAUTÉ [Normal]. When the oil is shimmering, add the onion, carrot, parsnip, and garlic. Cook, stirring constantly, 5 minutes or until tender. Turn off the cooker.

2. Add the beans, broth, thyme, salt, pepper, tomatoes, and bay leaf. Lock the lid; turn Pressure Valve to "Venting." SLOW COOK [Normal] for 9 hours.

3. Remove the bay leaf. Combine the breadcrumbs, cheese, and butter in a small bowl; toss with a fork until moist. Stir the breadcrumb mixture and sausage into the bean mixture; sprinkle with the parsley.

6-QUART

MOROCCAN CHICKPEA TAGINE WITH APRICOTS

SERVES 6 | HANDS-ON: 10 MINUTES | SLOW COOK: 4 HOURS, 30 MINUTES | SOAK: 8 HOURS

- 1 cup dried chickpeas (garbanzo beans)
- 2½ cups vertically sliced onion
- 2 cups organic lower-sodium vegetable stock
- 1 cup water
- 1 tablespoon grated peeled fresh ginger
- 1½ teaspoons ground cumin
- ½ teaspoon table salt
- ½ teaspoon ground cinnamon
- 8 garlic cloves, minced
- 8 dried apricots, halved
- 4 medium carrots, cut into 1-inch pieces
- 3 saffron threads, crushed
- 1 (¾- x 3-inch) strip fresh lemon rind
- ½ cup chopped fresh parsley
- ¼ cup slivered almonds, toasted
- 2 (8.8-ounce) pouches microwaveable pre-cooked whole-grain brown rice (such as Uncle Ben's Ready Rice)

1. Sort and wash the chickpeas; place in the inner pot of a 6-quart Instant Pot®. Cover with water to 2 inches above chickpeas. Lock the lid; turn Pressure Valve to "Venting" or Sealing." Let soak 8 hours. Drain the chickpeas.

2. Combine the drained chickpeas, onion, stock, 1 cup water, ginger, cumin, salt, cinnamon, garlic, apricots, carrots, saffron, and lemon rind; stir well. Return the pot to the cooker. Lock the lid; turn Pressure Valve to "Venting." SLOW COOK [More] for 4 hours and 30 minutes. (Cook additional time or until chickpeas are tender.) Sprinkle with the parsley and almonds; discard the lemon rind.

3. Heat rice according to package directions. Spoon the chickpea mixture over the rice.

8-QUART

SOUTHERN-STYLE "BAKED" MACARONI AND CHEESE

SERVES: 4 | HANDS-ON: 10 MINUTES | UNDER PRESSURE: 21 MINUTES
QUICK PRESSURE RELEASE

The Instant Pot® quickly cooks the pasta for this rich version of mac and cheese, more commonly served south of the Mason Dixon Line. The macaroni is baked in a cheese custard instead of stirred into a sauce. Serve with a side of steamed broccoli for a kid-friendly comfort food fix.

4½ cups water
1 cup macaroni noodles
1 large egg
½ teaspoon table salt
1¼ cups milk
6 ounces shredded sharp Cheddar cheese
Cooking spray
Freshly ground black pepper

1. Place 2½ cups of the water in the inner pot of an 8-quart Instant Pot®. Stir in the macaroni, spreading into an even layer. Close the lid; turn Pressure Valve to "Sealing." PRESSURE COOK [High Pressure] for 3 minutes. Open the cooker using Quick Pressure Release (page 7). Drain the pasta. Rinse the inner pot, and return it to the cooker. Pour the remaining 2 cups of the water into the pot.

2. While the pasta cooks, whisk together the egg and salt in a medium bowl until the egg is well blended. Whisk in the milk. Shred the cheese.

3. Coat a 1½-quart oven-proof casserole or soufflé dish with a glass lid with the cooking spray. Layer one third of the cooked pasta in the bottom of the dish. Sprinkle with one third of the cheese. Repeat layering the pasta and cheese once. Top with the remaining pasta, reserving the remaining one third of the cheese. Pour the milk mixture over the pasta mixture.

4. Set the dish on the Steam Rack of the cooker. Carefully lower the rack with the dish into the pot, gently squeezing the handles together to secure the dish. Cover the dish with the glass lid. Lock the lid of the Instant Pot®; turn Pressure Valve to "Sealing." PRESSURE COOK [High Pressure] for 18 minutes. Open the cooker using Quick Pressure Release (page 7). Immediately remove the dish from the pot, gently squeezing the handles together to secure the dish; uncover and sprinkle with the remaining cheese. Cover and let stand 5 minutes or until the cheese melts. Uncover and let stand 5 more minutes. Sprinkle with the black pepper before serving.

NOTE: Do not use preshredded cheese in this dish. It doesn't blend well into the custard because of additives.

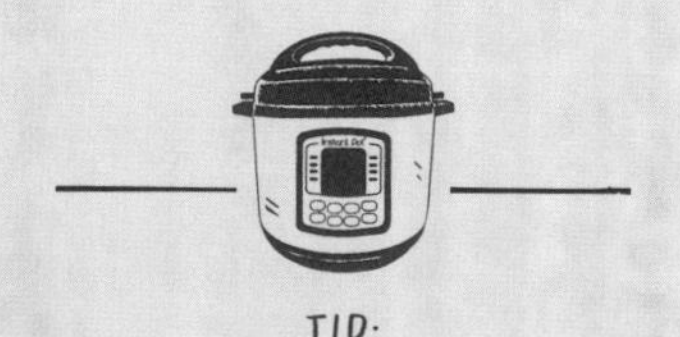

TIP:

You may prepare this recipe in a 6-quart Instant Pot®. However, only round 1½-quart dishes will fit. If you don't have a lid for your dish, you can cover it with foil, but the cook time may be a bit different.

6-QUART

THREE-CHEESE MACARONI AND CHEESE

SERVES 6 | HANDS-ON: 38 MINUTES | UNDER PRESSURE: 3 MINUTES | 5-MINUTE NATURAL PRESSURE RELEASE

1 tablespoon olive oil
⅔ cup panko (Japanese-style breadcrumbs)
8 ounces uncooked elbow macaroni (about 2 cups)
2½ cups water
Butter-flavored cooking spray
1 tablespoon butter
1 cup finely chopped onion (about 1 medium)
2 tablespoons all-purpose flour
1 garlic clove, minced
1½ cups 1% low-fat milk
1 bay leaf
2 ounces Gorgonzola cheese, crumbled (about ½ cup)
3 ounces Parmigiano-Reggiano cheese, grated (about ¾ cup)
¼ teaspoon table salt
⅛ teaspoon freshly ground black pepper
2½ ounces part-skim mozzarella cheese, shredded (about ⅔ cup)

1. Add the oil to the inner pot of a 6-quart Instant Pot®. Press SAUTÉ [Normal]. When the oil is shimmering, add the panko, and cook, stirring constantly, 1 minute or until golden brown. Turn off the cooker. Remove the panko from the pot; set aside. Wipe the pot clean with a paper towel; return the pot to the cooker.

2. Add the macaroni and 2½ cups water to the pot; stir. Lock the lid; turn Pressure Valve to "Sealing." PRESSURE COOK [High Pressure] for 3 minutes. Allow a 5-minute Natural Pressure Release (page 10). Turn Pressure Valve to "Venting" to release remaining pressure. Drain the pasta, and place in a bowl. Cover and keep warm. Wipe the pot dry with paper towels, and return it to the cooker. Coat the pot with the cooking spray.

3. With the lid off, add the butter to the pot. Press SAUTÉ [Normal]. When the butter melts, add the onion; cook 3 to 5 minutes or until tender, stirring occasionally. Add the flour and garlic; cook 1 minute, stirring constantly. Gradually stir in the milk, and add the bay leaf; bring to a boil, stirring constantly with a whisk. Cook, stirring constantly, 3 to 5 minutes or until thickened. Add the Gorgonzola, ½ cup of the Parmigiano-Reggiano, salt, and pepper; stir until cheeses melt. Discard the bay leaf.

4. Add the pasta to the cheese mixture, stirring constantly until thoroughly heated. Sprinkle evenly with the mozzarella. Turn off the cooker. Remove the pot from the cooker. Cover and let stand 2 minutes or until the cheese melts.

5. Combine the remaining ¼ cup of the Parmigiano-Reggiano and the panko; sprinkle evenly over the pasta mixture. Serve immediately.

6-QUART

CHEDDAR-FONTINA PENNE

SERVES 6 | HANDS-ON: 21 MINUTES | UNDER PRESSURE: 3 MINUTES | QUICK PRESSURE RELEASE

1 tablespoon plus 1 teaspoon extra-virgin olive oil
½ cup panko (Japanese breadcrumbs)
3¾ cups water
1 (14.5-ounce) package multigrain penne (tube-shaped pasta)
⅔ cup evaporated low-fat milk
¾ teaspoon garlic powder
¾ teaspoon table salt
¼ teaspoon freshly ground black pepper
¼ teaspoon ground red pepper
2 teaspoons all-purpose flour
3 ounces sharp white Cheddar cheese, shredded (about ¾ cup)
3 ounces fontina cheese, shredded (about ¾ cup)
1 cup grape tomatoes, halved
¼ cup chopped scallions

1. Place 1 tablespoon of the oil in a 6-quart Instant Pot®. Press SAUTÉ [Normal]. Add the panko; cook, stirring constantly, 1 minute or until golden brown. Turn off the cooker. Remove the panko from the pot; set aside. Wipe the pot clean with a paper towel.

2. Add 3½ cups of the water and the pasta to the pot. Lock the lid; turn Pressure Valve to "Sealing." PRESSURE COOK [High Pressure] for 3 minutes. Open the cooker using Quick Pressure Release (page 7).

3. Remove the pasta with a slotted spoon; place in a medium bowl. Add the milk, garlic powder, salt, black pepper, and red pepper to the cooking liquid. Combine the remaining ¼ cup water and the flour in a small bowl; gradually whisk into the milk mixture. With the lid off, press SAUTÉ [Normal]. Bring to a boil; cook 5 minutes or until slightly thick. Turn off the cooker. Add the cheeses, stirring until melted. Stir in the cooked pasta, tossing gently to coat.

4. Heat a medium nonstick skillet over medium-high. Add the remaining 1 teaspoon oil to the pan; swirl to coat. Add the tomatoes; sauté 2 minutes or until soft. Top the pasta mixture with the tomatoes and scallions; sprinkle with the panko.

6-QUART

TOFU LASAGNA

SERVES: 6 TO 8 | HANDS-ON: 42 MINUTES | UNDER PRESSURE: 20 MINUTES
NATURAL PRESSURE RELEASE

You won't miss the meat in this vegetarian rendition of classic lasagna. Mushrooms and toasted wheat germ lend a meatlike texture to the sauce, and tofu substitutes for ricotta cheese. If you have leftover wheat germ, stir a spoonful into Greek Yogurt (page 15) for an easy breakfast or snack.

1 (16-ounce) package firm tofu, well drained
2 ounces Parmesan cheese, shredded (about ½ cup)
1 (8-ounce) package pre-shredded Italian 5-Blend Cheese (such as Kraft)
¼ cup chopped fresh flat-leaf parsley
1 tablespoon olive oil
1 tablespoon butter
1 (8-ounce) package crimini mushrooms, chopped
3 garlic cloves, minced
¾ teaspoon table salt
½ teaspoon dried marjoram, crumbled
⅛ teaspoon freshly ground black pepper
2½ tablespoons extra-dry vermouth
2½ cups bottled marinara sauce (such as Ragu)
2 cups water
½ cup toasted wheat germ (such as Kretchmer's)
Cooking spray
16 no-boil lasagna noodles

1. Place the tofu in a bowl; mash with a fork until the consistency of cottage cheese. Add the Parmesan cheese, and toss well. Combine the Italian cheese blend and parsley in a separate bowl.

2. Add the olive oil and butter to the inner pot of a 6-quart Instant Pot®. Press SAUTÉ [Normal]. When the butter melts, add the mushrooms. Cook, stirring often, 5 minutes. Stir in the garlic, salt, marjoram, and pepper. Cook, stirring constantly, 30 seconds. Stir in the vermouth, and cook 1 minute. Stir in the marinara sauce, ½ cup of the water, and the wheat germ. Cook just until the sauce begins to bubble slightly. Stir well, and turn off the cooker. Remove the pot from the cooker. Set aside.

3. Coat 2 (7-inch x 2½-inch-deep) springform pans with the cooking spray. In the bottom of one pan, layer 2⅔ noodles, breaking the noodles into large pieces, as necessary, to fit the pan. Spread ⅔ cup sauce evenly over the noodles to completely cover. Layer ⅔ cup tofu mixture over the sauce. Sprinkle with ⅓ cup cheese mixture. Repeat the layers with noodles, sauce, tofu mixture, and cheese mixture. Repeat the layering procedure in the second pan with the remaining noodles, sauce, tofu, and cheese mixture.

4. Cover just the tops of the springform pans with aluminum foil coated with the cooking spray, coated side down. Crimp the edges to tightly secure the foil to each pan. Wash and dry the pot; return the pot to the cooker. Add the remaining 1½ cups water to the pot.

5. Place 1 pan on the Steam Rack. Using the rack handles, lower the pan into the pot. Carefully set the second pan directly on top of the first pan, ensuring that there is clearance between the sides of the pans and the pot all around.

6. Lock the lid; turn Pressure Valve to "Sealing." PRESSURE COOK [Normal] for 20 minutes. Open the cooker using Natural Pressure Release (page 7). Remove the pans from the cooker; remove the foil from the pans. Set the pans on a sheet pan lined with foil.

7. Preheat the broiler to high.

8. Broil in the top half of the oven 3 minutes or just until the cheese is lightly browned. Let stand 10 minutes. Remove the sides of each pan, and transfer each lasagna to a large plate. Cut into wedges, and serve hot.

8-QUART

BROWN RICE-STUFFED CABBAGE ROLLS WITH PINE NUTS AND CURRANTS

SERVES: 4 | HANDS-ON: 30 MINUTES | UNDER PRESSURE: 8 MINUTES
5-MINUTE NATURAL PRESSURE RELEASE

Pine nuts are pricey, but the 2 tablespoons in this recipe add maximum sweet, buttery flavor, so a little goes a long way. You can find small packages of pine nuts in the produce or baking aisle of your supermarket. Serve the cabbage rolls with slices of crusty bread to dip into the tomato sauce.

1 large head green cabbage, cored (3¾ pounds)
1 tablespoon olive oil
1½ cups finely chopped onion
½ cup dried currants
2 tablespoons pine nuts, toasted
2 tablespoons chopped fresh parsley
3 cups cooked Brown Basmati Rice (page 20)
3 ounces crumbled feta cheese (about ¾ cup)
½ teaspoon salt
¼ teaspoon freshly ground black pepper
½ cup apple juice
1 tablespoon cider vinegar
1 teaspoon brown sugar
1 (15-ounce) can crushed tomatoes, undrained
Additional chopped fresh parsley (optional)

1. Steam the cabbage head 8 minutes; cool slightly. Remove 16 leaves from the cabbage head; discard the remaining cabbage. Cut off the raised portion of the center vein of each cabbage leaf (do not cut out vein); set trimmed cabbage leaves aside.

2. Place the oil in the inner pot of an 8-quart Instant Pot®. Press SAUTÉ [Normal]. When the oil is shimmering, add the onion; cook, stirring constantly, 3 minutes or until tender. Turn off the cooker. Stir in the currants, pine nuts, and 2 tablespoons parsley. Stir in the brown rice, feta cheese, ¼ teaspoon of the salt, and ⅛ teaspoon of the pepper. Remove the inner pot from the cooker.

3. Place the cabbage leaves on a flat surface; spoon about ⅓ cup rice mixture into the center of each cabbage leaf. Fold in the edges of the leaves over the rice mixture; roll up. Wash and dry the inner pot. Place the pot in the cooker. Add the Steam Rack to the pot; position the handles upright.

4. Combine the remaining ¼ teaspoon salt, remaining ⅛ teaspoon pepper, apple juice, vinegar, brown sugar, and tomatoes in a bowl. Arrange half of the cabbage rolls on the rack in the pot. Pour half of the tomato mixture over the cabbage rolls. Repeat the procedure with the remaining half of cabbage rolls and half of the tomato mixture. Lock the lid; turn the Pressure Valve to "Sealing." PRESSURE COOK [High Pressure] for 8 minutes. Allow a 5-minute Natural Pressure Release (page 10). Turn Pressure Valve to "Venting" to release remaining pressure. Turn off the cooker. Transfer the cabbage rolls to a serving latter. Remove the rack. Press SAUTÉ [More]. Bring the sauce to a boil. Boil, stirring often, 3 minutes or until desired thickness. Spoon the sauce over the cabbage rolls. Sprinkle with the parsley, if desired.

8

VEGETABLES & SIDES

6-QUART

BACON-CIDER TURNIPS AND APPLES

SERVES: 8 | HANDS-ON: 15 MINUTES | UNDER PRESSURE: 3 MINUTES | QUICK PRESSURE RELEASE

Root vegetables like turnips are time consuming to cook, so they're a great fit for the Instant Pot®.

- **4 center-cut bacon slices**
- **2 pounds small turnips, peeled and each cut into 8 wedges (about 6 cups)**
- **1¾ cups vertically sliced onion**
- **2 Fuji apples, peeled and cut into wedges (about 1 pound)**
- **1 cup apple cider**
- **½ teaspoon table salt**
- **½ teaspoon freshly ground black pepper**
- **2 tablespoons chopped fresh parsley**

1. Remove the lid from a 6-quart Instant Pot®. Add the bacon to the pot. Press SAUTÉ [Normal]. Cook the bacon until crisp; remove from the pot, and drain on paper towels. Add the turnips, onion, and apple to the drippings in the pot; cook, stirring constantly, 2 minutes or until lightly browned. Stir in the cider, salt, and pepper. Turn off the cooker.

2. Lock the lid; turn Pressure Valve to "Sealing." PRESSURE COOK [High Pressure] for 3 minutes. Turn off the cooker. Open the cooker using Quick Pressure Release (page 7).

3. Place the turnip mixture in a serving dish. Sprinkle with the crumbled bacon and parsley.

6-QUART

BRAISED CABBAGE WITH APPLE AND BACON

SERVES: 6 TO 8 | HANDS-ON: 32 MINUTES | UNDER PRESSURE: 5 MINUTES
QUICK PRESSURE RELEASE

Pair this bacon-and-apple-studded side with pork chops for a fun twist on pork chops and applesauce.

- **Cooking spray**
- **4 thick bacon slices**
- **4 celery hearts, thinly sliced, leaves reserved**
- **1 medium onion, thinly sliced**
- **2 teaspoons fennel seeds (optional)**
- **½ cup white wine**
- **1 head red cabbage (about 2 pounds), thinly sliced**
- **1 cup reduced-sodium chicken broth**
- **1 cup unfiltered apple cider**
- **1 garlic clove, thinly sliced**
- **2 bay leaves**
- **1 Granny Smith apple, thinly sliced**
- **Table salt and black pepper**
- **1 tablespoon apple cider vinegar**

1. Coat the inner pot of a 6-quart Instant Pot® with the cooking spray. Place the bacon in the pot. Press SAUTÉ [Normal]. Cook about 8 minutes or until crisp, turning occasionally; remove the bacon from the pot, and drain on a paper towel. Turn off the cooker. Crumble the bacon, and set aside. Remove the pot from the cooker, and pour off excess drippings, reserving 3 tablespoons of the drippings in the pot. Wipe the rim of pot clean with a wet cloth. Return the pot to the cooker.

2. Press SAUTÉ [Normal]. Add the celery, onion, and if desired, fennel seeds; cook, stirring constantly, 6 minutes. Add the wine, and cook 2 minutes, stirring to remove brown bits from bottom of the pot.

3. Stir in the cabbage, broth, apple cider, garlic, bay leaves, and apple. Add the salt and black pepper to taste. Lock the lid; turn Pressure Valve to "Sealing." PRESSURE COOK [High Pressure] for 5 minutes. Open the cooker using Quick Pressure Release (page 7). Stir in the vinegar. Top with the reserved celery leaves and bacon.

6-QUART

CREOLE BRAISED CABBAGE

SERVES: 14 | HANDS-ON: 15 MINUTES | UNDER PRESSURE: 3 MINUTES
QUICK PRESSURE RELEASE

Chockful of flavor from a variety of spices, tomatoes, and bacon, this simple cabbage dish is so much more fun than a side salad.

4 center-cut bacon slices
1 medium onion, chopped
4 garlic cloves, minced
1 (2-pound) head green cabbage, halved, cored, and cut into ¼-inch-thick slices (about 12 cups)
⅔ cup fat-free, lower-sodium chicken broth
2 teaspoons chopped fresh oregano
2 teaspoons chopped fresh thyme
½ teaspoon crushed red pepper
¼ teaspoon freshly ground black pepper
1 (14.5-ounce) can diced tomatoes with green pepper, celery, and onion, drained
2 bay leaves
¼ cup chopped fresh parsley

1. Remove the lid from a 6-quart Instant Pot®. Press SAUTÉ [Normal]. Add the bacon to the inner pot, and cook 7 minutes or until crisp, turning occasionally. Remove the bacon from the pot, reserving 2 tablespoons drippings in pot; drain and crumble bacon. Add the onion and garlic to the drippings in the pot; cook, stirring constantly, 4 minutes. Stir in the cabbage; cook 2 minutes or until the cabbage begins to wilt, stirring frequently. Stir in the broth, oregano, thyme, red pepper, black pepper, tomatoes, and bay leaves. Turn off the cooker.

2. Lock the lid; turn Pressure Valve to "Sealing." PRESSURE COOK [High Pressure] for 3 minutes. Turn off the cooker. Open the cooker using Quick Pressure Release (page 7).

3. Remove the bay leaves; discard. Stir in the parsley and crumbled bacon.

6-QUART

SMOKY GREEN CABBAGE

SERVES: 4 TO 6 | HANDS-ON: 15 MINUTES | UNDER PRESSURE: 3 MINUTES
QUICK PRESSURE RELEASE

If you like your cabbage spicy, substitute a spicy-and-hot—smoked or Cajun-smoked sausage.

1 small green cabbage (about 1¾ pounds), cored and cut into 8 wedges
1 (3- to 4-ounce) piece cook-and-serve hickory-smoked sausage link (such as Conecuh)
Cooking spray
2 tablespoons butter
¾ cup water
¼ teaspoon table salt
¼ teaspoon freshly ground black pepper

1. Cut the cabbage wedges crosswise into ½-inch pieces. Halve the sausage lengthwise, then cut crosswise into ¼-inch-thick pieces.

2. Remove the lid of a 6-quart Instant Pot®, and coat the bottom of the inner pot with the cooking spray. Add the sausage pieces. Press SAUTÉ [Normal]. Cook uncovered, stirring often, until sausage is lightly browned, about 3 minutes. Add the butter. Cook and stir just until the butter begins to brown. Add the water, salt, and pepper, scraping with a wooden or plastic spatula until the bottom of the pot appears clean.

3. Add the cabbage, 1 handful at a time, stirring to moisten and distribute the sausage pieces. Turn off the cooker. Lock the lid; turn Pressure Valve to "Sealing." PRESSURE COOK [High Pressure] for 3 minutes. Open the cooker using Quick Pressure Release (page 7).
Serve immediately.

6-QUART

COLLARD GREENS WITH HAM HOCKS

SERVES: 4 | HANDS-ON: 15 MINUTES | UNDER PRESSURE: 46 MINUTES
QUICK PRESSURE RELEASE

Serve with Skillet Cornbread (page 47) to sop up the pot likker (pot liquor).

- **6 ounces smoked ham hocks**
- **2 cups water**
- **1 pound collard greens, stems removed and chopped**
- **1 tablespoon canola oil**
- **1 tablespoon chopped fresh garlic**
- **½ teaspoon table salt**
- **¼ teaspoon freshly ground black pepper**
- **⅛ teaspoon crushed red pepper**
- **1 (14.5-ounce) can fat-free, lower-sodium chicken broth**
- **1 small onion, chopped**
- **1 tablespoon brown sugar**
- **1 tablespoon cider vinegar**

1. Place the ham hocks and the water in the inner pot of a 6-quart Instant Pot®. Lock the lid; turn Pressure Valve to "Sealing." PRESSURE COOK [High Pressure] for 40 minutes. Turn off the cooker. Open the cooker using Quick Pressure Release (page 7).

2. Drain the ham hocks; discard the cooking liquid. Return the inner pot to cooker; return the ham to the pot. Add the greens, oil, garlic, salt, black pepper, red pepper, broth, and onion. PRESSURE COOK [High Pressure] for 6 minutes. Turn off the cooker. Open the cooker using Quick Pressure Release (page 7).

3. Remove the ham hocks; let stand until cool enough to handle. Remove the ham from the bones; coarsely chop. Discard the bones, skin, and fat. Stir the ham, brown sugar, and vinegar into the greens.

6-QUART

LEMONY STEAMED KALE

SERVES: 4 | HANDS-ON: 5 MINUTES | UNDER PRESSURE: 1 MINUTE
QUICK PRESSURE RELEASE

This flavorful but virtuous side is a great way to "eat your greens."

- 1 cup water
- 2 chicken bouillon cubes
- 2 small to medium bunches kale
- 4 teaspoons olive oil
- ½ teaspoon garlic powder
- ¼ teaspoon crushed red pepper
- 2 teaspoons grated lemon rind

1. Microwave the water and bouillon cubes in a 1-cup glass measuring cup at HIGH until hot, about 2 minutes.

2. Meanwhile, remove the stems from the kale. Chop the leaves, and place in cold water in a salad spinner. Wash and drain the leaves twice; spin to remove excess water, sand, and grit. Place the kale in the inner pot of a 6-quart Instant Pot®.

3. Stir the olive oil, garlic powder, and crushed red pepper into the hot bouillon; pour over the kale in the pot. Lock the lid; turn Pressure Valve to "Sealing." Press STEAM [High Pressure]; cook for 1 minute. Open the cooker using Quick Pressure Release (page 7). Turn the kale over with a pair of tongs until thoroughly coated with the cooking liquid. Transfer the kale to a serving bowl, using the tongs and allowing the excess cooking liquid to drain into the pot. Sprinkle with the lemon rind, and toss well. Serve immediately.

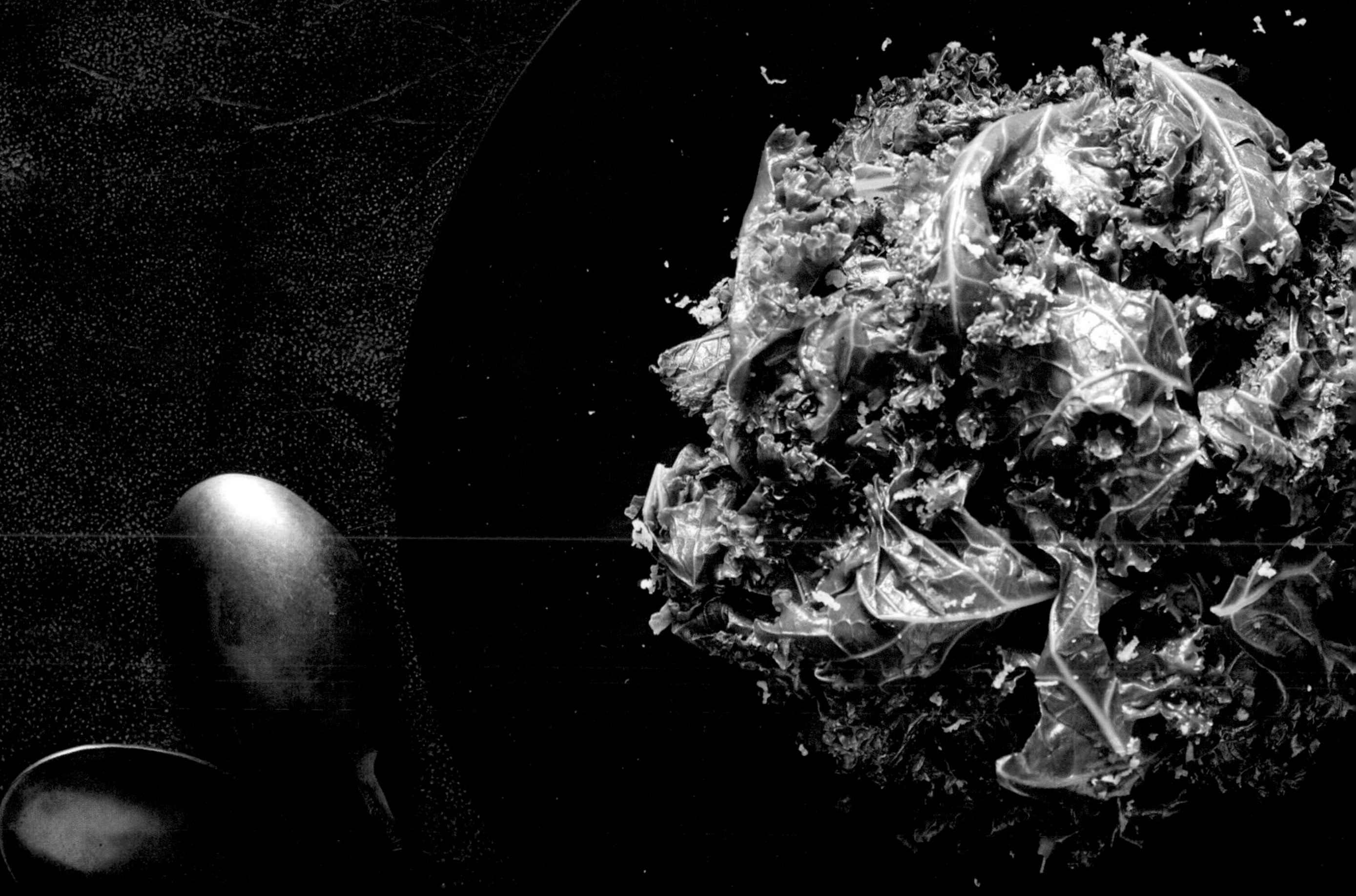

6-QUART

CAULIFLOWER AU GRATIN

SERVES: 5 | HANDS-ON: 10 MINUTES | UNDER PRESSURE: 2 MINUTES
QUICK PRESSURE RELEASE | BAKE: 5 MINUTES

Cauliflower is the low-carb answer to comfort food cravings. Here, the rich, cheesy flavors of traditional au gratin satisfy without the extra fuss.

1 cup water
1 large head cauliflower (2 pounds)
⅓ cup mayonnaise
1¼ teaspoons Dijon mustard
1 teaspoon curry powder
Cooking spray
⅔ cup (2.7 ounces) shredded sharp Cheddar cheese
Freshly ground black pepper
Chopped fresh parsley

1. Preheat the oven to 400°F.

2. Pour the 1 cup water in the inner pot of a 6-quart Instant Pot®. Insert the Steam Rack with the handles in the up position. Remove the leaves and core from the cauliflower. Set the cauliflower on the Steam Rack in an upright position. Lock the lid; turn Pressure Valve to "Sealing." Press STEAM [High Pressure], and cook 2 minutes. Open the cooker using Quick Pressure Release (page 7). Remove the cauliflower from the pot using the handles of the Steam Rack.

3. While the cauliflower cooks, stir together the mayonnaise, mustard, and curry powder in a small bowl until blended. Coat a medium-size baking dish that fits the cauliflower with the cooking spray.

4. Place the steamed cauliflower in the prepared dish. Spread the mayonnaise mixture over the top of the cauliflower; sprinkle with cheese, pressing to adhere.

5. Bake at 400°F for 5 minutes or until topping is thoroughly heated and cheese melts. Sprinkle with black pepper and parsley.

6-QUART

CAULIFLOWER AND FENNEL WITH DIJON-CIDER VINAIGRETTE

SERVES: 6 | HANDS-ON: 10 MINUTES | UNDER PRESSURE: 2 MINUTES | QUICK PRESSURE RELEASE

If you prefer, try this recipe with broccoli instead of cauliflower.

1 cup water
1 large head cauliflower
1 cup sliced fennel
¼ cup olive oil
1 tablespoon chopped fresh fennel fronds
2 tablespoons cider vinegar
2 teaspoons Dijon mustard
1 teaspoon honey
¼ teaspoon kosher salt
¼ teaspoon freshly ground black pepper

1. Pour the 1 cup water in the inner pot of a 6-quart Instant Pot®. Insert the Steam Rack with the handles in the up position. Remove the leaves and core from the cauliflower. Set the cauliflower on the Steam Rack in an upright position. Lock the lid; turn Pressure Valve to "Sealing." Press STEAM [High Pressure], and cook 2 minutes. Open the cooker using Quick Pressure Release (page 7). Remove the cauliflower from the pot using the handles of the Steam Rack.

2. Chop the cauliflower into florets. Toss with the fennel. Whisk together the oil and remaining ingredients in a large bowl. Add the cauliflower mixture; toss to coat.

6-QUART

BACON AND ONION–DRESSED GREEN BEANS

SERVES: 4 | HANDS-ON: 15 MINUTES | UNDER PRESSURE: 0 MINUTES | QUICK PRESSURE RELEASE

The cooking technique in this recipe yields crisp-tender green beans. If you like your beans cooked more, skip the cold water rinse, or add reheating time while you toss the beans with the bacon mixture.

1 cup water
1½ pounds fresh green beans, trimmed
Cooking spray
3 bacon slices, cut crosswise into ¼-inch pieces
½ cup finely chopped red onion
¼ teaspoon freshly ground pepper

1. Pour the 1 cup water into the inner pot of a 6-quart Instant Pot®. Place the Steam Rack in the pot with the handles up. Place the green beans in a wire-mesh steamer basket, and set on the Steam Rack. Lock the lid; turn Pressure Valve to "Sealing." Press STEAM [High Pressure]; set to 0 minutes. Open the cooker using Quick Pressure Release (page 7). Remove the steamer basket from the pot using the handles. Rinse briefly under cold running water to stop the cooking process; drain and set aside.

2. Dry the pot, and return it to the cooker; coat the pot with the cooking spray. Add the bacon. Press SAUTÉ [Normal] and cook 2 minutes, stirring often. Add the onion; cook, stirring constantly, until onion is tender and bacon is crisp. Turn off the cooker.

3. Remove the bacon mixture from the pot with a slotted spoon, and place in a small bowl, reserving 2 tablespoons of the bacon drippings in the pot. Stir the pepper and bacon mixture into the reserved drippings. Return the green beans to the pot. Press SAUTÉ [Less], and cook, tossing the beans with the bacon mixture until thoroughly heated. Serve immediately.

NOTE: If your steamer basket has feet, you will not need to use the Steam Rack.

6-QUART

CORN ON THE COB WITH SEASONED BUTTER

SERVES: 4 | HANDS-ON: 5 MINUTES | UNDER PRESSURE: 5 MINUTES | QUICK PRESSURE RELEASE

1 cup water
4 ears fresh corn, shucked
Lemon-Curry-Spice Butter, or Honey-Chipotle Butter (recipes at right)
Garnishes: freshly ground black pepper, chopped fresh chives, sliced fresh basil (optional)

1. Pour the 1 cup water into the inner pot of a 6-quart Instant Pot®. Place the Steam Rack in the pot. Place the corn on the rack. Lock the lid; turn Pressure Valve to "Sealing". Press STEAM [High Pressure], and cook 5 minutes.

2. Turn off the cooker. Open the lid using Quick Pressure Release (page 7). Remove the corn from the pot. Brush with desired butter mixture. Garnish, if desired.

LEMON-CURRY-SPICE BUTTER

HANDS-ON: 3 MINUTES

1 tablespoon unsalted butter, melted
1 teaspoon extra-virgin olive oil
1 teaspoon fresh lemon juice
½ teaspoon kosher salt
½ teaspoon Madras curry powder
⅛ teaspoon ground turmeric

Whisk together all ingredients in a small bowl until blended.

HONEY-CHIPOTLE BUTTER

HANDS-ON: 3 MINUTES

1 tablespoon unsalted butter, melted
1 teaspoon honey
½ teaspoon grated lime rind
1 teaspoon fresh lime juice
½ teaspoon kosher salt
½ teaspoon ground chipotle chile powder

Whisk together all ingredients in a small bowl until blended.

3- OR 6-QUART

OKRA CREOLE

SERVES: 6 | HANDS-ON: 12 MINUTES | UNDER PRESSURE: 3 MINUTES | QUICK PRESSURE RELEASE

Spice up okra and corn with allspice and hot salsa-style tomatoes.

Cooking spray
4 bacon slices, cut crosswise into ¼-inch pieces
½ cup chopped onion
1 (14½-ounce) can seasoned fire-roasted salsa-style diced tomatoes, undrained
2½ cups sliced fresh or frozen okra
1½ cups fresh or frozen corn kernels
1 cup chopped green bell pepper
¼ teaspoon table salt
¼ teaspoon ground allspice

1. Coat the bottom of the inner pot of a 3-quart or 6-quart Instant Pot® with the cooking spray. Add the bacon, and press SAUTÉ [Normal]. Cook until crisp, about 5 minutes, stirring occasionally. Remove the bacon with a slotted spoon, and drain on paper towels, reserving about 2 tablespoons of the drippings in the pot.

2. Add the onion; cook, stirring often, 3 minutes. Turn off the cooker. Stir in the tomatoes, scraping with a wooden or plastic spatula until the bottom of the pot feels smooth. Stir in the okra, corn, bell pepper, salt, and allspice. Lock the lid; turn Pressure Valve to "Sealing." PRESSURE COOK [High Pressure] for 3 minutes.

3. Open the cooker using Quick Pressure Release (page 7). Serve the okra mixture topped with the bacon.

6-QUART

PICKLED BEETS

SERVES: 6 | HANDS-ON: 17 MINUTES | UNDER PRESSURE: 11 MINUTES
QUICK PRESSURE RELEASE | CHILL: OVERNIGHT

A tangy garlicky yogurt mixture made from Greek Yogurt (page 15) accompanies these beets.

21 bunches fresh beets
1½ cups water
1½ cups apple cider vinegar
½ cup water
¼ cup sugar
1 tablespoon kosher salt
2 whole allspice berries
2 whole cloves
1 teaspoon coriander seeds
1 bay leaf
1 cup plain Greek Yogurt (page 15)
2 small garlic cloves, minced
¼ teaspoon kosher salt
Chopped fresh flat-leaf parsley
Chopped fresh mint
Fresh pomegranate seeds
Olive oil

1. Trim the beets, leaving 1 inch of the stems, and scrub.

2. Open a collapsible vegetable steamer, and place it in the inner pot of a 6-quart Instant Pot®. Pour the 1½ cups water into the pot. Place the beets in the steamer.

3. Lock the lid; turn Pressure Valve to "Sealing." Press STEAM [High Pressure], and cook 11 to 13 minutes or until tender.

4. Turn off the cooker. Open the cooker using Quick Pressure Release (page 7). Remove the steamer and beets from the pot. Pour out the water; rinse the pot, and dry thoroughly before returning the pot to the cooker.

5. Peel the beets, and cut into quarters; place in a large bowl. Combine the vinegar, ½ cup water, sugar, salt, allspice berries, cloves, coriander seeds, and bay leaf in the pot. With the lid off, press SAUTÉ [Normal], and bring the mixture to a boil. Reduce the temperature to SAUTÉ [Less], and simmer 15 minutes. Turn off the cooker. Add the vinegar mixture to the beets in the bowl. Cool to room temperature. Place in the refrigerator until thoroughly chilled, at least 4 hours.. Remove the bay leaf.

6. Combine the yogurt, garlic, and salt; cover and chill until ready to use.

7. Spread the yogurt mixture evenly onto a serving platter. Top with the drained beets, parsley, mint, and pomegranate seeds. Drizzle with the olive oil.

6-QUART

RATATOUILLE

SERVES: 6 | HANDS-ON: 14 MINUTES | UNDER PRESSURE: 2 MINUTES
QUICK PRESSURE RELEASE

This French vegetable mélange is delicious hot, room temperature, or even chilled with crusty bread, cheese, and red wine. It's good served over hot cooked couscous or pasta and can be used as a filling for omelets, too.

1 tablespoon extra-virgin olive oil
1½ cups chopped onion
2 large garlic cloves, minced (about 1 tablespoon)
1 (14.5-ounce) can diced tomatoes in sauce, undrained (such as Hunt's)
1 (¾-pound) eggplant, cut into ¾-inch cubes (3 cups)
1 medium zucchini, cut into ⅓-inch half-moon slices (2 cups)
1 large red bell pepper, cut into strips (2 cups)
1 large yellow bell pepper, cut into strips (2 cups)
1 small green bell pepper, cut into strips (1 cup)
1 teaspoon sugar
1½ teaspoons dried basil
¾ teaspoon table salt
½ teaspoon dried Italian seasoning
½ teaspoon freshly ground black pepper

1. Place the olive oil in the inner pot of a 6-quart Instant Pot®. Press SAUTÉ [Normal]. When the oil is shimmering, distribute it evenly over the bottom of the pot with a wooden or plastic spatula. Add the onion. Cook, stirring constantly with the spatula, 4 minutes. Add the garlic; cook, stirring constantly, 30 seconds. Turn off the cooker. Add the tomatoes, scraping with a wooden or plastic spatula until the bottom of the pot feels smooth. Add the eggplant and remaining ingredients; stir and lift the tomatoes up from the bottom of the pot to distribute throughout the vegetable mixture.

2. Lock the lid; turn Pressure Valve to "Sealing." PRESSURE COOK [High Pressure] for 2 minutes. Open the cooker using Quick Pressure Release (page 7). Transfer the vegetables from the pot to a large bowl with a slotted spoon, allowing vegetables to drain well over the pot.

3. Press SAUTÉ [Normal]. Bring the vegetable juice to a boil. Cook, stirring constantly, 5 to 10 minutes or until juice is thick and a clean track can be seen when the spatula is drawn through the thickened juice. Turn off the cooker, and transfer the pot from the cooker to a heatproof surface. Return the vegetables to the pot, stirring to coat with the thickened juice. Serve hot, room temperature, or chilled.

TIP:

Use a plastic pancake spatula instead of a wooden spoon to quickly spread oil in the domed bottom of the inner pot. The plastic spatula also does a great job of stirring the onions and bringing up the tomatoes and distributing them evenly throughout the vegetable mixture.

6-QUART

LEMON-SAGE SPAGHETTI SQUASH

SERVES: 4 | HANDS-ON: 15 MINUTES | UNDER PRESSURE: 9 MINUTES | QUICK PRESSURE RELEASE

Spaghetti squash has a subtle taste that pairs easily with other flavors, from the delicate butter and sage in this recipe to bold tomatoes and herbs in Italian meat sauces.

1 (2-pound) spaghetti squash, washed and cut in half

1 cup water

2 tablespoons butter

¼ cup chopped onion

2 garlic cloves, minced

2 tablespoons grated fresh Parmesan cheese

2 teaspoons small fresh sage leaves, chopped

1 teaspoon grated lemon rind

½ teaspoon table salt

¼ teaspoon freshly ground black pepper

1. Scrape the membranes from the squash halves with a spoon, reserving the seeds to roast, if desired.

2. Place the Steam Rack, with the handles in the up position, in the inner pot of a 6-quart Instant Pot®; pour in the 1 cup water. Place the squash halves, cut sides up, on the rack.

3. Lock the lid; turn Pressure Valve to "Sealing." PRESSURE COOK [High Pressure] for 9 minutes. Open the cooker using Quick Pressure Release (page 7). Lift the squash from the pot using the rack handles. Set aside on the rack to cool.

4. While the squash cools, pour out the water from the pot; rinse with hot water, and dry thoroughly. Return the pot to the cooker.

5. When the squash is cool enough to handle, use a fork to remove the spaghetti-like strands, and place in a bowl.

6. Add the butter to the pot. Press SAUTÉ [Normal]. When the butter melts, add the onion and garlic to the pot; cook, stirring constantly, 2 minutes or until tender. Turn off the cooker. Add the squash strands to the pot; stir 2 minutes or until thoroughly heated. Return the squash to the bowl; add the Parmesan cheese and remaining ingredients. Toss well.

6-QUART

SPICED CARROTS WITH OLIVES AND MINT ▸

SERVES: 5 | HANDS-ON: 12 MINUTES | UNDER PRESSURE: 4 MINUTES | QUICK PRESSURE RELEASE

Oil-cured black olives plus mint, cinnamon, and coriander transform sliced carrots into a lively Moroccan side dish.

2 cups water
5 cups (1-inch) sliced carrots (about 2 pounds)
1½ tablespoons honey
1 tablespoon fresh lemon juice
½ teaspoon sea salt
½ teaspoon coriander seeds
¼ teaspoon red pepper flakes
1 (5-inch) mint sprig
1 (2-inch) cinnamon stick
1 garlic clove, minced
¼ cup oil-cured black olives, pitted and coarsely chopped
1 teaspoon rice vinegar
1 teaspoon extra-virgin olive oil
1 teaspoon chopped fresh mint
Garnish: mint sprigs (optional)

1. Place the 2 cups water in the inner pot of a 6-quart Instant Pot®. Stir in the carrots, honey, lemon juice, salt, coriander seeds, red pepper, mint, cinnamon stick, and garlic. Lock the lid; turn Pressure Valve to "Sealing." PRESSURE COOK [High Pressure] for 4 minutes. Open the cooker using Quick Pressure Release (page 7).

2. Remove the carrots from the pot with a slotted spoon, reserving the cooking liquid in the pot. Press SAUTÉ [Normal]. Bring the cooking liquid to a boil; reduce to ¼ cup, stirring often. Turn off the cooker.

3. Return the carrots to the pot, stirring to coat. Stir in the olives, vinegar, and oil. Let stand in the pot 1 minute or until thoroughly heated. Sprinkle with the chopped mint. Garnish with the mint sprigs, if desired.

6-QUART

CURRIED CARROTS AND PARSNIPS

SERVES: 8 | HANDS-ON: 15 MINUTES | UNDER PRESSURE: 4 MINUTES | QUICK PRESSURE RELEASE

This quick side dish is on the table in less than 20 minutes.

1 tablespoon olive oil
1 pound carrots, peeled and cut into 1-inch pieces
1 pound parsnips, peeled and cut into 1-inch pieces
2 teaspoons curry powder
1 teaspoon ground cumin
¼ teaspoon ground cinnamon
¼ teaspoon table salt
⅛ teaspoon ground red pepper
1 cup organic vegetable broth
½ cup golden raisins
2 tablespoons chopped fresh cilantro

1. Place the oil in the inner pot of a 6-quart Instant Pot®. Press SAUTÉ [Normal]. When the oil is shimmering, add the carrots, parsnips, curry powder, cumin, cinnamon, salt, and red pepper. Cook, stirring constantly, 1 minute or until the spices are lightly toasted. Stir in the broth and raisins. Turn off the cooker. Lock the lid; turn Pressure Valve to "Sealing." PRESSURE COOK [High Pressure] for 4 minutes. Turn off the cooker. Open the cooker using Quick Pressure Release (page 7).

2. Remove the vegetables from the pot a slotted spoon, and place on a platter; discard the cooking liquid. Sprinkle the vegetables with the cilantro.

6-QUART

CREAMY PARMESAN GRITS

SERVES: 4 TO 6 | HANDS-ON: 6 MINUTES | UNDER PRESSURE: 18 MINUTES
SLOW PRESSURE RELEASE

Cheese grits are often made with Cheddar cheese, but Parmesan adds an extra umami flavor.

- **4 cups water**
- **1 cup stone-ground grits**
- **2 teaspoons kosher salt**
- **1 ounce Parmesan cheese, grated (about ¼ cup)**
- **2½ tablespoons butter**
- **2 tablespoons heavy cream**

1. Combine the water, grits, and salt in the inner pot of a 6-quart Instant Pot®.

2. Lock the lid; turn Pressure Valve to "Sealing." Press PORRIDGE [High Pressure]. Cook for 18 minutes. Turn off the cooker. Open the cooker using Slow Pressure Release (page 10). Remove the inner pot from the cooker.

3. Stir in the cheese and butter. Stir in the cream, and serve immediately.

6-QUART

CHEDDAR MASHED POTATOES

SERVES: 9 | HANDS-ON: 14 MINUTES | UNDER PRESSURE: 9 MINUTES | QUICK PRESSURE RELEASE

Whip up these creamy potatoes when you have a craving for loaded baked potatoes but need a side ready in less than 30 minutes.

- **2 pounds peeled russet potatoes, cut into ½-inch-thick slices**
- **1 cup water**
- **1 teaspoon table salt**
- **1 teaspoon freshly ground black pepper**
- **4 ounces extra-sharp Cheddar cheese, shredded (about 1 cup)**
- **¼ cup plus 2 tablespoons 2% reduced-fat milk**
- **½ cup chopped scallions**
- **2 tablespoons reduced-fat sour cream**
- **4 center-cut bacon slices, cooked and crumbled (drained)**

1. Place the potatoes, 1 cup water, ½ teaspoon of the salt, and ½ teaspoon of the pepper in the inner pot of a 6-quart Instant Pot®. Lock the lid; turn Pressure Valve to "Sealing." PRESSURE COOK [High Pressure] for 9 minutes. Turn off the cooker. Open the cooker using Quick Pressure Release (page 7).

2. Add the cheese and milk to the potato mixture in the pot; mash to desired consistency. Press SAUTÉ [Normal]. Cook, stirring constantly, 1 minute or until thoroughly heated. Turn off the cooker. Stir in the remaining ½ teaspoon salt, remaining ½ teaspoon pepper, scallions, sour cream, and bacon.

6-QUART

GARLIC AND CHIVE MASHED POTATOES

SERVES: 5 | HANDS-ON: 8 MINUTES | UNDER PRESSURE: 9 MINUTES | QUICK PRESSURE RELEASE

Whole cloves of garlic simmer with the potatoes and then melt right into the mash. You can leave the peels on your potatoes for a more rustic texture.

2 cups lower-sodium chicken stock
2 pounds peeled Yukon gold or red potatoes, cut into 1-inch-thick slices
4 garlic cloves, peeled
1 cup Greek Yogurt (page 15)
½ cup whole milk
½ teaspoon table salt
¼ cup chopped fresh chives

1. Combine the first 3 ingredients in the inner pot of a 6-quart Instant Pot®. Lock the lid; turn Pressure Valve to "Sealing." PRESSURE COOK [High Pressure] for 9 minutes. Open the cooker using Quick Pressure Release (page 7). Turn off the cooker.

2. Mash potato mixture with a potato masher to desired consistency. Stir in the yogurt, milk, and salt. Stir in the chives just before serving.

6-QUART

STUFFED POTATOES WITH CHEESE AND SOUR CREAM

SERVES: 4 | HANDS-ON: 18 MINUTES | UNDER PRESSURE: 18 MINUTES | QUICK PRESSURE RELEASE

Blue cheese adds an unexpected punch of flavor to these rich potatoes.

1 cup water
4 (8-ounce) russet potatoes
Canola oil
3 ounces sharp Cheddar cheese, shredded (about ¾ cup)
½ cup sour cream
¼ cup finely chopped green onions
½ teaspoon table salt
¼ teaspoon freshly ground black pepper
1 ounce crumbled blue cheese (about ¼ cup)
½ cup grape tomatoes, quartered

1. Pour the 1 cup water into the inner pot of a 6-quart Instant Pot®. Remove the center post from a collapsible vegetable steamer, and place the steamer in the bottom of the pot. Scrub the potatoes, and pat dry. Rub the potatoes lightly with canola oil. Arrange the potatoes in the steamer. Lock the lid; turn Pressure Valve to "Sealing." STEAM [High Pressure] for 18 to 20 minutes, or until tender. Open the cooker using Quick Pressure Release (page 7).

2. Remove the potatoes from the pot with tongs; cool slightly. Cut a 2-inch wedge out of the top of each potato (do not cut all the way to the bottom of the potato). Scoop out the pulp, leaving a ¼-inch-thick shell, and place in a bowl.

3. Add the Cheddar cheese, sour cream, 2 tablespoons of the green onions, ⅜ teaspoon of the salt, and pepper; mash with a potato masher until coarsely mashed. Spoon about ⅔ cup potato mixture into each shell; top each with about 1 tablespoon blue cheese and 1½ teaspoons green onions.

4. Preheat the broiler.

5. Place the stuffed potatoes on a small aluminum foil-lined baking sheet. Broil 3 to 5 minutes or until the cheese melts and is lightly browned. Top the potatoes with the tomatoes, and sprinkle with the remaining ⅛ teaspoon salt.

TIP:

Start with the lower cook time. Check tenderness, and if potatoes are not tender, replace the lid, reset steam release handle, and cook for an additional 2 minutes.

6-QUART

SMOKY SWEET POTATO MASH ▸

SERVES: 4 | HANDS-ON: 10 MINUTES | UNDER PRESSURE: 11 MINUTES | QUICK PRESSURE RELEASE

Sweet and salty both work well with sweet potatoes. Choose potatoes that are the same size to ensure even cooking.

1 cup water

3 medium sweet potatoes (1½ pounds), scrubbed

2 ounces (¼ cup) butter, melted

¼ cup packed light brown sugar

½ teaspoon smoked paprika

¼ teaspoon table salt

4 cooked and crumbled bacon slices

1. Place the Steam Rack, with handles in the up position, in the inner pot of a 6-quart Instant Pot®. Pour in the 1 cup water. Place the potatoes on the rack.

2. Lock the lid; turn Pressure Valve to "Sealing." Press STEAM [High Pressure], and cook 11 to 14 minutes or until potatoes are tender when pierced with a fork. Open the cooker using Quick Pressure Release (page 7). Remove the potatoes from the pot.

3. When cool enough to handle, peel the potatoes and place in a large bowl. Mash roughly with a potato masher. Stir in the butter, brown sugar, paprika, and salt. Sprinkle with the crumbled bacon, and serve immediately.

TIP:

Sweet potatoes need to be very tender to mash well. If your potatoes are on the larger size, set your timer toward the longer end of the cooking range.

6-QUART

ROSEMARY POTATO WEDGES

SERVES: 5 | HANDS-ON: 10 MINUTES | UNDER PRESSURE: 7 MINUTES | QUICK PRESSURE RELEASE

Stir the potatoes very frequently while sautéing to prevent sticking.

2 tablespoons olive oil

1 pound small red potatoes, quartered

1 cup organic vegetable broth

2 teaspoons chopped fresh rosemary

2 tablespoons grated fresh Parmesan cheese

¼ teaspoon kosher salt

¼ teaspoon freshly ground black pepper

1. Add 1 tablespoon of the oil to the inner pot of a 6-quart Instant Pot®. Press SAUTÉ [Normal]. When the oil is shimmering, add the potatoes. Cook, stirring constantly, 5 minutes or until lightly browned. Add the broth, scraping with a wooden or plastic spatula until the bottom of the pot feels smooth. Sprinkle the potato mixture with the rosemary. Turn off the cooker.

2. Lock the lid; turn Pressure Valve to "Sealing." PRESSURE COOK [High Pressure] for 7 minutes. Turn off the cooker. Open the cooker using Quick Pressure Release (page 7). Drain the potatoes, discarding the cooking liquid.

3. Place the potatoes in a large bowl. Add the remaining 1 tablespoon oil, cheese, salt, and pepper; toss gently. Serve immediately.

TIP:

Any herb will work. Try basil, thyme, or parsley.

CLASSIC HUMMUS ▸

MAKES: 1⅔ CUPS | HANDS-ON: 5 MINUTES

Homemade hummus is made even easier with the Instant Pot®, which cooks the chickpeas quickly.

- **1 garlic clove**
- **¼ cup olive oil**
- **2 tablespoons lemon juice**
- **2 tablespoons tahini (sesame paste)**
- **½ teaspoon ground cumin**
- **¼ teaspoon table salt**
- **¼ teaspoon freshly ground black pepper**
- **1¾ cups drained cooked chickpeas (page 28)**
- **2 to 3 tablespoons reserved bean liquid**
- **Pita wedges, warmed, or pita chips**
- **Assorted vegetables**

With the processor running, drop the garlic through the food chute. Process until minced. Add the olive oil, lemon juice, tahini, cumin, salt, pepper, and chickpeas; process until smooth, adding some of the reserved bean liquid, if necessary, until desired consistency. Serve with the pita wedges or chips and assorted vegetables.

NOTE: You may substitute 1 (15-ounce) can chickpeas, drained, with the liquid reserved for the cooked dried chickpeas.

6-QUART

SWEET POTATO-CARROT TZIMMES

SERVES: 8 TO 10 | HANDS-ON: 18 MINUTES | UNDER PRESSURE: 1 MINUTE
QUICK PRESSURE RELEASE

Tzimmes is a traditional Jewish sweet stew. This version combines sweet potatoes with carrots, apricots, and golden raisins.

- **1 cup water**
- **2 large sweet potatoes (2 pounds), scrubbed**
- **1 cup (¼-inch-thick) carrot slices**
- **½ cup ginger ale**
- **¼ cup cranberry juice cocktail or apple cider**
- **3 tablespoons canola oil**
- **2 tablespoons fresh orange juice**
- **½ cup packed brown sugar**
- **¼ teaspoon table salt**
- **¼ teaspoon freshly ground black pepper**
- **½ cup dried apricots, cut into ¼-inch strips**
- **¼ cup golden raisins**

1. Open a collapsible vegetable steamer and place it in the inner pot of a 6-quart Instant Pot®; pour in the 1 cup water. Peel the sweet potatoes, and cut in half crosswise; cut each half lengthwise into 8 wedges. Place the potato wedges in the steamer. Sprinkle the carrot on top of the sweet potato.

2. Lock the lid; turn Pressure Valve to "Sealing." Press STEAM [High Pressure]; cook for 1 minute or just until the potato is tender but holds its shape. Open the cooker using Quick Pressure Release (page 7). Remove the steamer with the vegetables from the cooker. Place the potato and carrot in a large bowl.

3. Pour out the water from the pot; return the pot to the cooker.

4. Combine the ginger ale, juice cocktail, oil, orange juice, brown sugar, salt, and pepper in the pot, stirring to dissolve the sugar. With the lid off, press SAUTÉ [Normal], and cook 7 minutes or until syrupy, stirring often. Stir in the apricots and raisins. Turn off the cooker, and immediately pour the sauce over the vegetables. Stir gently to coat.

6-QUART

HOT TEXAS CAVIAR

MAKES: 8 CUPS | HANDS-ON: 30 MINUTES | UNDER PRESSURE: 12 MINUTES
10-MINUTE NATURAL PRESSURE RELEASE AND SLOW PRESSURE RELEASE

"Hot" here refers to temperature, but this party dip turned side dish is spicy, too.

1 pound dried black-eyed peas, sorted, washed, and drained
6 cups water
Cooking spray
3 bacon slices, cut crosswise into ¼-inch pieces
1 (14½-ounce) can seasoned fire-roasted salsa-style diced tomatoes, undrained
2¼ cups Chicken Bone Broth (page 24)
1 cup frozen corn kernels
½ cup chopped red bell pepper
½ cup chopped green bell pepper
½ teaspoon table salt
¼ teaspoon ground cumin
4 scallions, chopped
¼ cup chopped fresh cilantro

1. Place the washed peas and the 6 cups water in the inner pot of a 6-quart Instant Pot®. Lock the lid; turn Pressure Valve to "Sealing." PRESSURE COOK [High Pressure] for 2 minutes. Open the cooker using a Slow Pressure Release (page 10). Drain the peas; rinse and drain.

2. Wash the inner pot; dry thoroughly, coat with the cooking spray, and return to the cooker. Add the bacon, and press SAUTÉ [Normal]. Cook, stirring often, until crisp, about 5 minutes. Turn off the cooker. Remove the bacon with a slotted spoon, and drain on paper towels, reserving the drippings in the pot.

3. Stir the tomatoes into the drippings, scraping to loosen the browned bits from the bottom of the pot with a wooden or plastic spatula until the bottom of the pot appears clean. Stir in the peas, broth, corn, red and green bell peppers, salt, and cumin. Lock the lid; turn Pressure Valve to "Sealing." PRESSURE COOK [High Pressure] for 10 minutes. Crumble the bacon. Allow a 10-minute Natural Pressure Release (page 10). Turn Pressure Valve to "Venting" to release the remaining pressure. Stir in the scallions. Spoon into bowls, and sprinkle with the bacon and cilantro.

NOTE: You may substitute 1 (14.5-ounce) can fat-free, reduced-sodium chicken broth plus ½ cup water for the Chicken Bone Broth.

6-QUART

HERBED LIMA BEANS

SERVES: 4 | HANDS-ON: 6 MINUTES | UNDER PRESSURE: 5 MINUTES | QUICK PRESSURE RELEASE

No need to thaw the frozen lima beans; they go directly into the Instant Pot®.

- **1 (16-ounce) package frozen baby lima beans**
- **2 cups water**
- **2 tablespoons butter**
- **¼ cup chopped fresh flat-leaf parsley**
- **¼ cup chopped green onions**
- **2 teaspoons chopped fresh rosemary**
- **½ teaspoon table salt**
- **¼ teaspoon freshly ground pepper**

1. Combine the lima beans and 2 cups water in the inner pot of a 6-quart Instant Pot®. Lock the lid; turn the Pressure Valve to "Sealing." PRESSURE COOK [High Pressure] for 5 minutes. Turn off the cooker. Open the cooker using Quick Pressure Release (page 7). Quickly drain the beans, and return to the inner pot.
2. Add the butter and remaining ingredients, stirring until the butter melts.

6-QUART

REFRIED BEANS

SERVES: 10 | HANDS-ON: 17 MINUTES | UNDER PRESSURE: 15 MINUTES
10-MINUTE NATURAL PRESSURE RELEASE | SOAK: AT LEAST 8 HOURS

You can vary the texture of the beans by mashing to your liking as they cook.

1 pound dried pinto beans
Water for soaking
2 tablespoons canola oil
½ cup chopped onion
2 garlic cloves, minced
6 cups cold water
2 teaspoons table salt
½ teaspoon ground cumin
¼ teaspoon ground chipotle chile powder
2 ounces diced cooked ham
6 ounces sharp Cheddar cheese, shredded (about 1½ cups)
Garnish: cilantro sprigs (optional)

1. Sort and wash the beans; place the beans in the inner pot of a 6-quart Instant Pot®. Cover with water to a depth of 2 inches above the beans. Lock the lid; turn Pressure Valve to "Sealing" or "Venting", and let soak 8 hours or overnight. Drain the beans, discarding the soaking water.

2. Wash and dry the inner pot, and return it to the cooker. Press SAUTÉ [Normal]. When the word "Hot" appears, swirl in the oil. Add the onion, and cook, stirring constantly, 3 minutes. Add the garlic; cook, stirring constantly, 30 seconds. Add the 6 cups water, scraping with a wooden or plastic spatula until the bottom of the pot feels smooth. Stir in the beans and salt.

3. Lock the lid; turn Pressure Valve to "Sealing." PRESSURE COOK [High Pressure] for 15 minutes. Allow a 10-minute Natural Pressure Release (page 10). Turn the valve to "Venting" to release remaining pressure.

4. Drain the beans, reserving the cooking liquid. Return the beans to the pot. Add 1 cup of the reserved cooking liquid, the cumin, and chipotle chile powder. Mash the beans with a potato masher. Return the pot to the cooker. Press SAUTÉ [Normal], and cook, stirring constantly, 5 minutes. Stir in up to ½ cup additional cooking liquid, and mash until desired consistency. (Beans will thicken as they cool.) Turn off the cooker. Add the ham, and stir until thoroughly heated. Remove the pot from the cooker. Spoon the beans into a serving dish. Sprinkle with the cheese and, if desired, garnish with the cilantro.

6-QUART

ROSEMARY-GARLIC WHITE BEAN MASH

SERVES: 4 | HANDS-ON: 17 MINUTES | UNDER PRESSURE: 15 MINUTES
10-MINUTE NATURAL PRESSURE RELEASE | SOAK: AT LEAST 8 HOURS

Although the Instant Pot® can cook dried beans without soaking, soaked beans yield a creamier product in this recipe.

1¾ cups dried Great Northern beans
Water for soaking
4 cups water
2 tablespoons olive oil
2¼ teaspoons table salt
2 garlic cloves, minced
¼ cup sour cream
1 teaspoon chopped fresh rosemary
½ teaspoon grated lemon rind
¼ teaspoon freshly ground black pepper

1. Sort and wash the beans; place in the inner pot of a 6-quart Instant Pot®. Cover with water to a depth of 2 inches above beans. Lock the lid; turn Pressure Valve to "Sealing" or "Venting", and let soak 8 hours or overnight. Drain the beans, discarding the soaking water. Return the beans to the pot. Add the 4 cups water, 1 tablespoon of the oil, and 1¾ teaspoons of the salt.

2. Lock the lid; turn Pressure Valve to "Sealing." PRESSURE COOK [High Pressure] for 15 minutes. Allow a 10-minute Natural Pressure Release (page 10). Turn the valve to "Venting" to release remaining pressure.

3. Drain the beans, reserving the cooking liquid. Rinse the beans under cold, running water; drain. Wash and dry the pot; return to the cooker.

4. Add the remaining 1 tablespoon of the oil to the pot. Press SAUTÉ [Normal]. When the oil is shimmering, add the garlic, and cook, stirring constantly, 30 seconds. Add the beans; cook 3 minutes or until thoroughly heated, stirring often. Turn off the cooker. Remove the pot from the cooker. Coarsely mash the beans with a potato masher or fork. Stir in the remaining ½ teaspoon salt and 2 tablespoons of the reserved cooking liquid, reserving the remaining cooking liquid for another use. Stir in the sour cream, rosemary, lemon rind, and pepper.

5. Return the pot to the cooker. Press SAUTÉ [Normal]; cook, stirring constantly, 2 minutes or until the beans are thoroughly heated. Turn off the cooker, and remove the pot from the cooker.

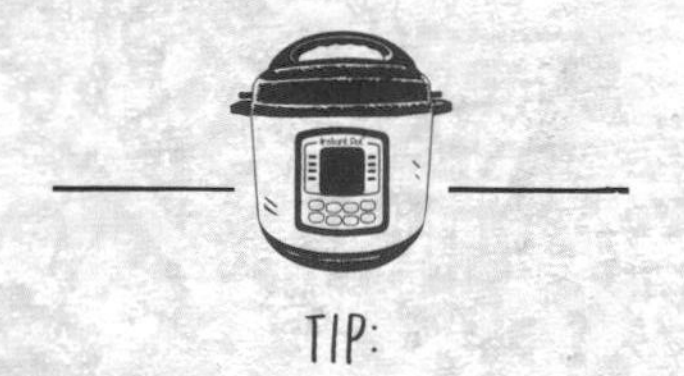

TIP:

Use leftover cooking liquid (not the soaking water) from dried beans as part of the liquid in soups to add nutrients.

6-QUART

SWEET AND SPICY BAKED BEANS

SERVES: 12 | HANDS-ON: 32 MINUTES | UNDER PRESSURE: 55 MINUTES
15-MINUTE NATURAL PRESSURE RELEASE | SOAK: AT LEAST 8 HOURS

To make the beans less spicy, remove the seeds from the jalapeños.

1 pound dried navy beans
Water for soaking
Cooking spray
4 bacon slices, cut crosswise into ¼-inch pieces
1 cup chopped onion (1 small)
3 cups water
⅓ cup light molasses
6 tablespoons packed dark brown sugar
3 tablespoons minced jalapeño chiles (about 1)
4 teaspoons Worcestershire sauce
2 teaspoons mustard
1¾ teaspoons table salt
¼ teaspoon cayenne pepper
¼ teaspoon liquid hickory smoke flavoring
⅛ teaspoon ground allspice
¾ cup ketchup

1. Sort and wash the beans; place in the inner pot of a 6-quart Instant Pot®. Cover with water to 2 inches above the beans. Lock the lid; turn the Pressure valve to "Sealing" or "Venting", and let soak 8 hours or overnight. Drain the beans, discarding the soaking water.

2. Wash and dry the pot. Coat the pot with the cooking spray. Return the pot to cooker; add the bacon. Press SAUTE [Normal]. Cook until almost crisp, stirring often; turn off the cooker. Continue stirring until the bacon is crisp. Remove the bacon from the pot with a slotted spoon. Discard all but 1 tablespoon of the drippings in the pot. Add the onion to the drippings. Press SAUTÉ [Normal], and cook, stirring constantly, 3 to 5 minutes or until almost tender. Turn off the cooker. Add ½ cup of the water, scraping with a wooden or plastic spatula until the bottom of the pot feels smooth. Stir in the molasses, brown sugar, chiles, Worcestershire sauce, mustard, salt, cayenne pepper, smoke flavoring, and allspice. Stir in the remaining 2½ cups water.

3. Lock the lid; turn Pressure Valve to "Sealing." PRESSURE COOK [High Pressure] for 55 minutes. Allow a 15-minute Natural Pressure Release (page 10). Turn the valve to "Venting" to release the remaining pressure.

4. Stir in the ketchup. Press SAUTÉ [Normal]; simmer 10 to 15 minutes or until desired consistency, stirring often. (As the beans thicken, it may be necessary to reduce the temperature to SAUTE [Less] to prevent sticking.) Beans will thicken more as they cool.

6-QUART

SPICY BLACK BEANS

MAKES: 6 CUPS | HANDS-ON: 10 MINUTES | UNDER PRESSURE: 10 MINUTES
10-MINUTE NATURAL PRESSURE RELEASE | SOAK: AT LEAST 8 HOURS

Use these fragrant black beans to get a head start on black beans and rice, black bean soup, or tostadas.

1 pound dried black beans
5 (10½-ounce) cans low-sodium chicken broth
1 cup chopped onion
½ cup chopped green bell pepper
½ teaspoon table salt
½ teaspoon freshly ground black pepper
¼ teaspoon ground cumin
¼ teaspoon ground coriander
¼ teaspoon cayenne pepper
2 large garlic cloves, minced
1 bay leaf
Garnishes: chopped bell pepper and sliced red onion (optional)

1. Sort and wash the beans; place the beans in the inner pot of a 6-quart Instant Pot®. Cover with water to 2 inches above the beans. Lock the lid; turn Pressure Valve to "Sealing" or "Venting", and let soak 8 hours or overnight. Drain the beans, discarding the soaking water.

2. Return the beans to the pot. Place the pot in the cooker. Add the broth and remaining ingredients. Lock the lid; turn Pressure Valve to "Sealing." PRESSURE COOK [High Pressure] for 10 to 15 minutes or until beans are tender. Allow a 10-minute Natural Pressure Release (page 10). Turn the valve to "Venting" to release the remaining pressure. Remove and discard the bay leaf. Use immediately, or divide the cooked beans into 1-cup rigid freezer containers, and add cooking liquid just to the fill line to allow for expansion. Freeze up to 6 months. Garnish with chopped bell pepper and sliced red onion, if desired.

9

RICE & GRAINS

6-QUART

BULGUR PILAF

SERVES: 4 TO 6 | HANDS-ON: 6 MINUTES | UNDER PRESSURE: 12 MINUTES
QUICK PRESSURE RELEASE

Bulgur wheat, a tasty alternative to rice, is high in soluble fiber. The flavor of this recipe is reminiscent of Thanksgiving cornbread dressing.

---

1 tablespoon olive oil
1 tablespoon butter
3 tablespoons finely chopped onion
2 tablespoons finely chopped celery
1 cup uncooked medium bulgur wheat
2 cups chicken broth
½ teaspoon table salt
½ teaspoon Italian seasoning

1. Remove the lid from a 6-quart Instant Pot®. Add the olive oil and butter to the inner pot. Press SAUTÉ [Normal]. Cook until the butter melts. Add the onion and celery. Cook, stirring constantly, 2 minutes. Add the bulgur, stirring to coat with oil. Stir in the chicken broth, salt, and Italian seasoning.

2. Turn off the cooker. Lock the lid; turn Pressure Valve to "Sealing." Press RICE [Low Pressure], and cook for 12 minutes.

3. Open the cooker using Quick Pressure Release (page 7). Fluff pilaf with a fork.

MUSHROOM-ALMOND BARLEY

SERVES: 4 | HANDS-ON: 15 MINUTES | UNDER PRESSURE: 25 MINUTES
QUICK PRESSURE RELEASE

Fresh parsley, toasted almonds, and hearty crimini mushrooms add flavor and texture to nutritious barley. To make this an easy one-bowl meal, top with Pressure Cooker Rotisserie-Style Chicken (page 26).

1 tablespoon olive oil
1 tablespoon butter
1 cup coarsely chopped crimini mushrooms
⅓ cup finely chopped shallots
¼ cup chopped celery
1 cup uncooked whole-grain hull-less barley
2⅔ cups beef stock
¼ teaspoon freshly ground black pepper
½ cup coarsely chopped toasted almonds
¼ cup chopped fresh parsley

1. Remove the lid from a 6-quart Instant Pot®. Add the olive oil and butter. Press SAUTÉ [Normal]. When the butter is melted, add the mushrooms, shallots, and celery. Cook, stirring constantly, 2 minutes. Add the barley; cook, stirring constantly, 2 minutes. Turn off the cooker.

2. Add the beef stock and pepper, scraping the pot with a wooden or plastic spatula until the bottom feels smooth. Lock the lid; turn Pressure Valve to "Sealing." PRESSURE COOK [Low Pressure] for 25 minutes. Open the cooker using Quick Pressure Release (page 7). Turn off the cooker. Press SAUTÉ [Normal]. Cook, stirring constantly, 2 minutes or until any excess liquid is almost evaporated and very slightly creamy. Turn off the cooker. Stir in the almonds and parsley. Serve immediately.

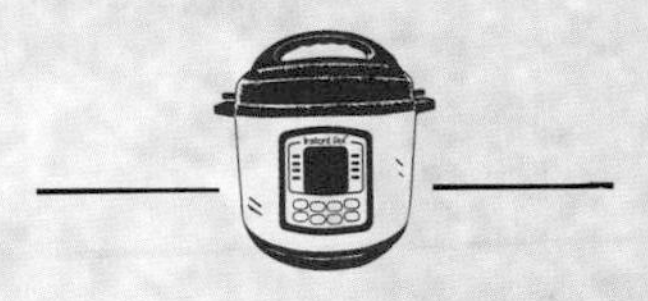

TIPS:

Hull-less barley is best here. It has a nutty flavor and doesn't soak up as much liquid as pearl barley does, so do not substitute pearl barley.

...

To save time, start with sliced mushrooms, then coarsely chop.

3- OR 6-QUART

FRUITED BROWN RICE PILAF

SERVES: 6 | HANDS-ON: 7 MINUTES | UNDER PRESSURE: 20 MINUTES
10-MINUTE NATURAL PRESSURE RELEASE

For pressure cooker rice success, measure veggies with high water content, like carrots, along with the cooking liquid.

1 cup brown basmati rice
½ cup coarsely shredded carrot
Chicken Bone Broth (page 24), or chicken broth (about 1 cup)
⅛ teaspoon table salt
¼ cup golden raisins
¼ cup coarsely chopped dried apricots
¼ cup thinly sliced scallions
¼ cup chopped salted macadamia nuts

Place rice in the inner pot of a 3- or 6-quart Instant Pot®. Place the carrot in a large glass measuring cup. Add broth to measure 1¼ cups. Stir the broth mixture and salt into the rice. Lock the lid; turn Pressure Valve to "Sealing." PRESSURE COOK [High Pressure] for 20 minutes. Allow a 10-Minute Natural Pressure Release (page 10). Turn the valve to "Venting" to release remaining pressure. Add the raisins, apricots, and scallions; fluff with a fork. Cover and let stand 3 minutes. Sprinkle with macadamia nuts.

TIP:

If you substitute toasted natural, slivered almonds, or sliced almonds, or chopped toasted pecans for the macadamia nuts, the salt may need to be increased to ¼ teaspoon.

6-QUART

CITRUS-SCENTED RICE WITH FRESH BASIL

SERVES: 4 | HANDS-ON: 5 MINUTES | UNDER PRESSURE: 12 MINUTES | QUICK PRESSURE RELEASE

The fresh orange and lemon flavors in this dish pair well with fish and seafood.

1½ cups chicken broth
2 tablespoons butter
1 tablespoon grated orange rind
2 tablespoons fresh orange juice
1 teaspoon grated lemon rind
1 cup uncooked basmati rice
3 tablespoons chopped fresh basil
Garnishes: orange and lemon slices, grated orange rind, grated lemon rind (optional)

1. Combine the chicken broth, butter, orange rind, orange juice, lemon rind, and rice in the inner pot of a 6-quart Instant Pot®.
2. Lock the lid; turn Pressure Valve to "Sealing." Press RICE [Low Pressure], and cook for 12 minutes. Open the cooker using Quick Pressure Release (page 7).
3. Add the basil; fluff the rice with a fork. Garnish, if desired.

6-QUART

BUTTERNUT SQUASH RISOTTO

SERVES: 6 TO 8 | HANDS-ON: 21 MINUTES | UNDER PRESSURE: 12 MINUTES
QUICK PRESSURE RELEASE

To save prep time, look for cubed butternut squash in the produce or freezer aisle of your supermarket.

- **2 teaspoons olive oil**
- **½ cup finely chopped yellow onion**
- **1½ cups arborio rice or other short-grain rice**
- **1 cup water**
- **½ teaspoon table salt**
- **¼ teaspoon freshly ground black pepper**
- **3 cups (¾-inch) cubed peeled butternut squash (about 1 pound)**
- **2 (14¼-ounce) cans low-sodium beef broth**
- **2 ounces Parmigiano-Reggiano cheese, grated (about ½ cup)**
- **3 tablespoons unsalted butter**
- **2 tablespoons finely chopped fresh parsley**

1. Add the oil to the inner pot of a 6-quart Instant Pot®. Press SAUTÉ [Normal]. When the oil is shimmering, add the onion, and cook, stirring constantly, 3 minutes. Add the rice; cook, stirring constantly, 1 minute or until rice is coated with oil.
2. Add ½ cup of the water, the salt, and pepper. Cook, stirring constantly, until the water is absorbed. Stir in the remaining ½ cup water, squash, and broth.
3. Lock the lid; turn Pressure Valve to "Sealing." Press RICE [Low Pressure], and cook for 12 minutes.
4. Open the cooker using Quick Pressure Release (page 7). Turn off the cooker.
5. Add the cheese, butter, and parsley, stirring until creamy. Serve immediately.

6-QUART

QUICK PARMESAN RISOTTO

SERVES 6 | HANDS-ON: 10 MINUTES | UNDER PRESSURE: 12 MINUTES | QUICK PRESSURE RELEASE

Practically hands-free risotto? You bet. Stir just for a bit after pressure cooking to develop the characteristic creaminess.

- **1½ tablespoons butter**
- **⅔ cup finely chopped shallots**
- **3 garlic cloves, minced**
- **1⅓ cups uncooked arborio rice**
- **4 cups chicken broth**
- **2 ounces fresh Parmigiano-Reggiano cheese**
- **1 teaspoon fresh thyme leaves**
- **½ teaspoon grated lemon rind**
- **¼ teaspoon freshly ground black pepper**

1. Add the butter to the inner pot of a 6-quart Instant Pot®. Press SAUTÉ [Normal]. When the butter melts, add the shallots; cook, stirring constantly, 2 minutes. Add the garlic; cook, stirring constantly, 30 seconds. Add the rice; cook, stirring constantly, 1 minute until the rice is coated with butter. Add ½ cup of the chicken broth; cook, stirring constantly, 1 minute or until the liquid is absorbed. Stir in the remaining broth.
2. Lock the lid; turn Pressure Valve to "Sealing." Press RICE [Low Pressure], and cook for 12 minutes.
3. Open the cooker using Quick Pressure Release (page 7). Turn off the cooker.
4. Grate 1¾ ounces of the cheese; add to the rice mixture. Add the thyme, lemon rind, and pepper; stir until desired consistency. Shave the remaining ¼ ounce cheese, and top the rice with the shavings. Serve immediately.

6-QUART

◂ CHEESY SAUSAGE, BROCCOLI, AND QUINOA CASSEROLE

SERVES: 12 | HANDS-ON: 37 MINUTES | BAKE: 18 MINUTES

- **1½ tablespoons olive oil**
- **½ cup chopped yellow onion**
- **½ cup chopped carrot**
- **4 (4-ounce) links sweet Italian chicken sausage, casings removed**
- **¼ cup all-purpose flour**
- **2 tablespoons unsalted butter**
- **2 garlic cloves, chopped**
- **2 cups whole milk**
- **2 cups unsalted chicken stock (such as Swanson)**
- **6 cups chopped fresh broccoli florets**
- **1 tablespoon chopped fresh thyme**
- **½ teaspoon kosher salt**
- **½ teaspoon freshly ground black pepper**
- **¼ teaspoon red pepper flakes**
- **5⅓ cups hot Cooked Quinoa (page 22)**
- **Cooking spray**
- **½ cup whole-wheat panko (Japanese-style breadcrumbs)**
- **4 ounces Cheddar cheese, shredded (about 1 cup)**

1. Preheat the oven to 400°F. Place 1 tablespoon of the oil in the inner pot of a 6-quart Instant Pot®. Press SAUTÉ [Normal]. When the oil is shimmering, add the onion, carrot, and sausage; cook 7 minutes, stirring to crumble sausage. Transfer the mixture to a bowl with a slotted spoon.

2. Add the flour, butter, and garlic to the drippings in the pot; cook 2 minutes, stirring frequently. Add the milk and stock; bring to a boil. Cook 2 minutes, stirring constantly with a whisk. Stir in the broccoli, 2 teaspoons of the thyme, ⅜ teaspoon of the salt, ⅜ teaspoon of the black pepper, and the red pepper flakes. Cook 2 minutes, stirring constantly. Turn off the cooker. Stir in the quinoa and sausage mixture.

3. Coat 2 (8-inch) square microwave-safe glass or ceramic baking dishes with the cooking spray. Divide the quinoa mixture between the dishes. Combine the remaining 1½ teaspoons oil and panko in a bowl; add the remaining 1 teaspoon thyme, remaining ⅛ teaspoon salt, remaining ⅛ teaspoon black pepper, and Cheddar cheese. Sprinkle the cheese mixture evenly over the casseroles.

4. Bake at 400°F for 18 minutes or until browned.

6-QUART PICTURED ON PAGE 21

RISOTTO WITH TOMATO TOPPING

SERVES: 10 | HANDS-ON: 10 MINUTES | UNDER PRESSURE: 7 MINUTES
NATURAL PRESSURE RELEASE

TOPPING

- **1½ cups chopped seeded tomato**
- **2 tablespoons chopped scallions**
- **1½ teaspoons extra-virgin olive oil**
- **1 teaspoon balsamic vinegar**
- **¼ teaspoon crushed red pepper**
- **⅛ teaspoon sugar**
- **⅛ teaspoon table salt**
- **⅛ teaspoon freshly ground black pepper**

RISOTTO

- **2 tablespoons butter**
- **1 cup chopped onion**
- **1½ cups Arborio rice or other medium-grain rice**
- **2 garlic cloves, minced**
- **½ cup dry white wine**
- **4 cups fat-free, lower-sodium chicken broth**
- **½ teaspoon table salt**
- **¼ teaspoon freshly ground black pepper**
- **⅛ teaspoon ground nutmeg**
- **4 ounces grated fresh Parmesan cheese (about 1 cup)**
- **⅓ cup finely chopped fresh basil**
- **1 teaspoon grated lemon rind**
- **2 tablespoons fresh lemon juice**

1. Make the Topping: Combine the tomato, scallions, olive oil, vinegar, red pepper, sugar, salt, and black pepper in a bowl. Cover; let stand at room temperature.

2. Make the Risotto: Add the butter to the inner pot of a 6-quart Instant Pot®. Press SAUTÉ [Normal]. When the butter melts, add the onion; cook, stirring, constantly, 2 minutes. Add the rice and garlic; cook, stirring constantly, 2 minutes. Add the wine; cook 1 minute or until the liquid is absorbed, stirring often. Stir in the broth, salt, pepper, and nutmeg. Turn off the cooker.

3. Lock the lid; turn Pressure Valve to "Sealing." PRESSURE COOK [High Pressure] for 7 minutes. Turn off the cooker. Open the cooker using Natural Pressure Release (page 7). Stir in the cheese, basil, lemon rind, and juice. Serve the risotto with the tomato topping.

10 DESSERTS

WHITE CHOCOLATE-STRAWBERRY YOGURT ICE POPS

SERVES: 6 | HANDS-ON: 15 MINUTES | FREEZE: 6 HOURS

You don't have to wait for the ice-cream truck to make its summertime rounds. Enjoy these sweets all year.

1 cup sliced strawberries
⅓ cup superfine sugar
1 teaspoon vanilla extract
2 cups Plain Yogurt (page 14)
6 craft sticks
⅓ cup candy sprinkles
8 ounces white chocolate, finely chopped
¼ cup coconut oil

1. Combine the strawberries, sugar, and vanilla in a large bowl. Mash the berries with a fork until the sugar is dissolved. Stir in the yogurt.

2. Divide the mixture among 6 (4-ounce) ice-pop molds. Top with the lids. Insert a craft stick into each mold. Freeze for 6 hours or until frozen.

3. Place the sprinkles on a small plate. Combine the chocolate and coconut oil in a tall microwave-safe glass. Microwave at HIGH 1 minute or just until melted. Stir until smooth. Allow to cool to room temperature.

4. Remove the pops from the molds. Dip the ends in the melted chocolate, letting the excess drip off, and then quickly roll in the sprinkles. Serve immediately.

6-QUART

APPLESAUCE

MAKES: 2 QUARTS | HANDS-ON: 15 MINUTES | UNDER PRESSURE: 3 MINUTES
NATURAL PRESSURE RELEASE

Homemade applesauce is surprisingly easy to make, especially with the Instant Pot®. Unlike in the store-bought version, the sugar and spice amount is in your control.

¼ cup lemon juice
¼ cup fresh-pressed unfiltered apple cider
6 medium Granny Smith apples, peeled, cored, and quartered
6 medium-size Golden Delicious apples, peeled, cored, and quartered
¾ to 1 cup sugar
Ground cinnamon (optional)

1. Combine the lemon juice, apple cider, and apples in the inner pot of a 6-quart Instant Pot®. Lock the lid; turn Pressure Valve to "Sealing." PRESSURE COOK [High Pressure] for 3 minutes. Open the cooker using Natural Pressure Release (page 7).

2. Let the apple mixture cool slightly; stir or process with an immersion blender to desired consistency. Stir in the sugar and, if desired, cinnamon to taste. Cool completely. Transfer the applesauce to desired size of mason freezer jars or plastic freezer containers, leaving 1-inch headspace. Cover and store in the refrigerator up to 2 weeks, or freeze up to 1 year.

TIP:

Make sure glass containers are made specifically for freezing.

6-QUART

TROPICAL BANANAS FOSTER

SERVES: 7 | HANDS-ON: 5 MINUTES | SLOW COOK: 1 HOUR, 15 MINUTES

Sliced bananas and cubed pineapple meet soft vanilla ice cream and a smooth cinnamon-flavored sauce to give you a very decadent dessert.

Cooking spray
½ cup packed dark brown sugar
3 tablespoons butter
¼ cup light coconut milk
¼ cup dark rum
1 cup (1-inch) cubed fresh pineapple
¼ teaspoon ground cinnamon
4 ripe bananas, cut into ½-inch-thick slices
1¾ cups gluten-free vanilla reduced-fat ice cream

1. Coat the inner pot of a 6-quart Instant Pot® with cooking spray. Combine the brown sugar, butter, coconut milk, and rum in the pot. Lock the lid; turn Pressure Valve to "Venting." SLOW COOK [Normal] for 1 hour. Whisk until smooth.

2. Add the pineapple, cinnamon, and bananas to the sauce, stirring to coat. Lock the lid; turn Pressure Valve to "Venting." Set the cooker to SLOW COOK [Normal] for 30 minutes. After 15 minutes, turn off the cooker, and let stand covered 15 minutes. Serve immediately over the ice cream.

6-QUART

◂ MARSALA-POACHED PEARS

SERVES: 8 | HANDS-ON: 13 MINUTES | SLOW COOK: 2 HOURS

Sweet with a hint of spice, Bosc pears pair nicely with Gorgonzola's sharp flavor.

- **3 cups sweet Marsala or Madeira**
- **1 cup water**
- **¼ cup turbinado sugar or granulated sugar**
- **4 (3- x 1-inch) strips orange rind**
- **1 (3-inch) cinnamon stick**
- **8 peeled firm Bosc pears (about 3 pounds), cored**
- **8 teaspoons Gorgonzola Dolce cheese**

1. Combine the Marsala, 1 cup water, sugar, orange rind, and cinnamon stick in the inner pot of a 6-quart Instant Pot®; set the pears in the pot. Lock the lid; turn Pressure Valve to "Venting." SLOW COOK [Normal] for 2 hours. Turn off the cooker. Carefully remove the pears from the pot, reserving the cooking liquid in the pot; cool.

2. While the pears cool, press SAUTÉ [More]. Bring the cooking liquid to a boil; boil until reduced to 2 cups (about 30 minutes). Discard the cinnamon stick and orange rind strips. Serve pears with the cooking liquid and cheese.

TIP:

Use a melon baller to core the pears from the bottom (rather than cutting them in half first) so they can be served whole.

6-QUART

POMEGRANATE-POACHED PEARS

SERVES: 6 | HANDS-ON: 14 MINUTES | UNDER PRESSURE: 3 MINUTES | QUICK PRESSURE RELEASE

Tart pomegranate juice and dried cherries brighten up these poached pears.

- **6 firm ripe medium pears with stems**
- **1½ tablespoons fresh lemon juice**
- **1¾ cups pomegranate juice**
- **⅓ cup dried tart cherries**
- **6 tablespoons granulated sugar**
- **1 teaspoon vanilla extract**
- **2 (3-inch) cinnamon sticks, broken in half**
- **2 whole cloves**
- **¾ cup light sour cream**
- **4 teaspoons brown sugar**

1. Peel the pears, leaving the stems intact. Scoop the bottom of the core from each pear using the large end of a melon baller. With the small end, scoop out the seeds. If necessary, cut about ¼ inch from base of pears so they will sit flat. Squeeze the lemon juice over the pears.

2. Combine the pomegranate juice, cherries, sugar, vanilla, cinnamon, and cloves in the inner pot of a 6-quart Instant Pot®. Place the pears, stem ends up, in the pot.

3. Lock the lid; turn Pressure Valve to "Sealing." PRESSURE COOK [High Pressure] for 3 minutes. Turn off the cooker. Open the cooker using Quick Pressure Release (page 7).

4. Remove the pears with a slotted spoon, and place on a rimmed serving platter, reserving the cooking liquid in the pot. Press SAUTÉ [More]; bring the cooking liquid to a boil, and cook until reduced to 1 cup (about 10 minutes). Remove and discard the cinnamon sticks and cloves.

5. While the cooking liquid boils, combine the sour cream and brown sugar in a small bowl, stirring until the brown sugar dissolves. Spoon the pomegranate sauce over the pears, and serve with the sour cream mixture.

6-QUART

DECONSTRUCTED BLUEBERRY COBBLER

SERVES: 4 | HANDS-ON: 16 MINUTES | UNDER PRESSURE: 3 MINUTES | QUICK PRESSURE RELEASE

A traditional blueberry cobbler crust, if cooked in a pressure cooker, would be soggy from all the steam. Separating this dessert into its main parts solves the problem.

3 cups frozen blueberries
¾ cup sugar
2 teaspoons lemon juice
¼ teaspoon ground cinnamon
⅛ teaspoon table salt
Dash of ground nutmeg
3 tablespoons water
4 teaspoons cornstarch
Pastry Rounds (recipe at right), warmed
Toppings: Crème Fraîche (recipe at right), Greek Yogurt (page 15), or vanilla ice cream

1. Combine the blueberries, sugar, lemon juice, cinnamon, salt, nutmeg, and 2 tablespoons of the water in the inner pot of a 6-quart Instant Pot®. Stir well, and let stand 5 minutes or until juice begins to form. Stir well to coat the berries with sugar and juice.

2. Lock the lid; turn Pressure Valve to "Sealing," PRESSURE COOK [High Pressure] for 3 minutes. Open the lid using Quick Pressure Release (page 7). Turn off the cooker.

3. Combine the remaining 1 tablespoon water and cornstarch in a small bowl, stirring until smooth. Add 1 to 2 tablespoons of the hot berry liquid to the cornstarch mixture. Stir until blended. Stir the cornstarch mixture into the berry mixture in the pot.

4. Press SAUTÉ [Normal]. Bring to a boil, and cook 1 minute or until thickened and glossy, stirring often. Turn off the cooker. Remove the pot from the cooker, and set aside to cool.

5. Spoon the warm blueberry filling evenly into 4 dessert bowls. Top with 1 to 2 Pastry Rounds. Top with Crème Fraîche, Greek Yogurt, or vanilla ice cream.

PASTRY ROUNDS

Preheat the oven to 450°F. Unroll half of 1 (14.1-ounce) package refrigerated piecrust dough on a lightly floured surface. Cut into 4 rounds, using a 3½-inch round cutter. Place the rounds on an ungreased baking sheet. If desired, sprinkle lightly with bottled cinnamon-sugar, or sugar, pressing lightly to adhere. Repeat the procedure with the remaining half of the dough. Bake at 450°F for 8 to 10 minutes or until golden brown and crisp. Transfer the rounds to a wire rack to cool completely. Baked crusts may be placed in a rigid plastic freezer container and frozen up to 3 months. Reheat at 350°F in the oven or a toaster oven until hot and crisp. Makes 8 rounds.

CRÈME FRAÎCHE

Combine 1 cup heavy cream and 2 tablespoons cultured buttermilk in a glass container. Cover and let stand at room temperature (about 70°F) from 8 to 24 hours, or until very thick. Cover and chill at least 4 hours. Store in the refrigerator up to 10 days. Cream will thicken as it chills.

NOTE: Do not use ultra-pasteurized cream or cream with additives for this recipe.

6-QUART

WINTER FRUIT CRISP

SERVES: 8 | HANDS-ON: 19 MINUTES | UNDER PRESSURE: 2 MINUTES
10-MINUTE NATURAL PRESSURE RELEASE

Greek yogurt is a great topping for both sweet and savory dishes. Here, the tanginess balances the sweetness. You can also drizzle a bit of heavy cream over the crisp for added richness.

- **3 Rome apples (1½ pounds), unpeeled and sliced**
- **2 cups frozen cranberries (do not thaw)**
- **1 (8-ounce) can crushed pineapple in juice, undrained**
- **½ cup granulated sugar**
- **1 cup packed brown sugar**
- **6 tablespoons water**
- **2 tablespoons cornstarch**
- **2 tablespoons butter**
- **2⅔ cups Maple-Pecan Granola (page 33) Greek Yogurt (page 15), or whipped cream**
- **Ground cinnamon (optional)**

1. Combine the apples, cranberries, pineapple, granulated sugar, ½ cup of the brown sugar, and ¼ cup of the water in the inner pot of a 6-quart Instant Pot®, stirring to coat fruit with sugar. Let stand 5 minutes; stir to coat the fruit with juice. Lock the lid; turn Pressure Valve to "Sealing." PRESSURE COOK [High Pressure] for 2 minutes. Open the cooker using a 10-minute Natural Pressure Release (page 10). Turn off the cooker. Transfer the fruit to a bowl with a slotted spoon, reserving juice in the pot.

2. Combine remaining 2 tablespoons water and cornstarch in a small bowl, stirring until smooth. Spoon 1 to 2 tablespoons of the hot fruit juice into the cornstarch mixture, stirring until blended. Stir cornstarch mixture into the fruit juice in the pot.

3. Press SAUTÉ [Normal]. Bring mixture to a boil; cook, stirring constantly, 1 minute or until thick. Turn off the cooker. Add the butter; stir until the butter melts. Gently fold in the fruit. Remove the pot from the cooker, and set aside to cool.

4. To serve, spoon about ⅔ cup of the fruit mixture into each of 8 dessert or gratin dishes. Sprinkle each serving with about ⅓ cup Maple-Pecan Granola, and top with Greek Yogurt or whipped cream. Sprinkle lightly with cinnamon, if desired.

6-QUART

CHAI, MANGO, AND BROWN RICE PUDDING ▸

SERVES: 5 | HANDS-ON: 9 MINUTES | SLOW COOK: 4 HOURS

Make sure that you use medium or short-grain rice; a longer grain does not have the same starches necessary for thickening the pudding.

- 1 cup uncooked short-grain brown rice
- 2½ cups water
- ¼ cup chopped crystallized ginger
- ¼ cup packed light brown sugar
- 1 teaspoon ground cinnamon
- 1 teaspoon vanilla extract
- ¼ teaspoon ground fennel seeds
- ⅛ teaspoon ground cardamom
- ⅛ teaspoon ground cloves
- 1⁄16 teaspoon table salt
- 1 (13.66-ounce) can light coconut milk
- 1 cup chopped peeled mango (about 1 large)
- Ground cinnamon (optional)

1. Combine all ingredients, except the mango, in the inner pot of a 6-quart Instant Pot®; stir well.

2. Lock the lid; turn Pressure Valve to "Venting." SLOW COOK [More] for 4 hours. Uncover and cool 1 hour. Serve at room temperature, or cover and chill. Top with the mango before serving. Sprinkle with additional cinnamon, if desired.

6-QUART

ARBORIO RICE PUDDING WITH SAFFRON

SERVES: 8 | HANDS-ON: 5 MINUTES | UNDER PRESSURE: 12 MINUTES
10-MINUTE NATURAL PRESSURE RELEASE | SLOW COOK: 30 MINUTES

Extra creamy with subtle hints of saffron and cinnamon, this recipe is deliciously unique.

- 4 cups 2% reduced-fat milk
- 1½ cups water
- 1 cup uncooked arborio rice
- ½ teaspoon table salt
- ¼ teaspoon ground cinnamon
- ⅛ teaspoon crushed saffron threads
- ⅔ cup sugar
- ½ cup golden raisins
- 1 teaspoon vanilla extract
- Ground cinnamon (optional)

1. Combine 1½ cups of the milk, water, rice, salt, cinnamon, and saffron in the inner pot of a 6-quart Instant Pot®, stirring well. Lock the lid; turn Pressure Valve to "Sealing." Press RICE [Low Pressure], and cook 12 minutes.

2. Allow a 10-minute Natural Pressure Release (page 10). Turn Pressure Valve to "Venting" to release remaining pressure. Stir in the remaining 2½ cups milk, sugar, and raisins. Lock the lid; turn Pressure Valve to "Venting." SLOW COOK [Less] for 30 minutes.

3. Remove the lid. Press SAUTÉ [Less], and cook uncovered, stirring often, 3 to 5 minutes or just until pudding comes to a simmer. (Do not boil.) Immediately turn off the cooker. Stir in the vanilla, and let the pudding cool in the pot just until warm, stirring occasionally until creamy and slightly thick. (Pudding will continue to thicken after cooking as it stands.)

4. Serve the pudding warm or chilled in individual bowls. Sprinkle with additional ground cinnamon, if desired.

6-QUART

RICE PUDDING WITH PEARS AND RAISINS

SERVES: 6 | HANDS-ON: 15 MINUTES | UNDER PRESSURE: 4 MINUTES
10-MINUTE NATURAL PRESSURE RELEASE

Pressure cooking helps keep the rice from becoming hard when chilled.

- **3½ cups chopped peeled Bosc pears (about 4 pears)**
- **½ cup raisins**
- **¼ cup apple juice**
- **6 tablespoons sugar**
- **2 (3-inch) cinnamon sticks**
- **4 cups 2% reduced-fat milk**
- **1 cup uncooked arborio rice or other short-grain rice**
- **3 tablespoons nonfat dry milk**
- **¼ teaspoon ground nutmeg**
- **¼ teaspoon table salt**
- **1 (3-inch) piece vanilla bean, split lengthwise**
- **½ cup heavy cream**

1. Combine the pears, raisins, and apple juice in a small saucepan. Stir in 3 tablespoons of the sugar and 1 of the cinnamon sticks; bring to a boil. Reduce heat to low; simmer 10 minutes or until the pear is tender, stirring occasionally. Remove the cinnamon stick; discard.

2. While the pear cooks, combine the milk, rice, dry milk, nutmeg, and salt in the inner pot of a 6-quart Instant Pot®. Stir in the remaining 3 tablespoons sugar and remaining cinnamon stick. Scrape the seeds from the vanilla bean; add the seeds and bean to the rice mixture.

3. Lock the lid; turn Pressure Value to "Sealing." PRESSURE COOK [High Pressure] for 4 minutes.

4. Allow a 10-minute Natural Pressure Release (page 10). Turn Pressure Valve to "Venting" to release remaining pressure. Stir in the cream. Remove the pot from the cooker, and let the pudding cool in the pot just until warm, stirring occasionally until creamy and slightly thick (pudding will continue to thicken after cooking as it stands). Remove and discard the cinnamon stick and vanilla bean.

5. Serve the pudding warm or chilled in individual bowls. Top evenly with the pear mixture.

6-QUART

DATE-WALNUT BREAD PUDDING

SERVES: 8 | HANDS-ON: 20 MINUTES | UNDER PRESSURE: 34 MINUTES
QUICK PRESSURE RELEASE

Use lined rubber gloves, instead of pot holders, to easily remove the rack from the cooker.

4 large eggs, lightly beaten
1¼ cups 2% reduced-fat milk
¾ cup granulated sugar
¼ cup packed brown sugar
2 tablespoons orange-flavored liqueur
1 teaspoon vanilla extract
½ teaspoon ground cinnamon
8 ounces French bread, cut into 1-inch cubes
¾ cup chopped pitted Medjool dates
½ cup chopped walnuts, toasted
Cooking spay
5½ cups water
3 tablespoons water
¼ cup half-and-half

1. Combine the eggs, milk, ¼ cup of the granulated sugar, brown sugar, liqueur, vanilla, and cinnamon in a large bowl. Gently fold in the bread, dates, and walnuts. Pour the mixture into a 1½-quart soufflé dish coated with the cooking spray. Cover the dish with aluminum foil, making sure the foil fits tightly around sides and under bottom of the dish but leaving room for the pudding to puff during cooking.

2. Place the Steam Rack in the inner pot of a 6-quart Instant Pot®; position the handles upright. Carefully set the dish on the rack in the pot. Push the dish to one side, and carefully pour the 5½ cups water between the dish and the side of the pot. Center the dish on the rack.

3. Lock the lid; turn Pressure Valve to "Sealing." PRESSURE COOK [High Pressure] for 34 minutes. Turn off the cooker. Open the cooker using Quick Pressure Release (page 7). Blot the foil with a towel to remove any water that collected on the top. Wearing lined rubber gloves, grasp the handles of the rack, and carefully remove the dish from the cooker. Remove the foil, and let stand 15 minutes.

4. While the pudding stands, combine the remaining ½ cup granulated sugar and the 3 tablespoons water in a medium saucepan. Bring to a boil over medium (do not stir). Boil 4 minutes or until the sugar mixture is amber, swirling pan occasionally. Remove the pan from the heat. Gradually add the half-and-half, stirring with a whisk until smooth (be careful of the hot steam). If necessary, return the pan to low heat to dissolve the caramel, stirring until smooth. Serve the bread pudding with the caramel sauce.

6-QUART

GERMAN CHOCOLATE MINI CHEESECAKES

SERVES: 6 | HANDS-ON: 25 MINUTES | UNDER PRESSURE: 3 MINUTES | QUICK PRESSURE RELEASE CHILL: 8 HOURS

Successful cheesecakes depend on very soft cream cheese and not overbeating the filling. Beating too much air into the batter, especially after the egg is added, will result in cracking because the batter rises during cooking and then collapses as it cools.

1 cup water
6 silicone baking cups
Cooking spray

CRUST

⅔ cup finely crushed shortbread cookies without nuts (such as Keebler Sandies Classic Shortbread)
2 tablespoons butter, melted

FILLING

1 (8-ounce) package cream cheese, softened
¼ cup sugar
1 tablespoon unsweetened cocoa
1 teaspoon vanilla extract
1 large egg

TOPPING

1 tablespoon butter
3 tablespoons packed brown sugar
3 tablespoons heavy cream
¼ teaspoon vanilla extract
3 tablespoons chopped pecans, toasted
3 tablespoons sweetened flaked coconut
6 paper baking cups

1. Pour the 1 cup of water into the inner pot of a 6-quart Instant Pot®. Lower the Steam Rack into the pot using the handles. Lightly coat the 6 silicone baking cups with the cooking spray.

2. Make the Crust: Stir together the cookie crumbs and the 2 tablespoons melted butter until all crumbs are moistened. Divide the crumb mixture evenly among the prepared baking cups. Press the crumb mixture firmly into the bottom of the cups. Set aside.

3. Make the Filling: Beat the cream cheese, ¼ cup sugar, cocoa, and 1 teaspoon vanilla at medium speed with an electric mixer until blended. Add the egg; beat just until blended.

4. Spoon the filling evenly into prepared crusts. Set 3 cups on the Steam Rack in the pot. Insert a tall egg trivet with 3½-inch legs into the pot, and place the remaining 3 cups on top of the trivet. Lock the lid; turn Pressure Valve to "Sealing." Press STEAM [High Pressure]; set for 3 minutes. Open the cooker using Quick Pressure Release (page 7). (Do not let condensation drip onto the cakes when removing the lid.) Carefully remove the cheesecakes from the cooker. (Blot any condensation from the tops of the cheesecakes with the edge of a paper towel.) Let the cheesecakes cool to room temperature. Cover and chill thoroughly, at least 8 hours.

5. Make the Topping: Place the 1 tablespoon butter in a small microwave-safe bowl. Cover and microwave at HIGH 30 seconds or until melted. Stir in the brown sugar and cream. Cover and microwave at HIGH until bubbling vigorously, about 1 minute to 1 minute and 15 seconds. Add the ¼ teaspoon vanilla, and stir until mixture is smooth and slightly thickened. Stir in the pecans and coconut. Remove the cheesecakes from the refrigerator, and unmold; place each in the center of a paper baking cup on serving plates. Spoon topping evenly on top of the cheesecakes. Serve immediately, or chill.

TIP:

The Instant Pot® does a great job of softening cream cheese. Place the cream cheese on the opened package in the inner pot. Lock the lid; turn Pressure Valve to "Venting." Press YOGURT (Less). Let cream cheese stand in the pot 15 to 20 minutes or until very soft, turning over halfway through.

6-QUART

LEMON BURST CHEESECAKE WITH BLUEBERRY SAUCE

SERVES: 10 | HANDS-ON: 22 MINUTES | UNDER PRESSURE: 42 MINUTES
18-MINUTE NATURAL PRESSURE RELEASE | CHILL: 20 HOURS

YOGURT CHEESE

Cheesecloth
2⅓ cups nonfat Plain Yogurt (page 14), undrained
1½ cups water
Parchment paper
Butter-flavored cooking spray

CRUST

⅓ cup graham cracker crumbs (2 full cracker sheets)

FILLING

¼ cup (about 1.1 ounces) all-purpose flour
⅔ cup sugar
1½ teaspoons vanilla extract
2 teaspoons grated lemon rind
11 ounces ⅓-less-fat cream cheese, softened
¼ cup light sour cream
¾ cup egg substitute

BLUEBERRY SAUCE

½ cup sugar
1 tablespoon cornstarch
⅛ teaspoon ground nutmeg
Dash of table salt
½ cup water
1 cup fresh blueberries
½ teaspoon grated lemon rind
1½ tablespoons fresh lemon juice

1. Make the Yogurt Cheese: Place a colander in a 2-quart glass measure or medium glass bowl. Line the colander with 4 layers of cheesecloth, allowing the cheesecloth to extend over the outside edges of the bowl. Spoon the yogurt into the colander. Fold the edges of the cheesecloth on top of the yogurt. Cover the colander and bowl tightly with aluminum foil, and chill 12 hours.

2. Pour the 1½ cups water into the inner pot of a 6-quart Instant Pot®. Cut a round of parchment paper to fit the bottom of a 7-inch nonstick springform pan. Lightly coat the bottom and sides of the pan with the cooking spray. Fit the parchment paper in the pan, smoothing out any wrinkles. Lightly coat the parchment paper with the cooking spray.

3. Make the Crust: Firmly press the graham cracker crumbs into the bottom of prepared pan. Coat the crumbs with the cooking spray.

4. Make the Filling: Measure the yogurt cheese to equal 1¼ cups, reserving the whey for another use. Spoon the yogurt cheese into a large mixing bowl. Add the flour, sugar, vanilla, lemon rind, cream cheese, and sour cream to the yogurt cheese; beat at low speed with an electric mixer just until blended. Add the egg substitute, beating just until blended. Pour the batter into the prepared crust.

5. Gently tap the pan on a work surface to remove any air bubbles. Coat a 10-inch-long piece of aluminum foil with the cooking spray, and cover the pan, sprayed side down. Lightly crimp the edges of the foil to secure it to the top of the pan. Place the pan on the Steam Rack. Using the rack handles, gently lower the pan into the pot. Place the pot into the cooker.

6. Lock the lid; turn Pressure Valve to "Sealing." Turn off the KEEP WARM function of the Instant Pot®. PRESSURE COOK [High Pressure] for 42 minutes. Allow an 18-minute Natural Pressure Release (page 10). Turn Pressure Valve to "Venting" to release remaining pressure.

7. Carefully remove the lid, keeping it level to avoid dripping excess condensation onto the foil. Lightly blot the the foil to remove any condensation. Use the rack handles to remove the pan from the pot. Leave the pan on the rack. Carefully remove the foil. If necessary, lightly blot top of cheesecake with a paper towel to remove any excess cooking spray. Cool the cheesecake completely on the rack. Cover and chill at least 8 hours.

8. Make the Blueberry Sauce: Whisk together the sugar, cornstarch, nutmeg, and salt in a 2-cup glass measure or medium bowl. Gradually add the ½ cup water, whisking until smooth. Microwave at HIGH 2 minutes, whisking after 1 minute. Stir in the blueberries. Cover and microwave at HIGH 1 to 2 minutes or until thickened. Stir in the lemon rind and juice. Cool completely. Gently loosen the cheesecake from the sides of the pan with a plastic knife. Remove the sides of the pan, and transfer the cheesecake to a serving plate. Cut into wedges, and serve with the blueberry sauce.

NOTE: Store-bought plain nonfat yogurt may be substituted.

6-QUART

NEW YORK CHEESECAKE

SERVES: 10 | HANDS-ON: 15 MINUTES | UNDER PRESSURE: 42 MINUTES
18-MINUTE NATURAL PRESSURE RELEASE | CHILL: 8 HOURS

Thanks to a few easy substitutes, this cheesecake is just as dense and rich tasting as the original, but with fewer calories and less fat.

Parchment paper
Butter-flavored cooking spray
1½ cups water

CRUST

6 sugar-free pecan shortbread cookies (about 2¼ ounces), such as Murray

FILLING

2 (8-ounce) packages fat-free cream cheese, softened
11 ounces ⅓-less-fat cream cheese, softened
1 cup sugar
2 tablespoons all-purpose flour
2 teaspoons vanilla extract
1 vanilla bean, split lengthwise
⅛ teaspoon table salt
3 large eggs

TOPPING

1 (21-ounce) can cherry pie filling

1. Cut a round of parchment paper to fit the bottom of a 7-inch nonstick springform pan. Lightly coat the bottom and sides of the pan with cooking spray. Fit the parchment paper in the pan, smoothing out any wrinkles. Lightly coat the parchment paper with the cooking spray. Pour 1½ cups water into the inner pot of a 6-quart Instant Pot®.

2. Make the Crust: Break the cookies into the bowl of a food processor; process until finely ground. Sprinkle the crumbs in the bottom of the prepared pan; press firmly. Coat the crust with cooking spray. Freeze at least 10 minutes while preparing the filling.

3. Make the Filling: Combine the cream cheeses, sugar, flour, vanilla extract, vanilla bean, and salt in a food processor. Process just until blended. Add the eggs, 1 at a time, pulsing once after each addition. (Egg yolk may not be blended.) Do not overprocess.

4. Remove the crust from the freezer. Gently fold any visible egg yolk into the filling, and pour the filling into the crust, smoothing the top. Gently tap the pan on a work surface to remove any air bubbles. Coat a piece of aluminum foil just large enough to cover the top of the pan with cooking spray. Cover the pan with foil, sprayed side down. Lightly crimp the edges to secure the foil to the top of the pan. Place the pan on the Steam Rack. Using the rack handles, gently lower the pan into the pot. Place the pot in the cooker.

5. Lock the lid; turn Pressure Valve to "Sealing." Turn off the KEEP WARM function of the Instant Pot®. PRESSURE COOK [High Pressure] for 42 minutes. Allow an 18-minute Natural Pressure Release (page 10). Turn Pressure Valve to "Venting" to release remaining pressure.

6. Carefully remove the lid, keeping it level to avoid dripping condensation onto the foil. Lightly blot the top of the foil to remove any condensation. Use the rack handles to remove the pan from the pot. Leave the pan on the rack. Carefully remove the foil. Gently blot the top of the cheesecake with a paper towel to remove any excess cooking spray. Let the cheesecake cool completely on the rack. Cover and chill at least 8 hours. Gently loosen the cheesecake from the sides of the pan with a plastic knife. Remove the sides of the pan, and transfer the cheesecake to a serving plate. Cut into 10 wedges, and spoon the cherry pie filling evenly over the wedges.

6-QUART

TRIPLE-CHOCOLATE CHEESECAKE

SERVES: 10 | HANDS-ON: 26 MINUTES | UNDER PRESSURE: 44 MINUTES
20-MINUTE NATURAL PRESSURE RELEASE | CHILL: 8 HOURS

Parchment paper
Butter-flavored cooking spray
1½ cups water

CRUST

⅔ cup chocolate graham cracker crumbs (4 full cracker sheets)
1 tablespoon sugar
1 tablespoon butter, melted
1 tablespoon water

TOPPING

1 tablespoon sugar
2 teaspoons unsweetened cocoa
½ cup light sour cream

FILLING

3 tablespoons Kahlúa or other coffee-flavored liqueur
3 ounces semisweet chocolate, chopped
¼ cup chocolate syrup
1 (8-ounce) package fat-free cream cheese, softened
1 (8-ounce) package ⅓-less-fat cream cheese, softened
1 cup sugar
2 tablespoons unsweetened cocoa
¼ teaspoon table salt
1 teaspoon vanilla extract
2 large eggs
Garnishes: chocolate shavings, fresh raspberries (optional)

1. Cut a round of parchment paper to fit the bottom of a 7-inch nonstick springform pan. Lightly coat the bottom and sides of pan with cooking spray. Fit parchment paper in the pan, smoothing out any wrinkles. Lightly coat the parchment paper with the cooking spray. Pour the 1½ cups water into the inner pot of a 6-quart Instant Pot®.

2. Make the Crust: Combine the graham cracker crumbs and 1 tablespoon sugar. Stir in the butter and 1 tablespoon water, blending well. Firmly press the mixture into the bottom and ½ inch up sides of prepared pan. Freeze at least 10 minutes while preparing the topping and filling.

3. Make the Topping: Combine 1 tablespoon sugar and 2 teaspoons cocoa in a small bowl, stirring until well blended. Add the sour cream, stirring until well blended; cover and set aside.

4. Make the Filling: Combine the liqueur and chocolate in a small bowl. Microwave at HIGH 25 seconds; stir until smooth and glossy. Stir in the chocolate syrup.

5. Place the cheeses in a large bowl. Combine 1 cup sugar, 2 tablespoons cocoa, and salt, whisking until thoroughly blended; add to the cheeses. Add the vanilla, and beat at low speed with an electric mixer just until smooth. Scrape the sides of the bowl. Add both eggs at once; beat at low speed just until blended. Scrape the sides of the bowl, and stir by hand just until the batter is uniform in chocolate color.

6. Remove the crust from the freezer. Pour the filling into the crust, smoothing the top. Gently tap the pan on a work surface to remove any air bubbles. Coat a 10-inch-long piece of aluminum foil with the cooking spray, and cover the pan, sprayed side down. Lightly crimp edges to secure foil to the top of the pan. Place the pan on the rack. Using the rack handles, gently lower the pan into the pot.

7. Lock the lid; turn Pressure Valve to "Sealing." Turn off the KEEP WARM function of the cooker. PRESSURE COOK [High Pressure] for 44 minutes. Allow a 20-minute Natural Pressure Release (page 10). Turn Pressure Valve to "Venting" to release any remaining pressure.

8. Remove the lid, keeping it level to avoid dripping excess condensation onto foil. Lightly blot the top of the foil to remove any condensation. Use the rack handles to remove the pan from the pot. Leave the pan on the rack. Carefully remove the foil. If necessary, lightly blot the top of the cheesecake with a paper towel to remove any excess cooking spray.

9. Spoon the topping in small dollops around the edges and in center of the cheesecake. Using a small offset spatula, spread the topping over the cheesecake, being careful not to disturb the filling. Cool completely on the rack. Cover and chill at least 8 hours.

10. Gently loosen the cheesecake from the sides of the pan with a plastic knife. Remove the sides of the pan, and transfer the cheesecake to a serving plate. Cut into wedges, and garnish with the chocolate shavings and raspberries, if desired.

3- 6- OR 8-QUART

HOMEMADE DULCE DE LECHE

MAKES: 1½ CUPS | HANDS-ON: 3 MINUTES | UNDER PRESSURE: 30 MINUTES
NATURAL PRESSURE RELEASE | SLOW COOK: 10 HOURS

You can use either the Pressure Cook setting or the Slow Cook setting to make this easy caramel fondue–like sauce. Use it to make a Dulce de Leche Flan (page 241), or serve it over ice cream or as a dip for apple or banana slices.

1 (14-ounce) can fat-free sweetened condensed milk

SLOW COOK

1. Pour the milk into a 2-cup glass measuring cup; cover with aluminum foil. Place the Steam Rack in the inner pot of a 6-, or 8-quart Instant Pot®. Set the measuring cup on the rack. Carefully pour in very hot water to reach the level of the milk in the measuring cup.
2. Lock the lid; turn Pressure Valve to "Venting." SLOW COOK [Normal] for 10 hours. Cook additional time, if necessary, until the milk is caramel colored.

PRESSURE COOK

1. Pour the milk evenly into 3 (4-ounce) canning jars. Cover with the lids and screw on the bands finger tight. Set the jars on the Steam Rack in the inner pot of a 3-, 6-, or 8-quart Instant Pot®. Fill the inner pot with water to within ½ inch of the rim of the jars.
2. Lock the lid; turn Pressure Valve to "Sealing." PRESSURE COOK [High Pressure] for 30 minutes. Allow a complete Natural Pressure Release (page 7). Carefully remove the jars from the cooker using a canning jar lifter. Set the jars on a wire rack, and let cool 15 minutes. Remove lids, and stir until smooth. Recover and let stand until completely cool. Chill completely. Store in the refrigerator for up to 1 month.

6-QUART

DULCE DE LECHE FLAN

SERVES: 8 | HANDS-ON: 15 MINUTES | SLOW COOK: 2 HOURS, 30 MINUTES | CHILL: 6 HOURS

Make a batch of easy Homemade Dulche de Leche (page 240) and use it to flavor this flan.

¾ cup sugar
2 large eggs
4 large egg yolks
¾ cup canned fat-free dulce de leche or Homemade Dulce de Leche (page 240)
½ cup 1% low-fat milk
1 teaspoon vanilla extract
¼ teaspoon table salt
1 (12-ounce) can evaporated fat-free milk
5½ cups hot water
Whipped cream, blackberries, raspberries, mint sprigs (optional)

1. Place ½ cup of the sugar in a small skillet. Cook over medium 5 to 6 minutes or until amber in color (gently shaking the skillet occasionally until the sugar melts). Remove the pan from the heat, and carefully pour the hot caramel into a 1½-quart soufflé dish, tilting the dish to coat the bottom. Let stand 10 minutes.

2. Whisk together the eggs and egg yolks in a large bowl until well blended. Add the remaining ¼ cup sugar, ¾ cup dulce de leche, milk, vanilla, salt, and evaporated milk, whisking until blended. Pour the mixture through a wire-mesh strainer over the caramel in the dish; discard the solids. Cover the dish with aluminum foil.

3. Place the Steam Rack in the inner pot of a 6-quart Instant Pot®; position the handles upright. Carefully set the dish on the rack in the pot. Push the dish to one side, and carefully pour 5½ cups hot water between the dish and the side of the pot. Center the dish on the rack.

4. Lock the lid; turn Pressure Valve to "Venting." SLOW COOK [More] for 2 hours and 30 minutes. (When the time is up, the flan should be set, and a sharp knife inserted in the center should come out clean. Recover the dish, and cook additional time, if necessary.) Open the cooker. Blot excess moisture from the foil, if necessary, with a towel.

5. Remove the dish from the pot by carefully lifting out the rack, squeezing the handles toward each other to secure the dish. Remove the foil from the dish. Let stand on the rack until completely cool (about 1½ hours). Cover with foil, and chill at least 6 hours. Loosen the edges of the flan with a knife or rubber spatula. Place a plate upside down on top of the dish; invert the flan onto the plate. Serve with whipped cream, blackberries, raspberries, and mint sprigs, if desired.

6-QUART

VANILLA BEAN BAKED CUSTARD

SERVES: 4 | HANDS-ON: 10 MINUTES | SLOW COOK: 2 HOURS | CHILL: 6 HOURS

Using evaporated milk helps the custard stabilize and not curdle.

1 (12-ounce) can evaporated low-fat milk
½ cup 1% low-fat milk
1 teaspoon vanilla bean paste
1 large egg, lightly beaten
2 large egg yolks
⅓ cup sugar
Cooking spray
5½ cups hot water
Raspberries and blueberries (optional)

1. Combine the milks in a medium saucepan. Bring to a simmer over medium, about 4 minutes. Remove from heat; add the vanilla bean paste, stirring with a whisk until blended.

2. Whisk together the egg, egg yolks, and sugar in a medium bowl until blended. Gradually add the hot milk, whisking vigorously. Pour the egg mixture through a sieve into a 1½-quart soufflé dish coated with cooking spray; discard solids. Cover the dish with aluminum foil.

3. Place the Steam Rack in the inner pot of a 6-quart Instant Pot®. Position the handles upright. Carefully set the dish on the rack.

4. Push the dish to one side, and carefully pour 5½ cups hot water through the space created into the inner pot. Center the dish on the rack.

5. Lock the lid; turn Pressure Valve to "Venting." SLOW COOK [More] for 2 hours. (When the time is up, custard should be set, and a sharp knife inserted in center should come out clean. Recover the dish, and cook additional time, if necessary.) Remove the lid from cooker. Blot excess moisture from the top of the foil, if necessary, with a towel. Remove the foil from the dish.

6. Remove the dish from the cooker by carefully lifting out rack by the handles. Let custard stand on the rack until completely cool (about 1½ hours). Cover with foil, and chill at least 6 hours. Serve with raspberries and blueberries, if desired.

6-QUART

PUMPKIN PIE CUSTARDS WITH GINGERSNAP TOPPING

SERVES: 6 | HANDS-ON: 8 MINUTES | UNDER PRESSURE: 7 MINUTES | QUICK PRESSURE RELEASE
CHILL: 3 HOURS

3 large eggs, well beaten
1¼ cups canned unsweetened pumpkin
1 cup 2% reduced-fat evaporated milk
1 teaspoon vanilla extract
½ cup sugar
¼ teaspoon salt
¾ teaspoon ground cinnamon
¼ teaspoon ground nutmeg
¼ teaspoon ground ginger
2 cups water
½ cup frozen reduced-calorie whipped topping, thawed
8 teaspoons crushed gingersnaps

1. Whisk the eggs until blended in a 2-quart measuring cup. Stir in the pumpkin, milk, and vanilla. Combine the sugar, salt, cinnamon, nutmeg, and ginger; whisk into the pumpkin mixture. Pour the pumpkin mixture evenly into 6 (6-ounce) ramekins or custard cups.

2. Pour the 2 cups water into the inner pot of a 6-quart Instant Pot®. Fold the handles under the Steam Rack, and place it in the bottom of the pot. Tightly cover each ramekin with a 9- x 5-inch piece of aluminum foil, tucking the excess under the bottom. Center 3 ramekins on the rack in a cloverleaf pattern; stack the remaining 3 ramekins on top, offsetting the cloverleaf pattern for stability.

3. Lock the lid; turn Pressure Valve to "Sealing." PRESSURE COOK [High Pressure] for 7 minutes. Open the cooker using Quick Pressure Release (page 7).

4. Carefully remove the top 3 ramekins from the cooker; place on a wire rack, leaving the foil on. Remove the remaining 3 ramekins from the cooker, and remove the foil immediately. Let the top 3 ramekins stand covered at least 10 minutes or until a thin sharp knife inserted in the center through the foil comes out clean; uncover and cool completely. Cover and chill at least 3 hours. Top each custard with whipped topping and gingersnaps just before serving.

6-QUART

CHOCOLATE ALMOND CAKE

SERVES: 8 | HANDS-ON: 25 MINUTES | UNDER PRESSURE: 27 MINUTES
SLOW PRESSURE RELEASE

One package of the cake mix will make 2 (7-inch) cakes, but do not prepare them at the same time. The times listed here are for starting in a completely cool Instant Pot®. If prepared at the same time, the batter for a second cake would deflate while waiting for the first cake to cook. For best results, weigh the cake mix, and measure the water carefully.

CAKE

1½ cups water

1 (16-ounce) package angel food cake mix

½ cup plus 2 tablespoons water

FROSTING

⅓ cup toasted natural almonds, chopped

¼ cup sweetened flaked coconut

¾ cup semisweet chocolate chips

3 tablespoons Greek Yogurt whey (page 15)

1. Make the Cake: Pour the 1½ cups water into the inner pot of a 6-quart Instant Pot®. Weigh or lightly spoon ½ package (8 ounces; about 1½ cups) of the cake mix into dry measuring cups; level with a knife. Reserve the remaining cake mix for another use.

2. Place the cake mix in a large bowl. Add the ½ cup plus 2 tablespoons of water, and beat at low speed with an electric mixer for 30 seconds; beat at medium speed for 1 minute. Spoon the batter into an ungreased 7-inch tube pan with a removable bottom. Smooth out the top of the batter. Cover the pan with a piece of aluminum foil just large enough to fit over the top of the pan, and gently tuck the foil under the rim of the pan to secure. Do not cover the entire pan. Place the pan on the Steam Rack, and lower it into the pot using the handles. Lock the lid; turn Pressure Valve to "Sealing." PRESSURE COOK (High Pressure) 27 minutes. Open the cooker using a Slow Pressure Release (page 10). When removing the lid of the cooker, do not allow condensation to drip onto the foil.

3. Remove the cake from the pot, using the rack handles, and set the pan and rack on a work surface. Remove the foil. Invert the cake onto the feet of the pan (or place the center tube over a bottle) to cool completely.

4. Loosen the cake from the sides of the pan using a thin, narrow metal spatula. Invert the cake onto a second cooling rack, then invert the cake back onto a plate.

5. Make the Frosting: Use scissors to trim the top edges of the cake. Combine the chopped toasted almonds and coconut in a small bowl. Place the chocolate chips in a small microwave-safe bowl. Microwave at HIGH 2 minutes or until the chocolate softens and begins to melt, stirring after 1 minute. Stir the chocolate, and add the whey. (Chocolate may clump.) Microwave 15 to 20 seconds or just until warm. Stir until smooth, glossy, and slightly thickened, but still pourable. Allow the frosting to cool for a few minutes, while stirring constantly, to reach spreading consistency. (Frosting will become firmer when smoothed over the cake, so begin spreading while slightly thick, but still pourable.)

6. Working quickly, spread frosting over the top of the cake with a small offset spatula, beginning at the center hole and working outward. Spoon frosting along the outside rim of the cake, and use the spatula to smooth it downward over the sides.

7. While the frosting is still moist, carefully sprinkle the almond mixture over the top of the cake, pressing gently to adhere. Let the cake stand at room temperature until the frosting is firm.

6-QUART

BOURBON-PECAN CAKE

SERVES: 8 | HANDS-ON: 35 MINUTES | UNDER PRESSURE: 55 MINUTES
10-MINUTE NATURAL PRESSURE RELEASE

This spirited cake and glaze is for mature palates. You may substitute milk for the bourbon in the glaze and add 1/4 teaspoon vanilla extract. You can substitute milk for the bourbon in the cake, too.

CAKE

- **Butter-flavored cooking spray**
- **1½ cups all-purpose flour**
- **1½ cups water**
- **¼ cup packed light brown sugar**
- **3 tablespoons chopped toasted pecans**
- **¾ teaspoon ground cinnamon**
- **1 teaspoon baking soda**
- **½ teaspoon table salt**
- **¼ teaspoon ground nutmeg**
- **¾ cup granulated sugar**
- **4 ounces (½ cup) butter, softened and cut into 6 pieces**
- **1 teaspoon grated orange zest**
- **1 teaspoon vanilla extract**
- **¼ teaspoon almond extract**
- **¼ teaspoon maple flavoring**
- **2 large eggs**
- **¼ cup bourbon**
- **¼ cup Greek Yogurt (page 15)**
- **2 tablespoons Greek Yogurt whey (page 15)**

GLAZE

- **1 cup powdered sugar**
- **1 tablespoon softened butter**
- **3 to 4 teaspoons bourbon**

1. Coat a 6-cup nonstick Bundt pan with the cooking spray. Dust the bottom and sides of the pan with 2 teaspoons of the flour. Pour the 1½ cups water into the inner pot of a 6-quart Instant Pot®. Combine the brown sugar, pecans, and ¼ teaspoon of the cinnamon in a small bowl. Set aside.

2. Combine the remaining flour, baking soda, salt, nutmeg, and the remaining ½ teaspoon cinnamon in a bowl. Process the ¾ cup granulated sugar, butter, orange zest, extracts, and maple flavoring in a food processor 20 seconds or until smooth. Add the eggs through the food chute; process 15 seconds or until blended and creamy. Scrape down the sides. Process 10 more seconds. Add the flour mixture, the ¼ cup bourbon, yogurt, and whey; process 5 seconds. Scrape down the sides; pulse twice.

3. Spoon one-third of the batter into the prepared pan. Sharply tap pan on counter to remove air bubbles; smooth the top of the batter. Sprinkle the reserved pecan mixture over the batter, avoiding the area within ½ inch of the center of the pan. Spoon the remaining two-thirds of the batter over the pecan mixture, covering all of the pecan mixture completely with batter. Repeat tapping the pan to remove air bubbles, and smooth the top, sealing the batter to the edges and center of the pan. Cover the top of the pan with aluminum foil coated with the cooking spray, coated side down. Lightly crimp the edges to secure the foil to the top edge of the pan. Place the pan on the Steam Rack. Using the rack handles, lower the pan into the inner pot.

4. Lock the lid; turn Pressure Valve to "Sealing." PRESSURE COOK [High Pressure] for 55 minutes. Allow a 10-minute Natural Pressure Release (page 10). Turn the Pressure Valve to release the remaining pressure. Lift the pan and rack from the pot, using the handles. Remove the foil. Let the cake cool in the pan 5 minutes. Loosen the cake from the sides and center of the pan, using a plastic knife or narrow spatula. Invert the cake onto a wire cooling rack; cool completely.

5. Make the Glaze: Whisk together the powdered sugar, butter, and the 3 teaspoons bourbon, adding an additional 1 teaspoon of bourbon, if necessary, until thick, but still pourable. Spoon the glaze over the cake. Let stand until the glaze is firm.

6-QUART

BUTTER CAKE

SERVES: 8 | HANDS-ON: 10 MINUTES | UNDER PRESSURE: 55 MINUTES
10-MINUTE NATURAL PRESSURE RELEASE

Top with chocolate frosting and dust with powdered sugar, garnish with Chocolate Glaze (page 249), or use generous slices as a base for strawberry shortcake.

Butter-flavored cooking spray
1½ cups all-purpose flour
1½ cups water
½ teaspoon table salt
¼ teaspoon baking soda
1 cup sugar
4 ounces (½ cup) softened unsalted butter
1 teaspoon vanilla extract
½ teaspoon almond extract
2 large eggs
¼ cup Greek Yogurt whey (page 15)
¼ cup Greek Yogurt (page 15)

1. Coat a 6-cup nonstick Bundt pan with the cooking spray. Dust the bottom and sides of the pan with 2 teaspoons of the flour. Pour the 1½ cups water into the inner pot of a 6-quart Instant Pot®.

2. Combine the remaining flour, salt, and baking soda. Process the sugar, butter, and extracts in a food processor 20 seconds or until smooth. Add the eggs through the food chute; process 15 seconds or until blended and creamy. Scrape down the sides. Process 10 more seconds. Add the flour mixture, whey, and yogurt; process 5 seconds. Scrape down the sides; pulse twice.

3. Spoon the batter into the prepared pan. Sharply tap the pan on the counter to remove air bubbles; smooth the top of the batter. Cover the top of the pan with aluminum foil coated with the cooking spray, coated side down. Lightly crimp the edges to secure the foil to the top edge of the pan. Place the pan on the Steam Rack. Using the rack handles, lower the pan into the inner pot.

4. Lock the lid; turn Pressure Valve to "Sealing." PRESSURE COOK [High Pressure] for 55 minutes. Allow a 10-minute Natural Pressure Release (page 10). Turn the Pressure Valve to "Venting" to release the remaining pressure. Lift the pan and rack from the pot, using the handles. Remove the foil. Let the cake cool in the pan 5 minutes. Loosen the cake from the sides and center of the pan, using a plastic knife or narrow spatula. Invert the cake onto a wire cooling rack; cool completely.

NOTE: ½ cup buttermilk may be substituted for the yogurt whey and yogurt combination.

6-QUART

CHOCOLATE-ESPRESSO PUDDING CAKE

SERVES: 8 | HANDS-ON: 15 MINUTES | UNDER PRESSURE: 11 MINUTES
QUICK PRESSURE RELEASE

Pudding cake is good. Chocolate-espresso pudding cake is the best. Don't skip the ice cream on top—the combination of melting ice cream and warm cake is sublime.

2 cups water
Cooking spray
5 tablespoons sugar
4 ounces bittersweet chocolate, chopped
2 tablespoons butter
⅓ cup (about 1.5 ounces) all-purpose flour
¼ cup unsweetened cocoa
¼ teaspoon table salt
2 large eggs, separated
2 tablespoons coffee-flavored liqueur
2 teaspoons instant espresso granules
2 cups coffee or vanilla bean low-fat ice cream
Chocolate shavings (optional)

1. Pour the 2 cups water into the inner pot of a 6-quart Instant Pot®. Place the Steam Rack in the pot; position the handles upright. Coat a 6-inch round cake pan with the cooking spray; sprinkle with 1 tablespoon of the sugar, shaking gently to coat the bottom and sides of pan.

2. Combine the chocolate and butter in a small microwave-safe bowl. Microwave at HIGH 30 to 45 seconds or until melted.

3. Combine the flour, cocoa, and salt in a small bowl. Beat the egg whites with a mixer at high speed until soft peaks form; gradually add 2 tablespoons sugar, beating until stiff peaks form.

4. Combine the egg yolks and remaining 2 tablespoons sugar in a large bowl. Beat with a mixer at high speed until thick and pale. Gradually beat in the liqueur, espresso granules, and chocolate mixture. Fold the beaten egg whites into the egg yolk mixture. Gradually sift the flour mixture into the egg mixture, and fold in gently. Spoon the batter into the prepared pan, spreading gently (do not deflate the batter). Cover with aluminum foil, making sure the foil fits tightly around sides and under the bottom of the pan. Carefully set the pan on the rack in the pot.

5. Lock the lid; turn Pressure Valve to "Sealing." PRESSURE COOK [High Pressure] for 11 minutes. Open the cooker using Quick Pressure Release (page 7). Remove the pan from the pot using the rack handles. Remove the foil; cool 10 minutes. Spoon the warm cake into bowls, and serve immediately with the ice cream. Top with the chocolate shavings, if desired.

6-QUART

MEXICAN CHOCOLATE POUND CAKE

SERVES: 8 | HANDS-ON: 26 MINUTES | UNDER PRESSURE: 55 MINUTES
10-MINUTE NATURAL PRESSURE RELEASE

This cinnamon-scented cake has a fine, wonderfully moist texture. The Chocolate Glaze is just as glossy and elegant as ganache, but with much less fat, because it uses whey from Greek Yogurt (page 15) instead of heavy cream.

Butter-flavored cooking spray
1½ cups water

CAKE

⅔ cup semisweet chocolate chips
4 ounces (½ cup) butter, softened
¾ cup sugar
2 large eggs
¼ cup chocolate syrup
2 teaspoons vanilla extract
1¼ cups (about 5.6 ounces) all-purpose flour
1½ teaspoons ground cinnamon
¼ teaspoon baking soda
Dash of table salt
½ cup nonfat Greek Yogurt whey (page 15)

CHOCOLATE GLAZE

½ cup semisweet chocolate chips
2 tablespoons Greek Yogurt whey (page 15)

1. Coat a 6-cup nonstick Bundt pan with the cooking spray. Pour the 1½ cups water into the inner pot of a 6-quart Instant Pot®.

2. Make the Cake: Place ⅔ cup chocolate chips in a microwave-safe bowl. Microwave at HIGH 1 minute and 30 seconds or until the chocolate is melted and smooth, stirring after 1 minute.

3. Beat the butter at medium speed with an electric mixer until creamy. Gradually add the sugar, beating 5 to 7 minutes or until light and fluffy. Add the eggs, 1 at a time, beating just until the yellow disappears after each addition. Stir in the melted chocolate, chocolate syrup, and vanilla until blended.

4. Combine the flour, cinnamon, baking soda, and salt; add to the butter mixture alternately with the whey, beginning and ending with the flour mixture. Beat at low speed just until blended after each addition. Pour the batter into the prepared pan, smoothing the top. Tap the pan on a work surface to remove air bubbles. Cover the top of the pan with aluminum foil coated with cooking spray, coated side down. Lightly crimp the edges to secure the foil to the top edge of the pan. Place the pan on the Steam Rack. Using the rack handles, gently lower the pan into the pot. Place the pot in the cooker.

5. Lock the lid; turn Pressure Valve to "Sealing." Turn off the KEEP WARM function. PRESSURE COOK [High Pressure] for 55 minutes. Allow a 10-minute Natural Pressure Release (page 10). Turn Pressure Valve to "Venting" to release remaining pressure.

6. Use the rack handles to lift the pan from the pot. Leave the pan on the rack. Remove the foil. Let the cake cool 10 minutes in the pan. Loosen the cake from the sides and center of the pan, using a plastic knife or narrow spatula. Invert the cake onto a wire cooling rack; cool completely.

7. Make the Chocolate Glaze: Microwave ½ cup chocolate chips in a microwave-safe bowl at HIGH 2 minutes or until chocolate melts, stirring after 1 minute. Stir the chocolate, and add the whey. Microwave 15 to 20 seconds or just until warm (do not overheat); stir until smooth and glossy. Drizzle the glaze over cake. Let stand until firm.

8-QUART

PRUNE SNACK CAKE

SERVES: 8 | HANDS-ON: 12 MINUTES | UNDER PRESSURE: 30 MINUTES
15-MINUTE NATURAL PRESSURE RELEASE

To dress up for company, sift the powdered sugar through a lacy doily, and serve each wedge with a dollop of Sweetened Whipped Cream (recipe below) on the side.

1½ cups water
Cooking spray
Parchment paper
1½ cups all-purpose flour
12 pitted prunes
1 teaspoon baking soda
½ teaspoon table salt
1 teaspoon ground cinnamon
¼ teaspoon ground nutmeg
¾ cup granulated sugar
4 ounces (½ cup) unsalted butter, softened and cut into 6 pieces
1 teaspoon vanilla extract
2 large eggs
⅓ cup Greek Yogurt whey (page 15)
⅓ cup Greek Yogurt (page 15)
Powdered sugar
Sweetened Whipped Cream (optional)

1. Pour the 1½ cups of water into the inner pot of an 8-quart Instant Pot®. Coat an 8- x 3-inch round cake pan with the cooking spray. Line the bottom of the pan with parchment paper; coat the parchment paper with the cooking spray, and dust the bottom and sides of the pan with 2 teaspoons of the flour. Chop the prunes into ½-inch pieces, and combine with 2 teaspoons of the flour in a small bowl, tossing with a fork to coat. Set aside.

2. Combine the remaining flour, baking soda, salt, cinnamon, and nutmeg, stirring with a whisk. Process the sugar, butter, and vanilla in a food processor 20 seconds or until blended and creamy. Add the eggs through the food chute; process 5 seconds. Add the flour mixture, whey, and yogurt. Process 5 seconds; scrape down the sides. Add the prune mixture; pulse 3 times. Pour the batter into the prepared pan. Cover the top of the pan with aluminum foil, crimping the edges to seal. Set the pan on the Steam Rack of the Instant Pot®. Lower the pan into the pot using the rack handles. Lock the lid; turn Pressure Valve to "Sealing." PRESSURE COOK [High Pressure] 30 minutes. Allow a 15-minute Natural Pressure Release (page 10). Turn Pressure Valve to "Venting" to release the remaining pressure.

3. Lift the cake from the pot using the handles. Let cool in the pan on the rack 5 minutes. Invert the cake onto a wire rack; remove the parchment paper, and let cool completely. To serve, transfer the cake, still inverted, to a plate, and dust with the powdered sugar. Cut into wedges. Serve with Sweetened Whipped Cream, if desired.

NOTE: ⅔ cup buttermilk may be substituted for the yogurt and whey mixture.

TIP:

Measure the ⅓ cup whey in a 1-cup glass measuring cup. Spoon in yogurt to measure ⅔ cup.

SWEETENED WHIPPED CREAM

MAKES: 2 CUPS

1 cup heavy cream
2 tablespoon powdered sugar
½ teaspoon vanilla extract

Combine all ingredients in a chilled metal bowl. With chilled beaters, beat the mixture with an electric mixer until soft peaks form.

6-QUART

SPICED CARROT CAKE

SERVES: 8 | HANDS-ON: 10 MINUTES | SLOW COOK: 1 HOUR, 30 MINUTES

Serve slices of this spiced cake with tea or coffee.

CAKE

Cooking spray
Parchment paper
1 cup (about 4.5 ounces) all-purpose flour
⅓ cup golden raisins
⅓ cup granulated sugar
⅓ cup packed light brown sugar
1 teaspoon baking soda
1 teaspoon ground cinnamon
¼ teaspoon table salt
¼ teaspoon ground ginger
¼ teaspoon grated whole nutmeg
⅛ teaspoon ground cloves
⅛ teaspoon ground allspice
⅓ cup canola oil
1 teaspoon vanilla extract
2 large eggs, lightly beaten
1½ cups finely shredded carrot
1 cup water

FROSTING

3 ounces ⅓-less-fat cream cheese, softened
½ cup powdered sugar
½ teaspoon vanilla extract

1. Make the Cake: Coat an 8-inch round (thin-rimmed) cake pan with cooking spray. Line the cake pan with the parchment paper; coat the parchment paper with cooking spray, and dust with 1 tablespoon of the flour. Combine the raisins and a second tablespoon of the flour in a small bowl; toss well.

2. Whisk together the remaining flour, granulated sugar, brown sugar, baking soda, cinnamon, salt, ginger, nutmeg, cloves, and allspice in a large bowl. Combine the oil, vanilla, and eggs in a small bowl; add to the flour mixture, stirring until blended. Stir in the carrot and raisins. Pour the batter into the prepared pan. Cover the pan with aluminum foil coated with the cooking spray, coated side down.

3. Place the Steam Rack in the inner pot of a 6-quart Instant Pot®; fold the handles under the rack. Pour 1 cup water into the pot. Fold a 20-inch-long strip of foil lengthwise into thirds to make a sling. Set the cake pan in the center of the sling. Grasping the ends of the sling, lower the pan into the pot, and set it on the rack. Fold the sling over the top of the pan.

4. Lock the lid; turn Pressure Valve to "Venting." SLOW COOK [More] for 1 hour and 30 minutes. (Cook additional time, if necessary, until a wooden pick inserted in the center comes out clean.) Carefully remove the lid from the cooker. Blot any water that has collected on top of the foil with a towel. Carefully transfer the pan to a wire rack using the foil sling. Remove the sling and the foil from the cake, and lightly blot the top of the cake with a paper towel, if necessary, to remove any collected moisture. Cool the cake 10 minutes in the pan on a wire rack; remove the cake from the pan. Cool completely on a wire rack.

5. Make the Frosting: Beat the cream cheese with a mixer at medium speed until smooth; add the powdered sugar and vanilla, beating until smooth. Garnish slices of cake with the frosting.

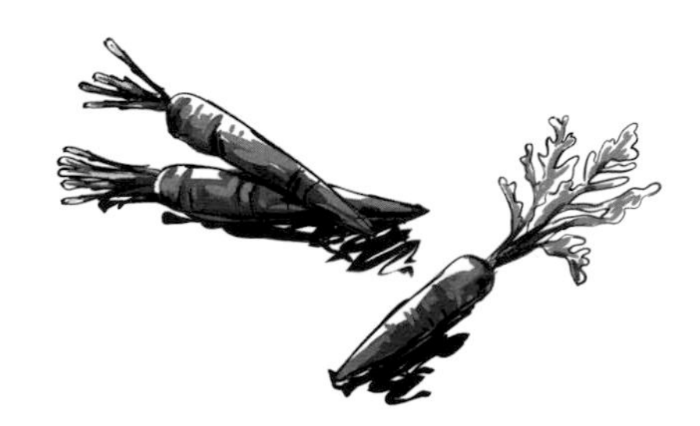

METRIC EQUIVALENTS

The information in the following chart is provided to help cooks outside the United States successfully use the recipes in this book. All equivalents are approximate.

COOKING/OVEN TEMPERATURES

	Fahrenheit	Celsius	Gas Mark
Freeze Water	32° F	0° C	
Room Temp.	68° F	20° C	
Boil Water	212° F	100° C	
Bake	325° F	160° C	3
	350° F	180° C	4
	375° F	190° C	5
	400° F	200° C	6
	425° F	220° C	7
	450° F	230° C	8
Broil			Grill

LIQUID INGREDIENTS BY VOLUME

¼ tsp					=	1 ml		
½ tsp					=	2 ml		
1 tsp					=	5 ml		
3 tsp	=	1 Tbsp	=	½ fl oz	=	15 ml		
2 Tbsp	=	⅛ cup	=	1 fl oz	=	30 ml		
4 Tbsp	=	¼ cup	=	2 fl oz	=	60 ml		
5⅓ Tbsp	=	⅓ cup	=	3 fl oz	=	80 ml		
8 Tbsp	=	½ cup	=	4 fl oz	=	120 ml		
10⅔ Tbsp	=	⅔ cup	=	5 fl oz	=	160 ml		
12 Tbsp	=	¾ cup	=	6 fl oz	=	180 ml		
16 Tbsp	=	1 cup	=	8 fl oz	=	240 ml		
1 pt	=	2 cups	=	16 fl oz	=	480 ml		
1 qt	=	4 cups	=	32 fl oz	=	960 ml		
				33 fl oz	=	1000 ml	=	1 l

DRY INGREDIENTS BY WEIGHT

(To convert ounces to grams, multiply the number of ounces by 30.)

1 oz	=	1⁄16 lb	=	30 g
4 oz	=	¼ lb	=	120 g
8 oz	=	½ lb	=	240 g
12 oz	=	¾ lb	=	360 g
16 oz	=	1 lb	=	480 g

EQUIVALENTS FOR DIFFERENT TYPES OF INGREDIENTS

Standard Cup	Fine Powder (ex. flour)	Grain (ex. rice)	Granular (ex. sugar)	Liquid Solids (ex. butter)	Liquid (ex. milk)
1	140 g	150 g	190 g	200 g	240 ml
¾	105 g	113 g	143 g	150 g	180 ml
⅔	93 g	100 g	125 g	133 g	160 ml
½	70 g	75 g	95 g	100 g	120 ml
⅓	47 g	50 g	63 g	67 g	80 ml
¼	35 g	38 g	48 g	50 g	60 ml
⅛	18 g	19 g	24 g	25 g	30 ml

LENGTH

(To convert inches to centimeters, multiply inches by 2.5.)

1 in					=	2.5 cm		
12 in	=	1 ft			=	30 cm		
36 in	=	3 ft	=	1 yd	=	90 cm		
40 in	=					100 cm	=	1 m

INDEX

D

E

F

G

S

T

V

W

Y